Hand-Painted POP American Art in Transition 1955-62

exhibition organized by
Donna De Salvo and Paul Schimmel

edited by
Russell Ferguson

with essays by
David Deitcher, Stephen C. Foster, Dick Hebdige, Linda Norden,
Kenneth E. Silver, and John Yau

THE MUSEUM OF CONTEMPORARY ART, LOS ANGELES

RIZZOLI INTERNATIONAL PUBLICATIONS, NEW YORK

This publication accompanies the exhibition
"Hand-Painted Pop: American Art in Transition, 1955-62,"
curated by Paul Schimmel and Donna De Salvo,
and organized by The Museum of Contemporary Art, Los Angeles

"HAND-PAINTED POP: AMERICAN ART IN TRANSITION, 1955-62"
IS SPONSORED BY PHILIP MORRIS COMPANIES INC.

Additional support for the exhibition has been provided by the National Endowment for the Arts, a federal agency,
the Pasadena Art Alliance and the Sondra & Charles Gilman Jr. Foundation

EXHIBITION SCHEDULE
The Museum of Contemporary Art, Los Angeles
December 6, 1992 - March 7, 1993

The Museum of Contemporary Art, Chicago
April 3 - June 20, 1993

Whitney Museum of American Art, New York
July 16 - October 3, 1993

Library of Congress Cataloging-in-Publication Data

Hand-painted pop : American art in transition, 1955– 62/exhibition
organized by Donna De Salvo and Paul Schimmel : with essays by David
Deitcher...[et al.] : edited by Russell Ferguson.
    p.   cm.
  ISBN 0-914357-29-8 (MOCA)
  ISBN 0-8478-1631-1 (Rizzoli)
  1. Pop art — United States — Exhibitions. 2. Art, Modern — 20th
century — United States — Exhibitions. I. De Salvo, Donna M.
II. Schimmel, Paul. III. Deitcher, David. IV. Ferguson, Russell.
V. Museum of Contemporary Art (Los Angeles, Calif.).
N6512.5.P6H36   1993   92-32102
759.13'09'04507479494 — dc 20   CIP

Edited by Russell Ferguson
Assistant Editor: Sherri Schottlaender
Designed by Lorraine Wild and Susan Parr, ReVerb/Los Angeles
Typeset by Continental Typographics, Chatsworth, California
Printed by Nissha Printing Co., Ltd., Kyoto, Japan

Copyright © 1992 The Museum of Contemporary Art, Los Angeles
250 South Grand Avenue, Los Angeles, California 90012

Distributed by
Rizzoli International Publications, Inc.
300 Park Avenue South
New York, New York 10010

Cover:
ROY LICHTENSTEIN
Sponge II, 1962
Oil on canvas, 36 x 36 inches
Collection of Peder Bonnier, New York

Sponsor's Statement

Pop art holds a special significance for Philip Morris. It marks the beginning of our company's commitment to experimental contemporary work. In 1965, in the early years of our arts support program, the first museum exhibition and tour funded by Philip Morris was entitled "Pop and Op."

Thirty-five years after the beginning of our arts program, it is timely and relevant that we support "Hand-Painted Pop: American Art in Transition, 1955-62," an exhibition that explores the immense contribution made by American artists in the second half of the twentieth century and establishes the early years of Pop art as a visionary period. In examining the origins of Pop art, and its complex relationship with Abstract Expressionism, important questions are raised which further the ongoing rethinking of the place of Pop in modern art.

In funding this exhibition, we hope to participate in the continuing reassessment of American art and to support the quest to look at familiar ideas and images in new ways.

MICHAEL A. MILES
Chairman of the Board and Chief Executive Officer
Philip Morris Companies Inc.

ANDY WARHOL
Icebox, 1960
Oil, ink, and pencil on canvas, 67 x 53 1/8 inches
The Menil Collection, Houston

Contents

ROY LICHTENSTEIN
Calendar, 1962
Oil on canvas, 48 1/2 x 70 inches
The Museum of Contemporary Art, Los Angeles
The Panza Collection

Director's Foreword

"Hand-Painted Pop" represents The Museum of Contemporary Art's commitment to the continuing scholarly re-examination of art since 1945. Pop art followed virtually on the heels of the worldwide success of Abstract Expressionism, yet it is conventionally seen as constituting a complete break with what went before. Pop sometimes seems to have leapt fully-formed to the forefront of American art. Despite the enormous popular enthusiasm which the movement aroused (perhaps in part because of it), the origins of what would be called Pop have received surprisingly little critical attention. "Hand-Painted Pop" seeks to change that situation, by focusing on the most crucial period of development: 1955-62. It is our hope that the works presented here, which include both famous masterpieces and rarely seen early works, will form the basis for an ongoing re-evaluation of this important period of transition in American art.

"Hand-Painted Pop" follows other important exhibitions on related themes organized by the curators, including Donna De Salvo's "'Success is a Job in New York': The Early Art and Business of Andy Warhol" at the Grey Art Gallery, New York University, and Paul Schimmel's "Action/Precision: The New Direction in New York, 1955-60" at the Newport Harbor Art Museum.

It would have been difficult for the curators to undertake such an ambitious project without the resources of the Panza Collection at MOCA to serve as a foundation. The acquisition of Dr. and Mrs. Panza's collection in 1983 brought the Museum an outstanding group of works by American artists of the period, many of which are included in the exhibition. For many in Chicago and New York, this will be their first encounter with the rich holdings of the Panza Collection. And for those in Los Angeles, this will be an opportunity to see MOCA's collection in the context of other major works of the period.

This catalogue, which accompanies the exhibition, represents a significant contribution to the scholarship of American art, including as it does major essays by David Deitcher, John Yau, Linda Norden, Stephen C. Foster, Kenneth E. Silver, and Dick Hebdige, as well as by the curators. It continues MOCA's tradition of important publications alongside our exhibition program. We are grateful to our colleagues at Rizzoli Publications for their collaboration on this project.

We would like to thank all the artists for their enthusiastic cooperation with the organizers of "Hand-Painted Pop," and the lenders for agreeing to part with their cherished works for the duration of the exhibition's presentations in Los Angeles, at the Museum of Contemporary Art in Chicago, and at the Whitney Museum of American Art in New York. We also owe a debt of gratitude to Philip Morris Companies Inc. for their generous support of "Hand-Painted Pop."

RICHARD KOSHALEK
Director
The Museum of Contemporary Art,
Los Angeles

Lenders to the Exhibition

Albright-Knox Art Gallery, Buffalo, New York
Dia Center for the Arts, New York
FAE Musée d'Art Contemporain, Pully/Lausanne
Hirshhorn Museum and Sculpture Garden, Smithsonian
    Institution, Washington, D.C.
Kunstsammlung Nordrhein-Westphalen, Düsseldorf
Los Angeles County Museum of Art
The Menil Collection, Houston
The Metropolitan Museum of Art, New York
The Minneapolis Institute of Arts
Moderna Museet, Stockholm
Musée National d'Art Moderne, Centre Georges Pompidou, Paris
The Museum of Contemporary Art, Los Angeles
Museum Ludwig, Cologne
The Museum of Modern Art, New York
National Museum of American Art, Smithsonian Institution,
    Washington, D.C.
Neuberger Museum of Art, State University of New York at Purchase
Newport Harbor Art Museum, Newport Beach, California
Philadelphia Museum of Art
Rose Art Museum, Brandeis University, Waltham, Massachusetts
The Saint Louis Art Museum
San Diego Museum of Contemporary Art
Staatsgalerie Stuttgart
University of Nebraska-Lincoln, Sheldon Memorial Art Gallery
The Andy Warhol Foundation for the Visual Arts, Inc., New York
Whitney Museum of American Art, New York

Thomas Ammann, Zurich
Betty Asher, Beverly Hills
Sarah Goodwin Austin, New York
Peder Bonnier, New York
Pontus Bonnier, Stockholm
Jean-Christophe Castelli, New York
Joyce and Jay Cooper, Phoenix
James Corcoran, Malibu, California
Barney A. Ebsworth, St. Louis
Stefan T. Edlis Collection, Chicago
Ralph and Helyn Goldenberg, Chicago
Foster and Monique Goldstrom, Oakland and New York
Guess, Inc., Marciano Collection, Los Angeles
Anne and William J. Hokin Collection, Chicago
Jasper Johns, New York
The Sydney and Frances Lewis Collection, New York
David Lichtenstein, New York
Mitchell Lichtenstein, New York
Claes Oldenburg and Coosje van Bruggen, New York
PaineWebber Group, Inc., New York
Kimiko and John Powers, *Carbondale, Colorado*
Skot Ramos, *Burbank, California*
Robert and Jane Rosenblum, *New York*
Tony Shafrazi, New York
Holly Solomon, New York
The Sonnabend Collection, New York
Marcia and Irving Stenn, Chicago
Nina and Michael Sundell, New York
Mr. and Mrs. Richard Titelman, Atlanta
The Marcia Simon Weisman Trust, Los Angeles
Mr. and Mrs. Bagley Wright, Seattle
Anonymous lenders

Gallery Bruno Bischofberger, Zurich
Frumkin/Adams Gallery, New York
James Goodman Gallery, New York
Galerie Karsten Greve, Cologne
Odyssia Gallery, New York
Salama-Caro Gallery, London
Allan Stone Gallery, New York

Acknowledgments

Without the Panza Collection, it would have been inconceivable for The Museum of Contemporary Art to have organized "Hand-Painted Pop." I would like to acknowledge here, therefore, the pioneering vision of Dr. and Mrs. Panza, who made their acquisitions long before the international recognition of Pop art as a movement, and of the Board of Trustees of MOCA, who secured the collection for the Museum.

In the organization of "Hand-Painted Pop," we are first and foremost indebted to the artists, who have cooperated in every way possible. Their willingness to participate in a reexamination of this period was crucial. Billy Al Bengston, Jim Dine, Joe Goode, Grace Hartigan, Robert Indiana, Jasper Johns, Allan Kaprow, Roy Lichtenstein, Claes Oldenburg, Mel Ramos, Robert Rauschenberg, Larry Rivers, James Rosenquist, Edward Ruscha, Peter Saul, Wayne Thiebaud, Cy Twombly, and John Wesley have all graciously contributed to the exhibition through loans from their own collections and in encouraging others to lend works. In addition, they have given endless hours to discussion with us about both their work in general and that period in particular.

The many lenders to this exhibition are gratefully acknowledged for their willingness to part with works which will be sorely missed from their collections, both private and public. The importance and value of these works made the decision to lend all the more significant. Their willingness to make these works available shows a great sense of responsibility to the public interest. A few lenders went to extraordinary lengths to help us realize this exhibition. We are particularly grateful to the Dia Center for the Arts, New York, Charles Wright, Director; the Musée National d'Art Moderne, Centre Georges Pompidou, Paris, Dominique Bozo, Director; The Museum of Modern Art, New York, Richard E. Oldenburg, Director, and Kirk Varnedoe, Director of the Department of Painting and Sculpture; Thomas Ammann, Zurich; Kimiko and John Powers, Carbondale, Colorado; and Ileana Sonnabend, New York.

At The Museum of Contemporary Art, Richard Koshalek, Director, enthusiastically embraced the idea of organizing an exhibition about the formative years of Pop art, and its relationship to the New York School. During the three years from the time the idea was first proposed until its realization, Richard has supported every aspect of its organization, from conceptualization to fundraising. Over a period of months, hours were spent every morning making phone calls to collectors and museums around the world to secure the significant loans so important to an exhibition of this scope. Sherri Geldin, Associate Director, has contributed counsel and advice for many crucial organizational and administrative aspects of the exhibition. Erica Clark, Director of Development, enthusiastically planned and executed a successful fundraising program for this exhibition; we also want to thank June Scott, Grants Manager, for her work on the grants. Thanks also go to Jack Wiant,

11

ROBERT RAUSCHENBERG
Inlet, 1959
Combine painting, 84 1/2 x 48 inches
The Museum of Contemporary Art, Los Angeles
The Panza Collection

Controller, who managed the financial aspects of this exhibition. Russell Ferguson, MOCA's Editor, in his first large-scale project since joining the Museum, has shown a great depth of understanding about the project. He had an active role in the selection of the catalogue's authors, and has skillfully edited their essays. Assistant Editor Sherri Schottlaender speedily and with great accuracy procured all photography, handled rights and reproduction issues, and assisted with myriad details of the editorial process. Mo Shannon, Registrar, and Rosanna Hemerick, Registrarial Assistant, have provided all of the highly specialized shipping and handling arrangements necessary to enable the lenders to entrust such important works to the exhibition. Conservation was needed on several works from the Panza Collection; we are grateful for the sympathetic and thorough job done by Sharon Shore, Tatyana Thompson, Mark Watters, and Glenn Wharton. John Bowsher, Exhibition Production Manager, has worked on all aspects of the exhibition and its tour. Much additional assistance with the exhibition has been provided by Alma Ruiz, Exhibitions Coordinator. Dawn Setzer, Press Officer, working with Sylvia Hohri, Assistant Director of Communications, developed and managed the public relations program. Vas Prabhu, Director of Education, Kim Kanatani, Associate Director of Education, and Caroline Blackburn, Art Talks Coordinator, developed and facilitated a series of lectures and talks, and organized a reading room for the exhibition. I also want to acknowledge the interest expressed by my curatorial colleagues at MOCA, Kerry Brougher, Ann Goldstein, Julie Lazar, and Elizabeth Smith. Our personal and professional thanks go to Diane Aldrich, Secretary to the Chief Curator, for constantly keeping the two curators in touch with each other, making all of our travel arrangements, and often clearing the decks of other work so we that we could concentrate on the exhibition at hand. More than any other staff person, however, it is former NEA intern and Research Assistant Heidi Nickisher who deserves our gratitude for her research into the exhibition, and, most importantly, for handling the daunting task of coordinating the numerous loan requests and endless revisions of the checklist in the process of organizing this exhibition. The research conducted by Lydia Yee in New York, and that of Simonetta Fraquelli, is greatly appreciated. Erin Bonner, former MOCA Librarian, along with Heidi Nickisher, compiled the bibliography, and is due our thanks. Thanks are also due to Susan Colletta and Colette Dartnall, Curatorial Assistants, and Brent Zerger, Curatorial Secretary.

The scholarly significance of this project has been greatly enhanced by the original contributions to the catalogue by David Deitcher, Stephen C. Foster, Dick Hebdige, Linda Norden, Kenneth E. Silver, and John Yau, which provide a range of fresh insights into this period. When the exhibition was in its formative stages, Rizzoli International exhibited a strong commitment to this project; the interest and enthusiasm of Gianfranco Monacelli and Charles Miers are greatly appreciated. Lorraine Wild and Susan Parr have created the book's sensitive and original design.

The early research underlying this exhibition was greatly augmented and facilitated by discussions with many art historians, museum professionals, and dealers. They include Martha Baer of Christie's, Dick Bellamy, Leo Castelli, James Corcoran, Jeffrey Deitch, Anthony Grant of Sotheby's, Henry Geldzahler, Antonio Homem, Ivan Karp, and Robert Rosenblum. Their insights into the period are greatly appreciated. Among the many others who helped with this complex project are Beverly Coe, Gretchen Corners, James di Pasquale, Karla Fox, Paula Goldman, Michael Harrigan, Cindy Hemstreet, Shelley Lee, Lawrence Lipkind, Cassandra Lozano, David Platzker, Pat Poncy, Paul Ruscha, David Sundberg, Sarah Taggart, Debbie Taylor, and Karen Tsujimoto.

This exhibition has been made possible through the generous support of Philip Morris Companies Inc. which has supported the visual arts for thirty-five years. Stephanie French, Karen Brosius, and

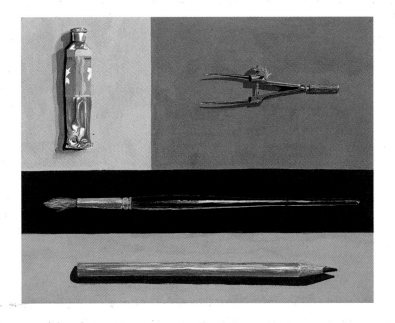

Marilynn Donini enthusiastically embraced the idea of this exhibition from the outset. Philip Morris has provided critical funding for the exhibition, its tour, and our ability to reach a wide public through educational brochures and public relations. They are more than just a corporate sponsor. Their expertise provides a partnership in reaching a wider audience. Additionally, the crucial initial support for this exhibition was received from the National Endowment for the Arts, a federal agency, and significant additional funds have also been provided by the Pasadena Art Alliance, and the Sondra & Charles Gilman Jr. Foundation.

The early and enthusiastic commitments of The Museum of Contemporary Art in Chicago, and the Whitney Museum of American Art in New York, were greatly appreciated. Not only have they become our partners in providing significant venues for this exhibition, but their staffs, under the leadership of Kevin Consey at the Museum of Contemporary Art, Chicago, and David Ross at the Whitney Museum, have provided guidance and support, both in the aims of this exhibition and in the form of some significant loans from their respective institutions and communities.

It has been a pleasure and a privilege to collaborate with my friend and colleague Donna De Salvo on "Hand-Painted Pop." Without Donna, it would have been a very different project. Although we both saw the core of the exhibition in a similar fashion, we also brought our individual perspectives to it: my own starting point was the 1950s, while Donna's background was mainly art of the 1960s. The fresh vision which Donna always brings to art and ideas has made "Hand-Painted Pop" richer, more varied, and more original.

Finally, I would like to dedicate this exhibition to the memory of Marcia Simon Weisman, a great collector, a generous patron, and a founder of MOCA, who contributed to its collection one of our most significant works, Jasper Johns's *Map* (1962), which is among the most important works included in this exhibition.

PAUL SCHIMMEL

Chief Curator

The Museum of Contemporary Art,

Los Angeles

The organization of an exhibition is never the work of any one person and this is no less so with "Hand-Painted Pop." In addition to seconding all that Paul Schimmel has said, I welcome the opportunity to add my own thanks. At The Museum of Contemporary Art, I would especially like to thank Richard Koshalek, Director, for the invitation to work with the museum on this important project, and to serve as an Ahmanson Curatorial Fellow. Russell Ferguson, the museum's Editor, has expertly shaped the catalogue and essays into an impressive publication, and his professionalism and patience made it a joy to work with him. Heidi Nickisher, former NEA intern, provided important organizational and research assistance throughout the project. In New York, Lydia Yee, Research Assistant, used her excellent skills to track down photographs and information for the catalogue.

It is a pleasure to see this exhibition travel to two important institutions, The Museum of Contemporary Art in Chicago and the Whitney Museum of American Art in New York. I am most grateful to those museums' directors, Kevin Consey and David A. Ross, for helping to realize this tour. Stephanie French of Philip Morris has been supportive of this project throughout, and I would like to extend my thanks to her for her personal efforts on the project's behalf. Many collectors and institutions have graciously agreed to lend their works of art to this exhibition. Without their cooperation and support, "Hand-Painted Pop" would never have been possible.

Throughout the organization of this exhibition, many artists have willingly opened their archives and memories to me, offering insights into the developmental stages of their work. They have also allowed us to exhibit works which have not been seen for many years. Without their cooperation, our rethinking of this period would have been much more difficult. I would especially like to thank those who took the time to meet with me personally: Jim Dine, Grace Hartigan, Jasper Johns, Allan Kaprow, Roy Lichtenstein, Claes Oldenburg, Larry Rivers, James Rosenquist, Edward Ruscha, Cy Twombly, and John Wesley. I would also like to extend my thanks to David Platzker, Coosje van Bruggen, Roslyn Drexler, Cassandra Lozano, James di Pasquale, Laurie Lambrecht, and Beverly Coe.

Many individuals have helped to locate the numerous loans required for this exhibition. My gratitude goes to Walter Hopps, Billy Kluver and Julie Martin, Larry Gagosian, Karsten Greve, Virginia Zabriskie, Horace Richter, Terry Myers, Melissa McGrath, Debbie Taylor, Leo Castelli, Susan Brundage, Mark Francis, Susan Hapgood, Jeffrey Deitch, Henry Geldzahler, Paul Winkler, and Nan Rosenthal. Trudy C. Kramer, Director of The Parrish Art Museum, supported this undertaking with great enthusiasm, allowing me the time needed to bring it to completion. I am grateful to her and the entire staff of the museum for their understanding and support.

There are several individuals whose intellectual advice and support, not just during the organization of this project, but over the years, have been especially important to me. My warmest thanks to Linda Norden, Maurice Berger, Danny Kaiser, Gary Kuehn, Barbara Moore, Neil Printz, and Barbara Kruger. I extend my warmest thanks to my family, Frances De Salvo and Peter De Salvo, for their belief and encouragement.

I would like to reserve my final thanks for Paul Schimmel, Chief Curator at The Museum of Contemporary Art, who first suggested that we work together on this exhibition. Throughout the months of organization, we have brought to the table many different readings of the period under investigation, and our discussions have been characterized by agreement as well as debate. Our individual investigations of high art and popular culture have sometimes followed different paths, but, in the end, we each returned to the works of art. I am indebted to Paul for the insights, dedication, and enthusiasm he brought to the project.

15

DONNA DE SALVO
Robert Lehman Curator
Parrish Art Museum, Southampton, New York
and Ahmanson Curatorial Fellow, 1992
The Museum of Contemporary Art, Los Angeles

Introduction

Abstract Expressionism and Pop art both had profound implications for subsequent artmaking in the United States and Europe. Each would introduce certain "nameable" features to the vocabulary of aesthetics —the marks and gestures of Abstract Expressionism, the signs and symbols of popular culture in Pop art—that continue to influence artists today. The period that fell between these two movements, however, remains perplexing, without a satisfactory "label," for the work produced during this time combines the stylistic attributes of both movements. This work, which we have chosen to call "hand-painted Pop," was a product of the intense experimentation taking place at a time when one movement was losing its momentum and another was just beginning.

There has been a tendency to think that Pop art emerged out of an abrupt break with Abstract Expressionism. The real relationship was, in fact, much more complex. This exhibition, "Hand-Painted Pop: American Art in Transition, 1955-62," focuses on the long and layered period of evolution which produced both Pop art and other tendencies. As the title suggests, the combination of "hand-painted" with "Pop" emphasizes the seemingly incongruous nature of this exploration. Pop art with its machine-like, industrially produced, seemingly cold, commercial orientation is juxtaposed to the notion of the hand-painted, the human mark and gesture, hot and emotionally charged. This either/or division does not accurately reflect the genesis of what we now know as Pop art. Nor does it embrace the complexity of the artists' intentions.

The exhibition covers only the years 1955-1962. Deciding just when to begin presented the greatest difficulty, because it could be argued that Pop tendencies in American art began even earlier in the century. The work of Stuart Davis, for instance, reflected the impact of popular culture and graphic design as early as the 1920s. The choice of 1955, however, was made because it marked the year in which Jasper Johns produced his first flag and target paintings, and in which Robert Rauschenberg shifted from his nostalgic collage work toward his proto-Pop pieces (*Rebus* and *Interview*), which fully engaged the material of popular culture. The inclusion in the show, however, of two versions of *Washington Crossing the Delaware* painted earlier, by Roy Lichtenstein (ca. 1951) and Larry Rivers (1953), reminds us of the impossibility of precisely pinpointing any exact moment of origin.

The last year to be considered was easier to decide upon, in that by 1962 Pop art had become an internationally recognized cultural phenomenon. Pop had been named as a movement, and a series of museum exhibitions helped to legitimize the term. By 1962, the Pop artists had, in fact, moved from their earlier, more painterly works, to a crisper, more commercially inspired approach. Artists had found a style and technique that had a greater coherence with the subject of their pictures. The hesitation was over.

We are fortunate that recent scholarship has contributed new understanding to this transitional period, helping to underscore the inadequacy of the term "Pop art." Exhibitions such as "Blam! The Explosion of Pop, Minimalism, and Performance," organized by Barbara Haskell for the Whitney Museum of American Art, "The Fifties: Aspects of Painting in New York," organized by Phyllis Rosenzweig for the

Hirshhorn Museum, and "Made in U.S.A.," organized by Sidra Stich for the University Art Museum, Berkeley, have unearthed unknown works and recontextualized them in fresh ways. "Hand-Painted Pop" hopes to further complicate the false clarity with which we have traditionally understood Pop art. Resisting the art historian's urge to organize art into neat categories, it reflects instead the messiness of the period.

In this publication, a number of scholars contribute their perspectives. David Deitcher focuses in particular on the impact of art and design education on the work of Roy Lichtenstein and Andy Warhol. John Yau takes as his starting point a key work by Jasper Johns and, through close examination, reveals the complexities behind this hybrid type of painting. Linda Norden makes a compelling case for looking at the work of Cy Twombly in the context of his American contemporaries. Stephen Foster examines the contemporary criticism of the new work as part of a general crisis of criticism. Kenneth Silver looks at the gay iconography in work by Johns and Warhol. Dick Hebdige focuses on the experiential quality of Pop, and its ideological implications.

Our decision to include only the work of American artists, and to focus primarily on painting, was made after much careful thought and research. Clearly, interest in popular culture was not new, and not limited to the United States. In Britain, Richard Hamilton and Eduardo Paolozzi had already begun their own investigations of the ideologies of popular culture, specifically American popular culture. Nevertheless, they experienced this culture from afar, as something "exotic," and thus quite differently from American artists living in America. It should be noted that in organizing an early exhibition on Pop art for the Guggenheim Museum in 1963, Lawrence Alloway, the British art critic and originator of the term "Pop Art," also chose to focus exclusively on Americans, perhaps recognizing the differences in their approach.

Along these same lines, the work being made simultaneously in Germany and France shows certain similarities with what was taking place in America. The "capitalist realism" of the German artists Sigmar Polke and Gerhard Richter was a direct response to American Pop art. Rather than really being part of Pop art, it is, instead, a critique of it. And although the process-oriented *affichiste* compositions of Mimmo Rotella, Jacques de la Villegle, and Raymond Hains bear some resemblance to the 1956 work of Allan Kaprow, and to that of Rauschenberg, their inclusion would be somewhat peripheral to our main investigation.

From this show's inception it was the relationship between the New York School and the emerging generation of Pop art painters that provided the focus. Although sculpture, assemblage, and collage all played a significant role in the development of this American vernacular, we felt that the theoretical underpinnings of Abstract Expressionism, expressed almost entirely in relation to painting, required our full attention. Thus the only sculptor included here is Claes Oldenburg, due to the strong painterly and two-dimensional qualities of many of the works from *The Store*. Oldenburg's work of the mid-1950s did, in fact, include many paintings.

There is no doubt that our investigation of this transitional period in American art will be incomplete. There are many artists whose work is germane to our discussion, but who are not included. The selection of artists, and of specific works, was undertaken with the intention of constructing a narrative that could help elucidate some of the period's important developments and concerns; this is not to imply that other narratives are illegitimate. Nor is it to imply that Pop art is the only destination to which the experimentation of the fifties and early sixties led.

One of the greatest pleasures in organizing this exhibition has been the opportunity to present lesser-known works by some of America's most well-known artists. Their evident starts, stops, and reformulations reveal the vulnerability of artists still working towards their mature styles. Their appearance alongside acknowledged masterpieces offers us compelling information about the personal roots of aesthetic choices, and reminds us that there is still much to learn about the development of artists whose work it is easy to imagine we know all too well. By keeping a tight focus on American painting between 1955 and 1962, "Hand-Painted Pop" aspires to provide a foundation for renewed discussion of what happened in this period.

DONNA DE SALVO and PAUL SCHIMMEL

18

LARRY RIVERS
Washington Crossing the Delaware, 1953
Oil, graphite, and charcoal on linen, 83 5/8 x 111 5/8 inches
The Museum of Modern Art, New York
Given anonymously

Paul Schimmel

The Faked Gesture:
Pop Art and the New York School

To start every day moving out from Pollock and de Kooning,
which is sort of a long way to have to go to start from. Robert Rauschenberg[1]

For a brief moment, sometime in the first half of the 1950s, there was a conviction among painters that a gesture could be pure and unencumbered, and reveal nothing but itself and the action of making a picture. Painting was an "act" that existed in time. Paintings themselves became viable when their real subject was their own making. It took only a short time, however, for that existential freedom to begin to become caricatured, copied, reproduced, appropriated, synthesized, and finally drained of conviction. Yet almost every artist we associate with Pop art had to go through their own battle with what remained of the New York School. The legacy of process and gesture was to have a profound effect on the formative years of Pop, and was both the object and subject of many works during this transitional period.

19

      It was not until 1962 that gestural painting finally became irrelevant to young artists. By that time the Pop artists had found a style consonant with their subject matter, and they were no longer in a dialogue with the artists of "the club" (the group that believed that either you are with us or against us). For a painter in the mid-1950s, it had been inconceivable not to acknowledge the "breakthrough" of the New York School, but ten years later that "triumph" was beginning to seem like a chest-pounding joke. The loyalty, or lack of it, of artists to the so-called "school of de Kooning" was simply not an issue by the time Pop entered its "classic" phase.

      The overthrow of the myth of the New York School was hard won. For art to comment about itself and its relationship to the commercial world was heresy. When artists used "the style" to comment about picture making, a devastating step had been taken in the demystification of art. For the Pop artist, expressionist technique was just that: a technique, a style, something that could be copied, altered, and even played with. No longer was painting seen as a subconscious tracing of emotional states of being. No longer did artists struggle to find the picture by making the picture.

      It has been an inaccurate oversimplification to see Pop art as representing a clean break from Abstract Expressionism. The numerous instances of comment upon, and continuity with, the art of the Abstract Expressionists is a clear indication of evolutionary change. If our goals are to understand this extraordinarily active period of transition between two great eras, then there is a need to throw out preconceived ideas. This exhibition thus includes work outside, in advance of, part of, and in response to "Pop art."

New York during the first half of the 1950s, although dominated by the first generation painters of the New York School, continued to be a battleground fought over by many concurrent and seemingly mutually exclusive ideologies and "schools." There was a complex and layered dialogue that included not only first and second generation gestural/action painters, but also the more purely abstract field painters, the continuing legacy of figurative painting, and Geometric Abstraction. Pop art, Happenings, Minimalism, and color field painting all had their foundations in the 1950s.

The complex and overlapping art movements of the fifties, from which we can now distinguish Pop, assemblage, collage, Beat, figuration, gestural and hard edge abstraction, Happenings, Abstract Impressionist, and color field painting, were far from distinct to contemporary viewers. The Jewish Museum's "Artists of the New York School, Second Generation" (1957) included the work of Grace Hartigan, Alfred Leslie, and Joan Mitchell, as one would expect from such a title, but also the color field paintings of Helen Frankenthaler, the figurative work of Elaine de Kooning, and, most surprisingly, the proto-Pop abstraction of Jasper Johns. When the Museum of Modern Art organized its "Americans" series in 1959, Dorothy Miller chose to concentrate on a younger generation from New York and the rest of the nation, including California and the midwest. Johns and Rauschenberg were now seen with die-hard gestural abstractionist Leslie and proto-minimalist Frank Stella, among others. In the same year the Stable Gallery mounted "School of New York," which included Rauschenberg, Johns, and Cy Twombly, along with figurative and Abstract Expressionist painters. Galleries such as Hansa, Castelli, Janis, Green, Martha Jackson and Stable all showed Pop artists in the late fifties and early sixties alongside second generation Abstract Expressionists and Figurative Expressionists.

Until 1947, Jackson Pollock continued to incorporate figurative elements in his work, and completely eliminated specific subject from his art for a period of only three years, between 1949 and 1952. Willem de Kooning, always a figurative artist, continued to work with figure-derived biomorphic forms through 1949, at which time he was already beginning to work towards the *Woman* series. Even more than Pollock's return to the figure, de Kooning's perceived retrenchments sent rumors through the art world that the hard-won purity of abstract painting had been lost at the hand of one of its supposed proponents. When de Kooning exhibited the *Woman* series at the Sidney Janis Gallery in March, 1953, questions surrounding the use of figurative content and popular sources were thrust into the forefront of the avant-garde.

By incorporating the collaged mouth from a Camel cigarette advertisement into *Study for Woman* (1950), de Kooning opened the door again for artists to engage with and respond to popular imagery. "Many younger artists, already in reaction to the rigorously intellectual climate of Abstract Expressionism, considered it a permission to revive figure painting."[2] De Kooning had always been interested in sources drawn from popular culture, and had in fact incorporated newspaper transfers, comic strip characters, billboard and mannequin figures in his work throughout the forties.

For Pollock, like de Kooning, the return to the figure and reference in 1951 was natural. "I've had a period of drawing on canvas with some of my old images coming through."[3] Although the impact that Pollock's black enamel paintings were to have on the return to subject matter was not as dramatic as that of the *Woman* series, they did further the growing suspicion that abstraction was not the only path.

De Kooning and Pollock's return to figuration had an immediate impact on the artists now associated with Figurative Expressionism, including Grace Hartigan, Lester Johnson, Alex Katz, George McNeil,

ALFRED LESLIE
Quartet #1, 1958
Oil on canvas, 82 x 99 inches
Courtesy of Allan Stone Gallery, New York

Jan Müller, Fairfield Porter, Larry Rivers, and Bob Thompson, among others. But even those who continued in abstraction were moving away from painting as an impromptu and intuitive process of action and reaction towards a more precise and predetermined practice. Lawrence Alloway has described in Pop art the notion of "process abbreviation," in which "the finished work of art is…separate from traces of its long involvement in planning and realizing, at least in appearance and sometimes in fact."[4] This significant shift was occurring to some degree with the generation of painters who were called the "new academy" or "school of de Kooning" because of their imitation of gestural painting. They, like the Pop artists, could no longer believe that an artist could get lost in a painting and that gestures were pure, unrehearsed expressions of the inner soul.

> What are the signs of crisis in the de Kooning style? The first is the way it has been rendered decorative by painters who have converted it into a formula and given it a "professional" finish and polish. This happens only after a style has passed its period of vitality, when the metaphor becomes the cliche.[5]

While the second generation produced increasingly predetermined gestural painting, the Pop artist isolated the gesture and made it an object distinct from the ground. The gesture became a question rather than an answer. Both Pop artists and younger New York School painters recognized their inability to make an "authentic" painting. As Harold Rosenberg put it, "There is no greater aesthetic virtue in copying a de Kooning [e.g., Leslie Goldberg et al.] than in copying the design on a beer can [Jasper Johns]. If you do either, you are talking to the audience about itself, not necessarily engaging in creation."[6] Rosenberg's lament indicates the shift to a new approach in art, in which originality and creativity were no longer possible in the purest sense. The new generation was posing and solving different problems, in a concerted effort to advance painting towards objecthood. The artist was no longer the creative soul lost in the rapture of artmaking. Artists in this era became strategists, planning their futures rather than stumbling into them.

All the artists coming to maturity during the latter half of the fifties and early sixties benefitted from a dramatically changed working and artistic environment. Pollock, de Kooning, Franz Kline, Mark Rothko, and Barnett Newman had all suffered through the Depression and World War II. All had evolved out of and in response to European modernist and Surrealist painting. All had languished in the backwater obscurity of New York, isolated from the mainstream of culture in Europe, and even from the more popular Regionalist art in the United States. For the younger generation of New York painters, whether working in painterly, figurative or proto-Pop modes, there was support and acceptance at an early age. New York had evolved into a sympathetic environment in which not only artists but dealers, museums, collectors, critics, and even the general public took an active interest in the avant-garde. The financial possibilities for an artist emerging in the latter half of the fifties and early sixties were unprecedented, and separated all these artists from their bitter predecessors, the Abstract Expressionists. This new generation was apolitical, college educated in art and design, knew what they wanted to become, and had no need for manifestos.

For classic Abstract Expressionist painting, the reality of the painting itself was its only subject. Its environment was the space created by the monumental scale of the work. For the Pop artists and the second generation Abstract Expressionists, environment began to mean something altogether different. For the second generation Abstract Expressionists (Mitchell, Goldberg, Hartigan, and Norman Bluhm), the space within the painting became landscape. For Müller, Katz, Thompson, et al., the figure reemerged in a variety of real and imagined environments, and for the Pop artists, the environment became the world outside the picture frame.

WILLEM DE KOONING
Woman, 1950
Oil and enamel on paper, with pasted color photoengraving
14 5/8 x 11 5/8 inches
From the collection of Thomas B. Hess, jointly owned by
The Metropolitan Museum of Art and the heirs of Thomas B. Hess, 1984

But Pop offered no solace to the surviving conservative advocates of traditional figure painting. *From the moment when it became plain in the late forties that the first significant American style had crystallized in abstract expressionism, a certain unhappy majority began to look forward to the day when its discomfort at the absence from art of references to external reality would be mollified by a return to figuration in painting and sculpture....the new art offers no solace at all to the advocates of figuration, who had something quite different in mind.*[7]

Or, as Lawrence Alloway stated,

There had been for some years a theoretical program to return art to the human figure as important subject matter, and it was a disappointment to its backers when Pop art, instead of an expressionist revival, developed. Not only was the human figure not a dominant feature of Pop art, there were formal correspondences to be detected between the tidier Pop artists and the systematically planned abstract paintings of the same generation.[8]

22

"Hand-Painted Pop" hopes to soften the hard edges that are widely perceived to exist between New York School painting and Pop. The Pop artists began to dismember the notion of process, to disassemble it into its component parts. This tended to be seen in emotional terms as a lack of compassion, although compassion had nothing to do with making a gestural painting in the first place.

Grace Hartigan and Larry Rivers (although of the same generation as Johns, Rauschenberg, and Twombly) were squarely in the realm of New York School figurative painters. However, their work *anticipates* and *foreshadows* some of Pop art's concern with subject and attitude (as does that of Stuart Davis and Gerald Murphy from the late twenties). Johns and Rauschenberg are proto-Pop and, more than the other artists in this exhibition, sit squarely between the world of Abstract Expressionism and Pop art. Jim Dine, Allan Kaprow, and Claes Oldenburg became associated with Pop art after their Happenings, and they are more justifiably included in a Pop context than all the aforementioned artists. Roy Lichtenstein, Edward Ruscha, James

LARRY RIVERS
The Studio, 1956
Oil on canvas, 82 1/2 x 193 1/2 inches
The Minneapolis Institute of Arts
John R. Van Derlip Fund

Rosenquist, and Andy Warhol are, finally, paradigmatic Pop artists. They were able to find,

...a coincidence of style and subject, that ... represents mass-produced images and objects by using a style which is also based upon the visual vocabulary of mass production....the real Pop artist not only likes the fact of his commonplace objects, but more important, exults in their commonplace look, which is no longer viewed through the blurred, kaleidoscopic lenses of Abstract-Expressionism....[9]

Rivers and Hartigan both came to artistic maturity in the era of classic Abstract Expressionism. They lived in New York during the late forties and early fifties, when action painting was in its heyday. They were very much a part of the New York School, both ideologically and socially. Significantly younger than the first generation, they were to search for a painting that extended the tradition of gestural painting into the realm of history and "scenes of everyday life." Combining the painterly initiatives of de Kooning with a Manet-like search for history and the commonplace, Rivers and Hartigan created a pre-Pop art which was to anticipate rather than define the next generation's concerns with American iconography, consumer goods, and recontextualized subject matter.

Rivers's *Washington Crossing the Delaware* (1953) is a key precursor of Pop art. Into the moody seriousness of the New York School, Rivers injected the banality of repainting a work known to every schoolchild in America at that time, Emanuel Leutze's *Washington Crossing the Delaware* (1851). It was an outrageous act of attention-getting to update this famous work in the painterly style of the New York School. It was a game, and one that Warhol would later acknowledge as liberating for him among others. In *Washington Crossing the Delaware*, Rivers's style has seemingly been lifted from an enlarged page of a sketch book, as Fairfield Porter, the painter, noted in a review at that time.[10]

The painting received a largely hostile response, largely because of its "inappropriate" subject. All the attacks on Rivers would be repeated about Pop art six years later. Rivers's defiant nature and his fascination with "unsuitable" subjects connects him with the anti-art spirit which was of significance to Johns, Rauschenberg, and subsequently to Pop art in general. "Within a few years, Washington's image and other stereotyped trappings of Americana, often taken from mass-media sources, had become familiar devices in the Pop repertory."[11]

It is, however, how he paints that most clearly separates Rivers from Pop art. Rivers's bravura painterliness and his sketchy, intuitive technique are drawn directly from the New York School tradition. Simultaneously with his reworking of the Leutze history painting he was also paraphrasing the "de Kooning style" in a darker, old master palette. Rivers's move away from old and modern masters to his immediate surroundings occurred in 1954-55. Continuing to work in a free and sketchy manner, Rivers's more colorful and lighter palette was applied to personal images of his ancestors (*Europe*, 1956), his mother-in-law (*Berdie*, 1955), and his friends and family (*The Studio*, 1956). Towards the end of the 1950s, Rivers's use of virtuoso painterly gesture became increasingly important in his work. His visible reworking of the surface stemmed from "an abundance of dissatisfactions," resulting in canvases covered in pentimenti and overlapping images for the viewer to relish. Clearly, from the standpoint of process and painterliness, Rivers remained tied to the Abstract Expressionists. Where he broke with them was in his use of popular and historic subject matter, and in his willingness to violate the canon of the unified field. "Rivers treated it in a piecemeal fashion, composing a montage of vignettes held together by a solid structure of design."[12] That sense of composed design rather than unified field was to become an important aspect of Pop art. Even Lawrence Alloway, in a compelling argument against seeing Rivers as a Pop artist, concedes that there are exceptions.

23

EMANUEL LEUTZE
Washington Crossing the Delaware, 1851
Oil on canvas, 149 x 255 inches
The Metropolitan Museum of Art, New York
Gift of John S. Kennedy, 1897

24

LARRY RIVERS
Europe I, 1956
Oil on canvas, 72 x 48 inches
The Minneapolis Institute of Arts
Anonymous gift

LARRY RIVERS
Buick Painting with P, 1960
Oil on canvas, 48 x 61 inches
Collection of Mr. and Mrs. Richard Titelman, Atlanta

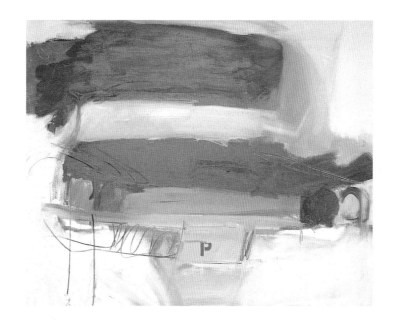

LARRY RIVERS
The Final Veteran, 1960
Oil on canvas, 81 3/8 x 51 inches
Albright-Knox Art Gallery, Buffalo, New York
Gift of The Seymour H. Knox Foundation, Inc., 1961

One point at which Rivers inarguably contributes to the Pop canon is in 1960 with three paintings of the new model Buick. The car is painted in long, low rectangular masses, giving the image of a Mark Rothko painting. The technological content and the levels of reference that conflate a car with an abstract painting have the locked balance of possible meanings characteristic of Pop.[13]

Grace Hartigan, like Rivers, was also to anticipate some aspects of Pop art in her painterly, figurative work of the mid-1950s. In her search for a subject, she turned both to her own neighborhood, and to the use of collaged material from the popular and commercial media. *Billboard* (1957) is a painterly push-pull composition based on a collection of photographs drawn from *Life* magazine advertisements. This patchwork quilt of color and image both exaggerated and recontextualized the source material. *Grand Street Brides* (1954), *Giftware* (1955), and *City Life* (1956), like *Billboard*, are all part of a series of work by Hartigan that brought urban life together with lessons she had learned from de Kooning and from older masters. Working from memory and from photographs that she asked Walter Silver to take of a bridal shop on Grand Street, Hartigan took a contemporary scene and remade it in a manner evocative of Velázquez's *Las Meninas* and Goya's

26

GRACE HARTIGAN
Billboard, 1957
Oil on canvas, 78 1/2 x 87 inches
The Minneapolis Institute of Arts
The Julia B. Bigelow Fund by John Bigelow

Family of Charles IV. As Rivers had in his use of Courbet in *The Studio* and Leutze in *Washington Crossing the Delaware*, Hartigan was extending the gestural painterly vocabulary of the day into the realm of history painting while taking her subjects from the everyday life around her.

She was, however, not a Pop artist. In her historicism and sentimentality, Hartigan's work was only to hint at the next decade's concerns. She recognized this in 1963, with some bitterness:

> *Pop art is not painting, because painting must have content and emotion. It must tell you what it is like to be a human being and have plastic qualities. Pop art is not like other reactions against abstract expressionism, such as the return to the figure, hard edge or even "dada" because they were serious attempts to express an opinion, a belief.*[14]

Hartigan and Rivers remained convinced of the inherent value of creative spontaneity. It was left to Rauschenberg and Johns to take the next and most dramatic leap of faith as to the meaning of painting at the end of the modern era. It was Rauschenberg who most eloquently commented on the nature of gesture and an artist's ability to fake spontaneity, improvisation, and action. The bringing together of the predetermined, controlled, and structured with the illusion of chance and risk is a defining characteristic of

Rauschenberg's work in the fifties and early sixties. On one hand Rauschenberg wants to get lost in the process of creating a work, and on the other hand he wants to make all the decisions.

> *I'd really like to think that the artist could be just another kind of material in the picture, working in collaboration with all the other materials. But of course I know this isn't possible, really. I know that the artist can't help exercising his control to a degree and that he makes all the decisions finally.*[15]

This duality was always clear in Rauschenberg, as Robert Rosenblum noted in 1956:

> Factum I, *for example, is a seemingly random assemblage of* Daily News *catastrophe and Presidential photographs, a dismembered calendar, a ragged fragment of upholstery, etc., all united by equally random paint daubs. But when one discovers its twin,* Factum II, *with its patient, scrupulous duplication of every dribble and tatter, one is forced to admit that the same combination of impulse and*

27

GRACE HARTIGAN
Giftwares, 1955
Oil on canvas, 63 x 81 inches
Neuberger Museum of Art, State University of New York at Purchase
Gift of Roy R. Neuberger

ROBERT RAUSCHENBERG
Factum I, 1957
Combine painting, 61 1/2 x 35 3/4 inches
The Museum of Contemporary Art, Los Angeles
The Panza Collection

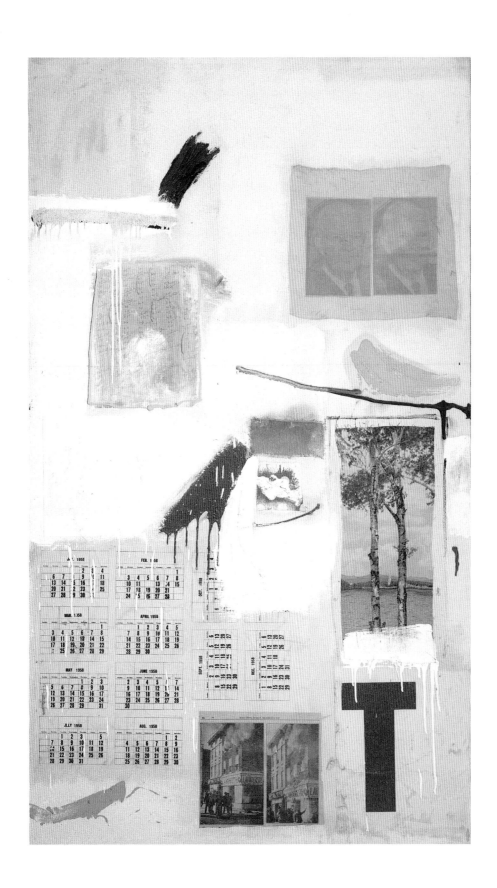

ROBERT RAUSCHENBERG
Factum II, 1957
Combine painting, 61 1/2 x 35 3/4 inches
The Morton G. Neumann Family Collection, Chicago

discipline that produces more conventional pictures is also operating here. And accepting these premises of unreasonable reason, one even finds further nonsensical sense in the paired but not quite identical photographs which recur in these paired but not quite identical paintings…. In fact, these serious practical jokes may yet enrich the very purified climate of painting in the 1950's.[16]

Factum I and *II* address New York School painting in a deliberate and didactically conceptual fashion. As in his previous assault on the New York School, *Erased de Kooning Drawing* (1953), Rauschenberg identified "the problem" and went about "constructing" a situation that best illustrated his point. In *Erased de Kooning Drawing*, one of the heroes of Abstract Expressionism is literally made invisible by the action of a younger artist in erasing his signature archetype, in this case a "woman."

While Rauschenberg's work does in some respects continue the painterly traditions of the 1950s, it does so in a controlled and intellectual manner. He was able to "purge" himself of "his teachers"[17] by placing their style into new non-aesthetic environments. The act of painting is isolated from the complete composition and is contained within the overall grid-like structure. Painting becomes a thing, an object, treated similarly to the collaged/assemblaged elements which are integrated into the dissonant composition. In Rauschenberg's work, objects, photographs, and painted areas are all combined on a non-hierarchial surface. Rauschenberg diagrams the experience of the process in making a painting. *Rebus* (1955), a representation of words or syllables by pictures of objects whose names resemble the intended words or syllables in sound, is also a riddle made up of such pictures or symbols. Rauschenberg was making up games about the New York School and action painting, using the strength and character of the older generation's work to metaphorically break the myth, enigma, and riddle of the New York School.

The control of the artist is implicit in the seriality which Rauschenberg employs in *Factum I* and *II*, *Rebus* (1955), and *Small Rebus* (1956). His repetition of objects, images and, most interestingly, brushstrokes or painterly accidents from one work to another, also implies seriality. *Summer Rental, Summer Rental + 1, Summer Rental + 2*, and *Summer Rental + 3* (all 1960), are four separate works all constituted of similar gestures and marks on identically sized canvases, with the addition of one color for each succeeding work. Rauschenberg knows that any mark or gesture repeated often enough loses its "originality." He takes the brushstroke and makes it one more collaged element, like his repeated use of pinup pictures, pieces of lace, or postcards. What infuriated the painters and critics of the New York School was that painting was now on the

ROBERT RAUSCHENBERG
Erased de Kooning Drawing, 1953
Traces of ink and crayon on paper with mat and hand-lettered
(ink) label in gold leaf frame, 25 1/4 x 21 3/4 inches
Collection of the artist

same level as a found object or collaged photo. What was really "inappropriate" about Rauschenberg's combine paintings was the combination of high abstract painterly style with the found object. If Rauschenberg had kept strictly to collage and assemblage like Joseph Cornell (in the Surrealist tradition) or Richard Stankiewicz (in the New York School tradition) that would have been fine.

Untitled Combine (Man with White Shoes) (1955) is a history painting bringing together a chronology of Rauschenberg's own oeuvre ca. 1950-54 and a nostalgic view of his friends and family while growing up in the South. Contained inside the multidimensional, freestanding painting is a black painting, (ca. 1951), and a combination of a white painting (1951) over a dirt painting (1952) with his own white shoes and socks. There is an outside panel that is reminiscent of the first mature collage and painted works of around 1953. This brief history of Rauschenberg's art is juxtaposed with intimate mementos of his life. Playing art history and personal history off each other, Rauschenberg includes a scrapbook of personal memories. A newspaper clipping of his sister being crowned Queen of the Louisiana Yam, news photos of his parents' silver wedding anniversary, and an article on the same event in which Milton (Robert) Rauschenberg is mentioned as

being an art student in New York City are juxtaposed with a personal letter. Drawings by Jack Tworkov and Cy Twombly, with whom Rauschenberg had traveled two years earlier in Europe and North Africa, are also part of a nostalgic remembrance. Rauschenberg was later to criticize his own work for this nostalgic quality, which he felt detracted from its immediacy.

Interview (1955) compartmentalizes commercial rugs, paisley and striped fabrics, doilies, and colored silks, which are added layer upon layer, with painted passages building up a heavily encrusted surface. *Interview* is a cornucopia of the options available to artists with regards to "style." It includes a rainbow of colors taken directly from paint tubes, juxtaposed with a red, orange, and white, Rothkoesque expanse of color. As in *Rebus*, there is a selection of color swatches (again, the options available to the artist) which form a

Left to right: Jasper Johns, Bill Giles, Ann Moreska,
Robert Rauschenberg, Merce Cunningham, John Cage, at Dillons Bar, New York, 1959
Photo: Fred W. McDarrah

ROBERT RAUSCHENBERG
Untitled Combine (Man with White Shoes), 1955
Combine painting, 86 1/2 x 37 x 26 1/3 inches
The Museum of Contemporary Art, Los Angeles
The Panza Collection
(2 views)

ROBERT RAUSCHENBERG
Interview, 1955
Combine painting, 72 3/4 x 49 1/4 inches
The Museum of Contemporary Art, Los Angeles
The Panza Collection

backdrop to one of the most poetic and magical passages to be found in any Rauschenberg combine, the floating softball with the green-encrusted, weightless fork.

With the creation of *Small Rebus*, one year after *Rebus*, Rauschenberg continues a commentary on his own art. *Small Rebus* is a simplified easel version of the heroically scaled *Rebus*. It is part of Rauschenberg's self-described "pedestrian series," where color and image jostle for attention as people do on a crowded street. Like *Rebus*, *Small Rebus* is divided exactly down the middle by the multicolor painted swatches. This compositional device, along with other formal aspects of *Small Rebus*, are what the two works have in common. Rauschenberg carries the abstract elements from one work to the next, but changes the iconography. In both works the strong horizontal orientation is enforced by the grid-like pattern in which the collaged photographs, postcards, map, fabrics, and diagrammatic drawing are placed. Unlike *Rebus*, *Small Rebus* has less open areas, and is dominated by images and painterly representations of action painting. As was common in several of Rauschenberg's combines, there is a preponderance of images of action and sports. The images include a bullfight, several photographs of gymnasts, and a track event which has been emphasized both

34

by scale and by a painted circle around the runner. The reproduction of a Baroque painting of a woman on the back of a bull is roughly mimicked in the newspaper photo of the bullfight. These two images may be interpreted as a wry commentary on the intersection of art and life, so important to Rauschenberg. Also demonstrated in *Small Rebus* is Rauschenberg's concern with the creative process and time. Included are three diagrammatic drawings — of a clock without hands, musical bars without notes, and a found diagram explaining sensory perception. It is the small diagram which most tellingly reveals Rauschenberg's concern with dismantling the riddle of the creative process.

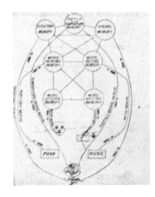

Small Rebus (detail)

ROBERT RAUSCHENBERG
Interior, 1956
Combine painting, 45 1/4 x 46 1/2 x 7 1/2 inches
The Sonnabend Collection, New York

ROBERT RAUSCHENBERG
Hymnal, 1955
Combine painting, 64 x 49 1/4 x 7 1/4 inches
The Sonnabend Collection, New York

ROBERT RAUSCHENBERG
Broadcast, 1959
Combine painting, 61 x 75 x 5 inches
Collection of Kimiko and John Powers, Carbondale, Colo.

In 1959, as gestural abstraction was increasingly perceived by critics as a dead end, both Rauschenberg and Johns, in reverse of the trend, increased the gestural and painterly qualities in their work. *Kickback* (1959) and *Inlet* (1959) are as close as Rauschenberg gets to painterly abstraction in the second half of the 1950s. Rauschenberg was reducing his use of objects. The works were moving from combines (the combination of painting and sculpture) back through collage towards two-dimensional painting. In *Canyon* (1959), an eagle is visually contained within the confines of the picture frame, and in *Inlet*, an egret is placed inside an electrical frame set within the composition. Rauschenberg is forever placing objects and images, marks and gestures, inside or in response to an overall geometric grid. Broad gestures of color don't just happen in response to a formal need but often in sardonic response to a previously placed collaged element. An open zipper bleeds green and black paint, or a white trouser leg becomes a bold slash of red.

36

It was Rauschenberg's neo-Dada junk aesthetic that provoked the loudest reaction, but it was his more measured dialogue between iconography and form that produced a revolutionary change in art's ability to comment on itself and its own making. It was with Jasper Johns that this change became fully evident. Rauschenberg, the artist of action and energy, and Johns, the artist of intellect and concentration, form the bridge between New York School painting and what came after.

Robert Rauschenberg and Laika in Broadway studio, New York, ca. 1961
Photo: Ugo Mulas, courtesy of the artist

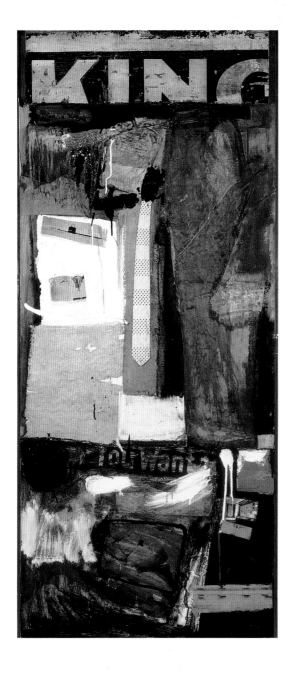

ROBERT RAUSCHENBERG
Kickback, 1959
Combine painting, 76 1/2 x 33 1/4 x 2 3/4 inches
The Museum of Contemporary Art, Los Angeles
The Panza Collection

ROBERT RAUSCHENBERG
Reservoir, 1961
Combine painting, 85 1/2 x 62 1/2 x 14 3/4 inches
National Museum of American Art,
Smithsonian Institution, Washington, D.C.
Gift of S. C. Johnson & Son, Inc.

ROBERT RAUSCHENBERG
Painting with Gray Wing, 1959
Combine painting, 31 x 21 inches
The Museum of Contemporary Art, Los Angeles
The Panza Collection

ROBERT RAUSCHENBERG
Photograph, 1959
Combine painting, 46 3/8 x 54 5/8 x 2 3/4 inches
Collection of Marcia and Irving Stenn, Chicago

ROBERT RAUSCHENBERG
Octave, 1960
Combine painting, 78 x 43 inches
Collection of Mr. and Mrs. Bagley Wright, Seattle

Harold Rosenberg, the critic who invented the term "action painting," understood both the significance of Abstract Expressionism to Johns and his ability to move beyond the breakthroughs of the New York School. "With the values of his predecessors turned inside out, he could make whatever use of their art he chose; to revolt against them became unnecessary."[18] Although Johns was still committed to painterly process, he was also able to announce a new relationship of the artist to process, subject, and the audience. Johns was never against Abstract Expressionism. He claims that early in his career, "he didn't know enough, hadn't seen enough, to make such a response."[19] Knowingly or not, Johns shared an emphasis on process with the Abstract Expressionist painters. While much has been rightly said about the radical break represented by his subject matter — the flags, targets, and numbers especially — less emphasis has been placed on the continuity shown in his revealing of process and his building up of the surface.

With de Kooning, reworking and hesitation signal spontaneity and the unconscious; with Johns, reworking and hesitation signal conceptual deliberation. Johns built up the surface on a predetermined grid,

using process to show the pointlessness of a search for a subject. The use of flags, targets, and numbers provided Johns with recognizable (but overlooked) subjects with which he could comment on issues of abstraction and representation. He avoided the pitfalls of more traditional subject matter (figure, landscape, and still life) — perceived by the avant-garde as a step back from pure abstraction — while still entering into a dialogue about abstract and representational modes. The painterly quality found in Johns's use of encaustic has much in common with the work of the first and second generation Abstract Expressionists.

During the mid-1950s, carefully nuanced paintings by Philip Guston and Milton Resnick had indicated a new direction for Abstract Expressionism. In these works, a more precisely controlled mark was used

JASPER JOHNS
Tango, 1955
Encaustic and collage on canvas with objects, 43 x 55 inches
Private collection

in the formation of Abstract Impressionist compositions. Guston's paintings of 1951-54 were "the sum of their *discrete* visible parts. In this structural candour he can be likened to Pollock in his open drip paintings...."[20] "The calligraphic lightness of these paintings was quickly perceived by other painters as an innovative mode of great promise."[21] However, while Guston's paintings were significant in technical method and surface, they remained essentially a variation on Abstract Expressionism. Their centrally weighted compositions seemed retrograde in comparison to both the allover field-like quality of classic Abstract Expressionism and the flatness of Johns's *Flag* and *Target* compositions. By choosing flat, two-dimensional man-made designs and signs, and having them fill the picture plane from edge to edge, Johns was able to reconnect with classic allover painting. He was able to revitalize an essential and revolutionary aspect of New York School painting while circumventing the issue of subject. By covering the entire picture plane with brushstrokes of equal regularity and intensity, Johns creates a random visual field with no focus. The white area below the flag in *Flag Above White* (1955) is as important as the image of the flag itself, and although the subject of *White Target* (1957) is centrally weighted, the painting is allover in its painterly attributes. Johns works against the central focus of the target to remind us that there is no subject other than the process: "The activity of the brushstrokes is not meant to represent the artist's state of mind while creating the painting; it is meant to provide 'possibilities for the changing focus of the eye.'"[22]

Johns's minimal and unconventional compositions are not arrangements of forms on the surface. They lack a traditional figure/ground relationship. There is no fixed point of reference. Johns's paintings, that is, "offer the awesome simplicity of irreducible colour and shape that presumes the experience of masters like Rothko, Still, and Newman."[23] While the field painters sought a quasi-religious, spiritual quality in their search for universal signs, Johns divorced himself from the basic tenet of Abstract Expressionism. "I didn't want my work to be an exposure of my feelings."[24] He did, nevertheless, paint his first flag after a dream, suggesting a link with Surrealism and early Abstract Expressionism.

In *Tango* (1955), Johns makes a revealing comment on action and field painting. He draws the viewer into the composition with the necessary action of turning the key to activate a music box. In this close proximity the painting becomes a field and the activator/viewer becomes lost in the composition (i.e., like Pollock lost in the action of his own paintings).

> *I wanted to suggest a physical relationship to the picture that was active. In the targets, one could stand back or one might go very close and lift the lids and shut them. In Tango, to wind the key and hear the sound, you had to stand relatively close to the painting, too close to see the outside shape of the picture.*[25]

There is another action in *Tango*; that is, Johns's willingness to reveal the process by which the brilliant blue encaustic was built up, by leaving a strip unfinished along the bottom edge. This suggestion of the artist's hand was an accident which Johns chose to leave. "In painting a large canvas, it was too hard to reach down to the bottom, to bend over. So I just didn't do it. Then when I noticed what I had done, I decided I liked it, and left it."[26] Subsequently, Johns was to employ an unfinished strip along the bottom edge in many pictures, but it was this initial accident that led to a significant pictorial device. Accidents may happen in Johns's work, but his choice to exploit and keep them is a deliberate act of painting. His attitude about accident is quite clear:

PHILIP GUSTON
The Room, 1954-55
Oil on canvas, 71 7/8 x 60 inches
Los Angeles County Museum of Art
Museum Purchase, Contemporary Art Council Fund

41

There are no accidents in my work. It sometimes happens that something unexpected occurs
—the paint may run—but then I see that it has happened, and I have the choice to paint it again or not.
And if I don't, then the appearance of that element in the painting is no accident.[27]

Is there such a world of difference between the "struggle" to find an image (Abstract Expressionism) and the choice to reveal one?

Canvas (1956) was the second painting by Johns to use an object (after *Tango*). The placement of the stretcher bars on the surface of the painting is a reference to making a painting as an object, and the construction, literally and metaphorically, of a picture. By covering the canvas and stretcher in a consistent gray surface, Johns made a painting about nothing except itself. He takes Rothko's square within a field and turns it into an ironic comment on support vs. image and the figure/ground relationship.

Johns skirts the issue of emotionalism implied in color by using his "favorite" color, gray. With Rothko, color connotes emotional state of mind; for Johns that was anathema.

I used gray encaustic to avoid the color situation. The encaustic paintings were done in gray because to
me this suggested a kind of literal quality that was unmoved or unmovable by coloration and thus
avoided all the emotional and dramatic quality of color. Black and white is very leading. It tells you what
to say or do. The gray encaustic paintings seemed to me to allow the literal qualities of the painting
to predominate over any of the others.[28]

Ironically, the gray works exhibit a greater gestural "freedom" than the compositions that use color. After 1958, Johns was to begin to isolate both gesture and color in a deliberate investigation into the properties that make up a picture.

On the heels of the overwhelming success of his first exhibition at the Leo Castelli Gallery in 1958, Johns significantly altered his style in his next body of work. He moved his focus of attention from field painting to gestural abstraction. Expanding his palette to include a wider range of color, the handling of the paint began to take on a dramatically more gestural quality. Increasingly, the work had dripped areas, unfinished edges, and the "free worked" mannerisms of de Kooning's painting.[29] But Johns was able to drain these colorfully "charged" paintings of emotion and outside reference. He was able to do to color what he had done to subject (*Flag*) and support (*Canvas*) previously. There is more to Johns's use of color than Michael Fried's suggestion that he "mocks, not in venom but in loving sadness, the mannerisms of abstract expressionism."[30] Color came to the forefront of Johns's thinking during this period. By placing labels on color, as he did in *False Start* (1958), and subsequently, he was able to retain "the objectness of the painting."[31] By using all the colors equally, without preference, and by literally naming them, Johns was able to find a predetermined method to apply color that was not dictated by the composition.

Johns's dismantling of the myth of spontaneity was furthered by the pairing of color versions with black, white, and gray versions of the same subject. In these paired works, which include *False Start* and *Jubilee* (1959); *Gray Painting with Ball* (1958) and *Painting with Two Balls* (1960); *Map* (1961) and *Map* (1962), it is the paintings without color that consistently appear to have a looser gestural quality, where the process of painting is revealed to a greater degree. Increasingly, as Johns's work became more gestural, it was drained of its emotive and personal potential by his repetition of marks and his inclusion of objects which make the marks, (e.g., a stick, a ruler); "there was an attempt to find a way that gestures would make up an image: the gestures would determine the boundaries."[32]

In *Gray Painting with Ball*, Johns literally split open the picture plane by the insertion of a ball. This act emphasizes the objectness of the canvas, the irony of an artist's desire "to open the picture plane" through pictorial means, and the widely held New York School dictum that "a painting should have balls." In the macho world of the Cedar Bar, a "good" painting had this masculine quality. As Rosalind Krauss notes,

42

The object undoubtedly refers to the myth of masculinity surrounding the central figures of Abstract Expressionism, the admiration for the violence with which they made their attack on the canvas, and the sexual potency read into their artistic acts.[33]

Fool's House (1962) is certainly a still life from an artist's studio, with its large brush-like broom, towel, stretcher-like canvas, and cup for mixing paints. The question Johns undeniably poses is: who's the fool? Johns has said the title of the painting was suggested by a friend's response to Johns's placement of the words "broom," "towel," "stretcher," and "cup" next to their respective objects. This friend stated, "Any fool knows it's a broom."[34] The broom, however, with its large gestural sweep, could also be a not-too-subtle comment on the excesses of New York School painting. Johns was systematically dismantling the heroic myths of the New York School (which nevertheless continued to fascinate him). As Rosenberg notes, "Johns has freely appropriated Abstract Expressionist devices: heavy impasto, impulsive brushing, broad paint strokes, emphasized contours, streaks, smears, drips, the vertical band, one color masses, scraps of newspaper and other matter mixed into the pigment," but in so doing "he turned it inside out" and forever changed the credibility of the New York school.[35] He used their tools to change the rules of the game.

For Johns the brushstroke of a Kline or a Guston is as external a "thing" as the flag or a target. The ends for which he employs Abstract Expressionist devices can be seen as a comment on the end of New York School painting, and the beginning of the end of modernism. Johns announces a new art without ever partaking in it. He anticipates Pop art, but remains a painter in dialogue with and about Abstract Expressionism and the nature of creativity. All of Johns's pictures continued to be hand-painted, unlike those of Rauschenberg, Lichtenstein, and Warhol, among others, who moved towards mechanical methods for imagemaking after 1962. Johns remained firmly committed to the artist's hand, to process, and to a dialogue with Modernism.

While Johns strove to make extraordinary art through "ordinary" objects, Allan Kaprow, the painter, sculptor, critic, and agitator for "unheard of happenings and events,"[36] wanted to use objects for non-aesthetic purposes. Kaprow called for a new artist to "discover out of ordinary things the meaning of ordinariness…not try to make them extraordinary. Only their real meaning will be stated."[37] Kaprow's vivid understanding of Pollock's significance to the next generation was as a "liberator." Pollock was significant for the action implicit in how the works were created. For Kaprow, Pollock's "entire painting comes out at the participant." In a prophetic statement, Kaprow concludes that "objects of every sort are materials for the new art: paint, chairs, food, electric and neon lights, smoke, water, old socks, a dog, movies, a thousand other things which will be discovered by the present generation of artists."[38]

Between 1956 and 1958, Kaprow progressed from New York School-inspired collages to environments and Happenings. Pollock's legacy was reconfigured in literal environments where actual gestures occurred in real time. Kaprow's Happenings keyed well into Claes Oldenburg's continuing interest in theater, which he had carried from Yale to Chicago, and finally to New York. Oldenburg's first Happening was concurrent with the showing of his environment *The Street* at Judson Gallery in February-March, 1960. That vital sense of action and gesture so important to Oldenburg's temporal investigations was also of great significance to the look and technique applied to the objects created for *The Store*. Oldenburg was doing more than mimicking the superficial mannerisms of Abstract Expressionism in his use of enamel paint, drips, splatters, and improvisation. He was imbuing his objects with a liveliness, an urgency, and a sense of their own making which reflected the temporality of a Happening.

Allan Kaprow at Reuben Gallery, New York, 1959
Photo: Fred W. McDarrah

44

ALLAN KAPROW
Caged Pheasant #1, 1956
Collage and paint on canvas, 72 x 60 inches
Collection of the artist

ALLAN KAPROW
Caged Pheasant #2, 1956
Collage and paint on canvas, 60 x 48 inches
Collection of the artist

In retrospect, it is clear that at the outset of his career, his formal conventions were those of Abstract Expressionism and its derivatives. For example, although his Store reliefs, like much of Pop Art, were based on mechanically drawn commercial ads, they bear hardly the slightest resemblance to them; whereas, with their restless contours rising and falling from fluttering, unstable edges, they have many similarities to "action painting."[39]

There is such a preponderance of painterly activity in these works that the action of the drips, splatters, and floods of paint nearly obliterates the highly personal and sometimes erotically charged objects.

The casual application of the paint roughly approximates the rapid and spontaneous method by which the armature/support was made. However, Oldenburg's method of applying paint was evolutionary rather than spontaneous. He would apply layer upon layer of paint, allowing the previous color to dry before applying the next, never allowing the colors to mix, only to show through. Significantly, there is no brushstroke visible on these gestural surfaces; the roughness of the plaster surface provided the "painterliness."

Lately I have begun to understand action painting that old thing in a new vital and peculiar sense —as corny as the scratches on a NY wall and by parodying its corn I have (miracle) come back to its authenticity! I feel as if Pollock is sitting on my shoulder, or rather crouching in my pants![40]

Oldenburg's style, a "realism which copies the posters and the ads instead of the thing itself,"[41] also copies the splashed, splattered, and dripped effect of his New York School predecessors.

Oldenburg and Jim Dine both had their first gallery exhibitions in New York City at Judson Gallery in 1958. Their subjects were commercial, consumer oriented, and popular, but were simultaneously personal, idiosyncratic, and subjective. Through objects drawn from the world, they sought highly charged, animistic, sexually evocative, psychologically loaded, and highly personal representations of themselves. Dine said in 1966, "I'm not a Pop artist [something every artist in this exhibition no doubt has said]. I'm not part of the movement because I'm too subjective... when I use objects, I see them as a vocabulary of feelings."[42] This younger generation of Kaprow, Oldenburg, and Dine had a less direct relationship with the New York School painters. For Oldenburg, the Abstract Expressionists were mythic figures whose telephone numbers he had cribbed and carried with him;[43] for Dine, who was only in his twenties when he had his first success, Kaprow was very influential, and Rauschenberg and Johns "were the most important artists alive."[44]

Dine's willingness to embrace the subjective was in distinction to Johns. His Happenings included dramatic and cathartic reenactments of events from his own life.[45] The emotion that the Abstract Expressionists sought in universal signs of abstraction, Dine sought in the commonplace. Possibly due to the increasingly liberal use of gestural techniques by Rauschenberg and Johns from 1959 on, Dine did not feel any inhibition about exploiting his technical facility to produce painterly effects. For Dine, the break with the New York School was a moot point. "I don't believe there was a sharp break and this [Pop art] is replacing Abstract-Expressionism."[46] And in fact Dine was subsequently to adopt the painterly attitude of the New York School and return to easel painting. For the Abstract Expressionists the delineation of object, figure, and space got in the way of revealing universal signifiers through pure painting. For Dine, the opposite became true. The objects carry the symbolism and expression, and the painterly qualities are the means once removed. "I tie myself to Abstract-Expressionism like fathers and sons.... I work with the vocabulary that I've picked up along the way, the vocabulary of paint application, but also the vocabulary of images."[47]

Unlike Dine and Oldenburg, Roy Lichtenstein had been an active and exhibiting painter since the early 1950s. After 1958 he made a dramatic move towards abstraction and a larger format. However, Lichtenstein could not just make a second generation Abstract Expressionist painting, and complained that "There were no spaces left between Milton Resnick and Mike Goldberg."[48] So with his "rag paintings" he made a painting about Abstract Expressionism. Previously, Lichtenstein had reinterpreted artistic traditions of the nineteenth century, and he was reinterpreting Abstract Expressionist painting before he broke through into a "commercial style" with which he reinterpreted advertising, cartoons, and modern masters.

In a perverse way, Lichtenstein's works of the early 1960s exhibit a keen interest in action. He paints about process and not with it. In *Like New* (1961), before and after views of a hole in a piece of cloth with its repair are presented side by side. The early cartoon paintings of romance and war are "action packed" with water, wind, and explosions. Seeing these works in the context of Lichtenstein's years of "desperate" struggle with an imitation of action painting provides an insight into this critical period of transition in his work. That transition is obviously represented in a series of drawings from 1958-59 that combine Lichtenstein's first use of cartoon characters with loose, freeworked gestural drawing. Like Andy Warhol, who did both hard-edge and painterly versions of his storm doors and Coca-Cola bottles, Lichtenstein was hedging his bets. He was not for the moment able to make the radical move to "low" subjects with commercial technique without at least some acknowledgement to "high" art, i.e., painterly painting.

> I began putting hidden comic images into those paintings, such as Mickey Mouse, Donald Duck, and Bugs Bunny. At the same time I was drawing little Mickey Mouses and things for my children and working from bubble gum wrappers, I remember specifically. Then it occurred to me to do one of these bubble gum wrappers, as is, large, [i.e., like his Abstract Expressionist painting] just to see what it would look like.[49]

Popeye (1961) was a breakthrough picture. Lichtenstein could have appreciated the theme of the skinny little guy, Popeye (i.e., the artist himself), punching out the giant Brutus (i.e., Abstract Expressionism).[50] Lichtenstein's paintings of comics and Warhol's similar work from the same period constitute the first true Pop art.

ROY LICHTENSTEIN
Mickey Mouse I, 1958
India ink and colored pencil on paper, 19 1/8 x 25 inches
Private collection

ROY LICHTENSTEIN
Mickey Mouse II, 1958
India ink on paper, 21 x 19 1/8 inches
Private collection

There is an extraordinary resemblance between the "cartoon" work of Lichtenstein and Warhol in 1960 and 1961, given the difference in their backgrounds, and the fact that they did not meet until 1962, when Lichtenstein had his first one-person exhibition at the Leo Castelli Gallery. They both did paintings of commercial goods and cartoons, including Popeye, and were still maintaining the last vestiges of painterly qualities in their styles. The decisive break with "the rituals of painting"[51] that occurred independently and almost simultaneously in Lichtenstein and Warhol between 1960-62 was the end of an era of transition.

There is an unresolved debate over whether this period of "painterliness" in Warhol's works is "a brief instance of hesitation" or "a parody of Abstract Expressionism,"[52] options that are not mutually exclusive. Warhol encouraged the confusion by keeping both the mechanical and painterly versions of the Coca-Cola and storm door pictures. Similarly, Lichtenstein chose to keep the gestural cartoon drawings of around 1958, although he did destroy a series of paintings from the same period which also included cartoon characters

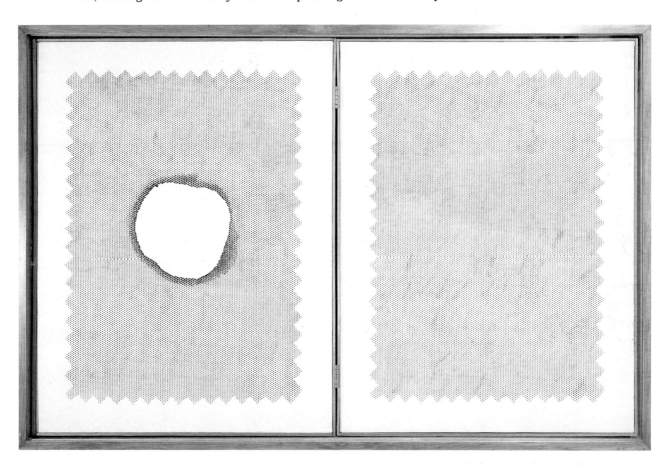

and painterly brushwork. Both Warhol and Lichtenstein were holding back their own desire to create works that had no painterly qualities; although the New York School was obviously on the wane, there remained a nagging need to show that these works were created by a painter.

Because of the missing (destroyed) Lichtensteins, there remains a gap between the gestural drawings with cartoons and the breakthrough works of 1961. This is not the case with Warhol, whose transition is remarkably coherent and linear. In both cases, however, the artists were able to resolve their search for an art that no longer was referential to the painterly and process-oriented tradition of the Abstract Expressionists.

ROY LICHTENSTEIN
Like New, 1962
Oil on canvas, Diptych: 36 x 28 inches each
Collection of Robert and Jane Rosenblum, New York

ROY LICHTENSTEIN
Popeye, 1961
Oil on canvas, 42 x 56 inches
Collection of David Lichtenstein, New York

JAMES ROSENQUIST
Astor Victoria, 1959
Billboard enamel on canvas, 67 5/16 x 82 3/4 inches
Collection of the artist

Schimmel

Lichtenstein and Warhol closed the door that Rivers had opened less than a decade earlier. Whereas Rivers wanted a new meaning to be brought to bear on art, Warhol and Lichtenstein wanted no meaning at all. They wanted to drain all reference to the artist and his struggle out of the composition, leaving the iconography of popular culture to speak for itself.

However, unlike Lichtenstein, whose work after 1962 increasingly eliminated all vestiges of process, Warhol continued to reveal the means by which he created his paintings. In fact, process became an increasingly important subject in his painting, although the process was now overtly mechanical. Through the use of multiple or repeated images, the inconsistency of the screen process was emphasized. Certainly, Warhol could have made a more uniform application of the silkscreened images. Instead, to impersonate paintings, the inconsistency was consciously emphasized. Warhol's continuing use of multiple and seemingly contradictory "styles" emphasized his willingness and ability to reproduce and illustrate style not as personal signifier but as commentary on the nature of painting. "How can you say one style is better than another? You ought to be able to be an Abstract-Expressionist next week, or a Pop artist, or a realist, without feeling you've given

49

up something."[53] It is just that kind of remark that emphasizes how far Warhol had come from the Abstract Expressionist search for style that was of the artist's own making. It was unheard of to think that an artist could "choose" a style and switch back and forth from opposing camps.

Unlike Lichtenstein and Warhol, James Rosenquist seems to have utterly abandoned his Abstract Expressionist "cross between Mark Tobey and Bradley Walker Tomlin"[54] overnight. While earning a living as a billboard painter during the day, at night Rosenquist would create thickly impastoed compositions of "straight and curving lines painted in tones of gray...."[55] Although he was not satisfied with his Abstract Expressionist pictures, this was, in his mind, what "the artist" did, as opposed to his commercial billboard work. Rosenquist would take home leftover paint from his day job and make Abstract Expressionist paintings, but

right: James Rosenquist in front of the Astor Victoria
billboard in Times Square, New York, 1958

far right: James Rosenquist and billboard workers
from the Artkraft Strauss Company, New York, 1958
Photos courtesy of the artist

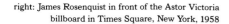

50

JAMES ROSENQUIST
Pushbutton, 1960
Magazine advertisement with tape, pencil, paper, and colored
paper, mounted on paper, 11 1/2 x 13 1/2 inches
Collection of the artist

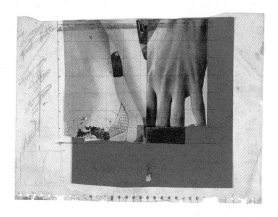

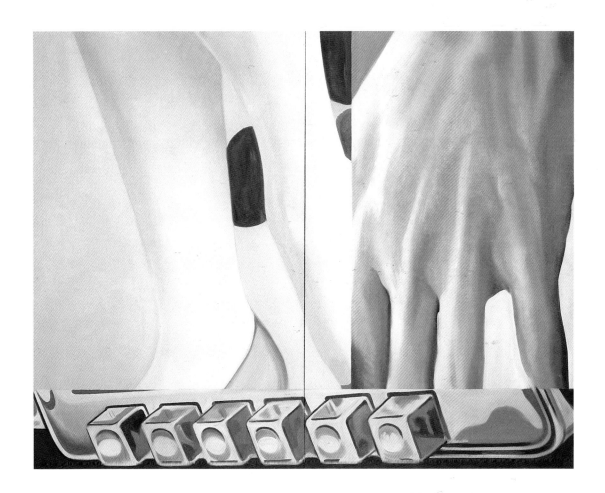

JAMES ROSENQUIST
Pushbutton, 1961
Oil on canvas, Diptych: 82 3/4 x 105 1/2 inches
The Museum of Contemporary Art, Los Angeles
The Panza Collection

JAMES ROSENQUIST
President Elect, 1960
Poster illustration and magazine advertisements with pencil,
paint, masking tape, and paper, mounted on paper, 17 1/2 x 32 inches
Collection of the artist

the memory of what the color had depicted during the day stuck with him. Although he was using the colors abstractly, the paint he had used to paint hops in a beer advertisement was still for him about the subject and not the color.

The first studio painting that Rosenquist executed with popular commercial subject matter was *President Elect*, which he began in 1960, concurrent with his Abstract Expressionist paintings.[56] In this work, he was closer both technically and in choice of subject to his commercial billboard work than he ever would be again. "Employing the sign-painter's techniques, he painted on masonite, used creamy paint, and scaled-up small magazine illustrations."[57] As much as Rosenquist had learned as a commercial artist, he was later to reject homogeneity and straightforward narrative nature in favor of more complex and abstract iconography.

Edward Ruscha's work in advertising, and his personal and professional interest in typography, were essential elements in the development of his style. Like many artists of his generation, Ruscha, while

52

studying "commercial art" at Chouinard Art Institute in Los Angeles, painted in an Abstract Expressionist style influenced by Franz Kline and Willem de Kooning. But for Ruscha, the myth of New York School painting lacked conviction. "They would say, face the canvas and let it happen, follow your own gestures, let the painting create itself. But I'd always have to think up something first. If I didn't, it wasn't art to me.... Whatever I'm going to do is completely premeditated...."[58] By 1957, Ruscha was already aware of Jasper Johns's *Target With*

James Rosenquist in his loft, 1963
Photo: Fred W. McDarrah

JAMES ROSENQUIST
President Elect, 1960-61
Oil on masonite, 84 x 144 inches
Musée National d'Art Moderne, Centre Georges Pompidou, Paris

54

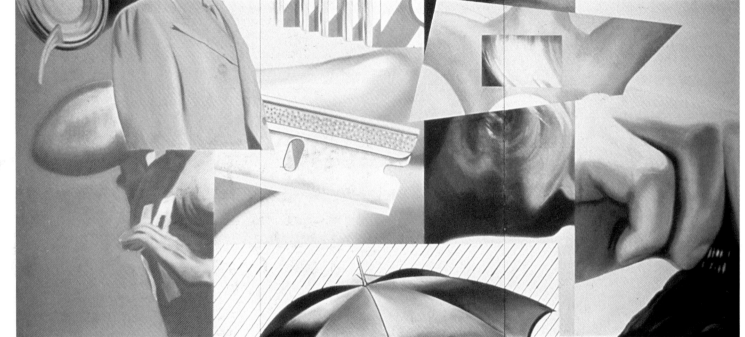

JAMES ROSENQUIST
A Lot to Like, 1962
Oil on canvas, Triptych: 93 x 204 inches
The Museum of Contemporary Art, Los Angeles
The Panza Collection

JAMES ROSENQUIST
I Love You with My Ford, 1961
Oil on canvas, 84 1/2 x 95 inches
Moderna Museet, Stockholm

EDWARD RUSCHA
Dublin, 1959
Wood, newspaper, and ink on paper, 13 1/2 x 13 inches
Collection of the artist

EDWARD RUSCHA
Dublin, 1960
Oil on canvas, 72 x 67 inches
Collection of the artist

Four Faces (1955) from a reproduction in *Print* magazine. Johns's successful evolution away from the New York School was the impetus for Ruscha to become a painter rather than a commercial artist. The notion of premeditation was essential in Ruscha's transformation of an "intuitive" collage, *Dublin* (1959), with its found wood object and cartoon, into a heroically enlarged hand-painted reproduction in 1960. Ruscha assaulted the myth of intuition and chance by his duplication of an intimate artistic meandering. In *E. Ruscha* (1959), a dense patchwork of brushstrokes forms a ground for the artist's name. Ruscha deliberately "premeditates" an accident that forces him to put the "ha" in Ruscha above, with an arrow pointing to his "mistake" that fills the canvas. In *Box Smashed Flat* (1960-61) and *Actual Size* (1962), Ruscha's premeditated methods are applied to illustrate the high velocity splatter of the gestural painters. In *Box Smashed Flat*, drips and splatters escape from under the flattened cardboard box. In *Actual Size*, the painterly splatter of blue in the upper half of the picture is allowed to drip down and create a star-like field across which shoots the flaming, comet-like can of Spam. *War Surplus* (1962) is a laboriously produced illustration of paint loss and cracks on a painted tarp in front of a war surplus store, perhaps again an ironic commentary on the faded glory of action painting.

Ruscha was not alone in creating a West Coast Pop art which incorporated aspects of the painterly influence of the New York School. Joe Goode created a series of field-like expanses of delicately nuanced, monochromatic color that were literally disrupted by the placement of a common object, a milk bottle, in front of the picture plane. The shadow or outline of the bottle is illustrationally inserted in the uniform color field, disrupting the homogenous purity of the otherwise abstract compositions. The influence of Johns on these early works cannot be underestimated. Although he did not have his first Los Angeles exhibition until 1960, the impact was immediate. The pump had been primed through reproductions. Johns's influence can also be seen in the painterly field on which Billy Al Bengston isolated his personal iconography of chevrons, hearts, and motorcycle parts.

EDWARD RUSCHA
Ice, 1961
Oil on paper, 10 3/4 x 12 inches
Collection of the artist

58

EDWARD RUSCHA
U.S. 66, 1960
Oil on paper, 13 1/16 x 13 inches
Collection of the artist

EDWARD RUSCHA
E. Ruscha, 1959
Oil on canvas, 43 1/2 x 43 1/2 inches
Collection of the artist

EDWARD RUSCHA
Heavy Industry, 1962
Oil on canvas, 67 x 71 5/8 inches
Collection of the artist

The impact of the New York School on the West Coast was not limited to Los Angeles. The dialogue between New York and San Francisco was, if anything, even more significant. Both Clyfford Still and Mark Rothko had a direct influence through their presence and teaching at the San Francisco Art Institute. Their pure abstraction was later rejected by a younger generation, including David Park and Richard Diebenkorn, who reintroduced the figure in conjunction with the painterly technique of the Abstract Expressionists. The influence of the Abstract Expressionists by way of the Bay Area Figurative artists was to have a profound impact on the early works of Wayne Thiebaud, who concentrated his love of paint on still life scenes of common objects.

The further we go, geographically and generationally, from the first generation Abstract Expressionists, the more allusive and indirect their influence becomes. The art of Johns and Rauschenberg was

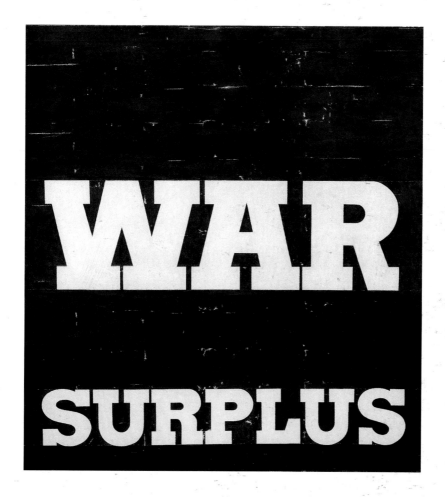

already of greater significance to the generation coming into their own in the early 1960s. No longer were de Kooning or Pollock the yardsticks by which all things were measured. Johns and Rauschenberg rapidly became the connective tissue between eras.

The development of Pop art in relationship to Abstract Expressionism was for the most part evolutionary; the revolutionary aspect of the transition was conceptually rather than stylistically or technically driven. The perceived chasm between these two eras was in fact bridged at many points in a variety of

EDWARD RUSCHA
War Surplus, 1962
Oil on canvas, 71 x 66 3/8 inches
Collection of the artist

EDWARD RUSCHA
Hotel, 1962
Oil on paper, 11 1/2 x 14 1/8 inches
Collection of the artist

EDWARD RUSCHA
Falling But Frozen, 1962
Oil on canvas, 72 x 67 inches
Collection of Tony Shafrazi, New York

EDWARD RUSCHA
Actual Size, 1962
Oil on canvas, 72 x 67 inches
Los Angeles County Museum of Art
Anonymous gift through the Contemporary Art Council

ways. Foremost was the continuing legacy of the painterly, spontaneous, gestural style, used both formally and as a subject in commenting on the process of painting by the emerging generation. For some Pop artists gestural abstraction was a painterly device used to decorate or design the surface; for others it was an illustration of process. For the Happening artists it stood simply for liberation. For Johns and Rauschenberg, gestural abstraction was used simultaneously as commentary on and as part of an abiding concern with the process of painting.

The simplistic view that all Abstract Expressionism is pure subjectivity, and that all Pop art is relentlessly objective and distant, seems myopic now. Just as we are learning to read the traces of specific references in the marks and gestures of the New York School, we are increasingly coming to understand the private and subjective significance of the "public signs" of the Pop artists, most of which were loaded with highly personal and charged meanings.

As the edge softens between these two "movements" in American art, one comes to realize how inadequate (of course) are the generalizations implicit in the very idea of "movements." The terms "Pop art" and "Abstract Expressionism" cover a host of far-ranging styles, qualities, and intentions. The chasm that separates Rosenquist from Johns is larger than that between Johns and de Kooning. The continuity between these seemingly opposite movements becomes increasingly clear with historical distance and more careful analysis of the transitional period.

PETER SAUL
Icebox, 1960
Oil on canvas, 69 x 58 1/2 inches
Courtesy of Frumkin/Adams Gallery, New York

1 Rauschenberg quoted in Calvin Tomkins, *The Bride and the Bachelors: Five Masters of the Avant-Garde* (New York: Penguin, 1976), p. 213.

2 Thomas Hess, *Willem de Kooning* (New York: The Museum of Modern Art, 1974), p. 74.

3 Letter to Alfonso Ossorio, June, 1951, quoted in *Jackson Pollock: Black Enamel Paintings* (New York: Gagosian Gallery, 1990), p. 23.

4 Lawrence Alloway, *American Pop Art* (New York: Macmillan, 1974), p. 16.

5 William Rubin, "Younger American Painters," *Art International* 4, no. 1 (1960): 25.

6 Harold Rosenberg, "The Game of Illusion," *The New Yorker* (November 24, 1962), p. 167.

7 Alan Solomon, "The New Art" (1963), in Carol Anne Mahsun, *Pop Art: The Critical Dialogue* (Ann Arbor, Mich.: UMI Research Press, 1989), pp. 49-50.

8 Alloway, *American Pop Art*, pp. 31-32.

9 Robert Rosenblum, "Pop Art and Non-Pop Art," *Art and Literature* 5, Summer 1964.

10 Fairfield Porter, "Larry Rivers," *Art News* 52, no. 43 (December 1953): 43.

11 Helen Harrison, *Larry Rivers* (New York: Harper and Row, 1984), p. 37.

12 Ibid., p. 42

13 Alloway, *American Pop Art*, p. 21.

14 Quoted in Robert Saltonstall Mattison, *Grace Hartigan: A Painter's World* (New York: Hudson Hills, 1990), from typescript of Hartigan lecture, University of Minnesota, Sept. 2, 1963, Hartigan Papers.

15 Quoted in Tomkins, *The Bride and the Bachelors*, p. 232.

16 Robert Rosenblum, review of Rauschenberg exhibition at Castelli Gallery in "In the Galleries," *Arts Magazine* 32, no. 6 (March 1958): 61.

17 De Kooning, conversation with the author, May 1976.

18 Harold Rosenberg, *The Anxious Object: Art Today and Its Audience* (New York: Horizon, 1964), p. 178.

19 Michael Crichton, *Jasper Johns* (New York: Abrams, in association with the Whitney Museum of American Art, 1977), p. 38.

20 Lawrence Alloway, "Notes on Guston," *Art Journal* 22, no. 1 (Fall 1962): 9.

21 Dore Ashton, *Yes, but . . .: A Critical Study of Philip Guston* (New York: Viking, 1976), p. 101.

22 Roberta Bernstein, *Jasper Johns' Paintings and Sculptures, 1954-1974: "The Changing Focus of the Eye"* (Ann Arbor, Mich.: UMI Research Press, 1985), p. 7. The phrase "the changing focus of the eye" is from Jasper Johns, "Statement," in *Sixteen Americans* (New York: The Museum of Modern Art, 1959), p. 22.

23 Robert Rosenblum, "Jasper Johns," *Art International* 4, no. 7 (September 25, 1960): 76.

24 Crichton, *Jasper Johns*, p. 41.

25 Quoted in ibid., p. 30.

26 Ibid.

27 Ibid., p. 46.

28 Joseph E. Young, "Jasper Johns: An Appraisal," *Art International* 13, no. 7 (September 1969): 50.

29 Castelli stated to the author that Alfred Barr, one of Johns's most significant champions, was surprised by the apparent retreat to the manner of Abstract Expressionism in the new work.

30 Quoted in Barbara Rose, "Pop Art at the Guggenheim," *Art International* 7, no. 5 (May 1963): 21

31 Johns quoted in Crichton, p. 39.

32 Johns quoted in ibid., p. 41.

33 Rosalind Krauss, "Jasper Johns," *Lugano Review* 1, no. 2 (1965): 97.

34 Alan R. Solomon, "Jasper Johns," in *Jasper Johns* (New York: The Jewish Museum, 1964), p. 16.

35 Harold Rosenberg, *The Anxious Object*, p. 178.

36 Allan Kaprow, "The Legacy of Jackson Pollock," *Art News* 57, no. 6 (October 1958): 56.

37 Ibid.

38 Ibid., pp. 55-56.

39 Barbara Rose, *Claes Oldenburg* (New York: The Museum of Modern Art, 1970), p. 9.

40 From Claes Oldenburg notebooks, 1961, quoted in Coosje van Bruggen, *Claes Oldenburg: Just Another Room* (Frankfurt: Museum für Moderne Kunst, 1991), p. 24.

41 Rose, *Claes Oldenburg*, p. 67.

42 John Gruen, "Jim Dine and the Life of Objects," *Art News* 76, no. 7 (September 1977): 38.

43 Van Bruggen, p. 9.

44 Gruen, p. 39.

45 Graham W. J. Beal, *Jim Dine: Five Themes* (Minneapolis: Walker Art Center, 1984), p. 12.

46 Interview by G. R. Swenson, "What is Pop Art?: Answers From Eight Painters, Part I," *Art News* 62, no. 7 (November 1963): 25.

47 Ibid.

48 John Coplans, "An Interview with Roy Lichtenstein" (1963), in John Coplans, ed., *Roy Lichtenstein* (New York and Washington: Praeger, 1972), p. 51.

49 Bruce Glaser, "Oldenburg, Lichtenstein, Warhol: A Discussion" (1966), in ibid., p. 55.

50 Diane Waldman, *Roy Lichtenstein* (New York: Abrams, 1971), p. 25.

51 Benjamin H. D. Buchloh, "Andy Warhol's One-Dimensional Art: 1956-1966," in Kynaston McShine, ed., *Andy Warhol: A Retrospective* (New York: Thames and Hudson, 1989), p. 44.

52 Ibid., p. 42.

53 Swenson, "What is Pop Art?," p. 26.

54 Judith Goldman, *James Rosenquist* (New York: Viking Penguin, 1985), p. 26.

55 Ibid.

56 Telephone conversation with the author, Spring 1991.

57 Judith Goldman, *James Rosenquist: The Early Pictures, 1961-1964* (New York: Rizzoli, in association with Gagosian Gallery, 1992) p. 15.

58 Dave Hickey and Peter Plagens, *The Works of Edward Ruscha* (New York: Hudson Hills Press, in association with the San Francisco Museum of Modern Art, 1982), p. 27.

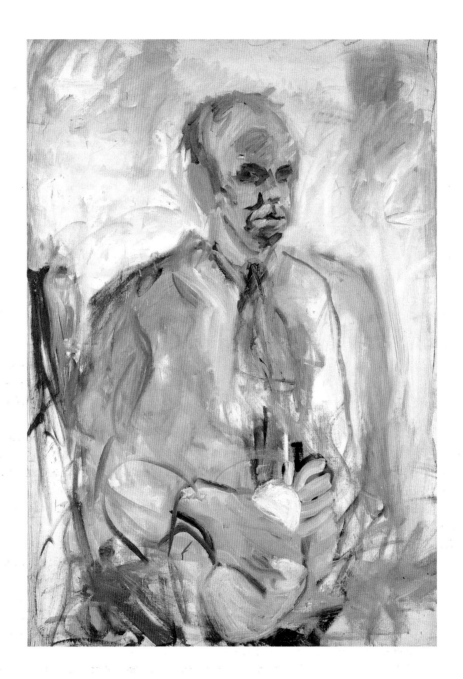

66

CLAES OLDENBURG
Self-Portrait, 1959
Oil on canvas, 68 x 47 1/2 inches
Collection of Claes Oldenburg and Coosje van Bruggen, New York

Donna De Salvo

"Subjects of the Artists": Towards a Painting Without Ideals

The painters of the New York School approached specific subject matter in the hope that it could deliver them from the dominance of European art and American regionalism. They also believed that myth held properties which would enable them to transcend the specifics of the everyday, reaching instead for something much more universal. This was expressed by Adolph Gottlieb and Mark Rothko in a June, 1943 statement in the *New York Times*:

> *It is a widely accepted notion among painters that it does not matter what one paints as long as it is well painted. This is the essence of academicism. There is no such thing as good painting about nothing. We assert the subject is crucial and only that subject matter is valid which is tragic and timeless. This is why we profess spiritual kinship with primitive and archaic art.*

Some time later, Gottlieb recalled

> *some conversations that I had with Rothko* [in 1941] *in which I said...that one of the ways to solve this is to find some sort of subject matter other than that which is around us. Because everyone was painting the American scene — Mark was painting people in subway stations...I said, well, why not try to find a good subject matter like mythological themes?*[1]

Many of the artists to emerge in the period after Abstract Expressionism, however, were to challenge some of the precepts of the New York School by using the subject matter of America itself, a subject matter legitimated by that very movement. By shifting the art world's center from Paris to New York, as Serge Guilbaut has observed, "the avant-garde artists took on both a prestigious past and an image of gravity and seriousness as well as a coherent native tradition, all the things that the new age required."[2] And as Allan Kaprow recalled recently:

> *The idea of American painting interested me because it signified that the model was my own experience as an American. That seemed to me perfectly legitimate instead of looking at models from afar which traditionally had been the case.*[3]

Although Pop art is conventionally seen as cold and distanced, the artists presented here in fact used the commercial symbols of American culture to create their own personal structures of meaning. One of the purposes of this exhibition, then, is an investigation of how the American environment became usable subject matter and of the shift in attitude that led to the emergence of Pop art.

Many of the New York School artists, from Jackson Pollock to Mark Rothko, had previously worked in the regionalist and social realist tradition. While Pollock had studied with Thomas Hart Benton, taking the American landscape as his subject matter in works such as *Going West* (1934-38), Mark Rothko's 1930s drawings of people in subways were inspired by the urban setting. Adolph Gottlieb had studied at New York's Art Students League with John Sloan, a leader of the Ashcan School of realism, as well as with Robert Henri.

Ultimately, these artists grew tired of the figurative and reportorial bases of regionalism; to produce a truly contemporary, truly American art they began to seek, instead, new subject matter — which they found in myth, ideas of the subconscious, and in Native American art (much as members of an earlier Parisian avant-garde had associated themselves with the naive painter Henri Rousseau, and had been fascinated by African and other "primitive" cultural objects in what is now the Musée de l'homme).

This led them, in 1948, to establish the Subjects of the Artists School, to explore primitive and archaic art, in the context of Jung's ideas about "archetypes" and the "collective unconscious." The study of myth and its cultural existence was not limited to artists; it was a subject on the minds of others during the 1940s and 1950s. Serious studies of popular culture and its mythology began to appear. Studies on the myths and rituals of other cultures were even incorporated into the curricula of some schools, such as the course in pictorial design given at the Carnegie Institute of Technology in Pittsburgh. As a student there, Andy Warhol was required to study Ruth Benedict's *Patterns of Culture* (1934), which investigated different "primitive civilizations."[4]

The platform of the Subjects of the Artists School, however, contained some contradictions. Gottlieb simultaneously affirmed the physical nature of the painted surface ("We are for flat forms because they destroy illusion and reveal truth") while at the same time elevating painting to a spiritual level by calling for subject matter "which is tragic and timeless." Given the horrors of World War II, it is not surprising that these artists might be attracted to something that held out the possibility of transcendence.[5]

From an examination of American art in the 1950s, it is clear that questions of subject matter, and especially the function of myth, were demanding increasing attention. It is also clear that while one generation was rising to international prominence, another was beginning the experimentation that would lead to a new language of art making.

Willem de Kooning, who was born in 1904 and emigrated to the United States in 1926, was a leading figure in New York School painting. In February, 1951, he was invited to present a paper for a symposium entitled "What Abstract Art Means to Me." Only two years later, however, in March of 1953, he was to exhibit his famous *Woman I*, the first of a series of five paintings in which he aggressively returned to the figure. His fascination with the advertising, commercial art, and consumer products of America, which he found "romantic, vulgar, and in its own way poignant," found expression in his collages which utilized a woman's mouth from a cigarette ad. "I put the mouth more or less in the place where it was supposed to be. It always turned out to be very beautiful and it helped me immensely to have this real thing. I don't know why I did it with the mouth. Maybe the grin — it's rather like the Mesopotamian idols."[6]

This, then, was the context, in 1953, for the appearance of Larry Rivers's *Washington Crossing the Delaware* — a painting that ushered in a new approach to subject matter by ironically upholding the mythological instincts of Abstract Expressionism. Rivers's painting was based on the 1851 work of the same name by the German academic painter, Emanuel Leutze. Leutze's painting was well known through reproductions in grammar school textbooks[7] and through a special exhibition in 1952 marking the 175th anniversary of the event, which received massive attention from the press. Rivers has said,

> *I wanted to make a work of art that included some aspects of national life, and so I chose* Washington Crossing the Delaware.... *Year after year, as a kid in school, you see these amateurish plays that are completely absurd but you know they represent patriotism — love of country, so there I am choosing something that everybody has this funny duality about.*[8]

Prior to embarking on his journey through the American past, Rivers had turned to European models. In 1951, he had painted *The Burial*, based on Courbet's *Burial at Ornans* (1859), as well as on memories of his own grandmother's funeral. His choice evolved from a desire to find American counterparts for his European heroes. He had read Leo Tolstoy's *War and Peace*, and remembered, "I tried to think of a work that would have that kind of general recognition to everybody and put some little thing that was personal on top."[9] Of his reasons for making the work, Rivers has said he

> *was angry enough to want to do something no one in the New York art world would doubt was disgusting, dead, and absurd. So, what could be dopier than a painting dedicated to a national cliche* —Washington Crossing the Delaware. *The last painting that dealt with George and the rebels is hanging in the Met and was painted by a coarse German nineteenth-century academician who really loved Napoleon more than anyone and thought crossing a river on a late December afternoon was just another excuse for a general to assume a heroic, slightly tragic pose. He practically put you in the rowboat with George. What could have inspired him I'll never know. What I saw in the crossing was quite different. I saw the moment as nerve-racking and uncomfortable. I couldn't picture anyone getting into a chilly river around Christmas time with anything resembling hand-on-chest heroics.*[10]

During the years of the Cold War there was a great desire for patriotic art. But Rivers was not interested in glorifying this event. Rather, he broke down the stereotypical view of Washington's river crossing—and also, one might say, of the idea of painting itself as a heroic act.

The response to the painting was mixed. In fact, Rivers equated his own act with the appearance of Marcel Duchamp's *Fountain* (ca. 1917), saying he had made it not to outrage the general public, "but for the painters."[11] Rivers's friend, the painter Grace Hartigan, commented that the difference between herself and Larry Rivers was that "Larry was an entertainer, he played to an audience."[12] This self-conscious awareness of the audience would play a major role in the art which developed during this period, especially in the work of Jasper Johns and Robert Rauschenberg. Clearly, the hermeticism of the New York School was being undermined by Rivers and these other artists.

69

It was not only Rivers's use of a figurative reference, however, that angered other painters. Willem de Kooning had already created his influential paintings of Women (1949-54), uniting representation with the painterly mark. It was the complete and total irreverence of Rivers's work, especially in the context of paintings that aspired to transcendental heights, which was so provocative. Gottlieb and Rothko thought World War II the single most important event in their lifetime, and had used mythological themes to create an art that spoke to some ancient form of the past as one way of dealing with the war's horror. Newman's attitude toward Northwest Coast Indian art was reverential. Rivers had deliberately turned to an American historical past and instead of finding it elevating, had discovered something corny and dumb.

This attitude toward the event as being less than ideal is seen in his decision to fragment, rather than unify, Washington and his men. By setting Washington apart from his troops, the painting takes on a disjunctive quality, each figure occupying a separate, but independent space. The once heroic figures appear rather bereft, if not comic, making possible a reading of the painting as a cartoon rather than as the bombastic history painting that was its model. Two years earlier, Roy Lichtenstein (who had been teaching in Ohio) had also produced a painting on the same theme; though his piece lacks the formal sophistication of Rivers's—at this point Lichtenstein was still using a style indebted to Pablo Picasso—he too felt the urge to call into question an American past through the symbols that represented it.[13]

Despite the choice of subject, however, there is some continuity between Rivers and other artists of the New York School. Aware of the avant-gardist dismissal of realism as retrograde, Rivers slightly obscured the painting in a field of expressive brushwork. The freshness with which he approached his subject, the

Larry Rivers in his studio, ca. 1959
Photo: Walt Silver

quickness of his brushstroke, the energy with which he articulates the surface, are decidedly and emphatically about the moment. It is part of the ironic texture of the painting that this spontaneous freshness is expended on a theme so rooted in the past, and so in tune in some ways with the years of McCarthyism.

Grace Hartigan was a close friend of Rivers and, like him, had studied with Hans Hofmann. (They also shared an interest in the work of poets such as Frank O'Hara). Although she was more interested in the notion of a European past (de Kooning was important to her not only because he showed "a new way to paint," but also because he represented something meaningful about the past), her work shows a clear desire to find subject matter in the specifics of everyday life. This was important to her, since "the notion of both continuation and invention, tradition and newness, had remained essential...."[14] She frequently used reproductions of old masters as she felt she "had to paint my way through art history."[15]

In 1954, she began the first of her paintings dealing with the urban environment, *Grand Street Brides*, which was based on another kind of reproduction, a photograph taken by a friend of a bridal shop window on Grand Street, on New York's Lower East side — a store Hartigan saw every time she left her studio. Although drawn from her city neighborhood, the painting pays homage to the School of Paris; Hartigan's brides have the appearance of primitive figures; they could even be compared with Picasso's *Les Demoiselles d'Avignon* (1907). She continued to use imagery taken from the street, and, in 1955, completed *Giftwares*, another store window that featured kitschy items, especially cheaply made household goods. This work signals a more abstract direction in her work, which would heighten in paintings such as *Billboard* (1957).

There were other ways in which artists were investigating subject matter. Jean Follett was clearly interested in certain notions of the primitive as practiced by the Abstract Expressionists, but towards decidedly different ends. Though her name is little known today, her work is remembered with enthusiasm by a number of artists, including James Rosenquist, Allan Kaprow, and Jim Dine, all of whom found her work highly original, especially because of her use of objects.[16] Follett, like Kaprow, exhibited regularly at the Hansa Gallery in the 1950s and, like Rivers and Hartigan, had studied with Hans Hofmann.

Also like Kaprow, and later Dine, Follett would come to violate the purity of the painting surface by making wall pieces — "painting-objects" — of tools, machine parts, pieces of wood, cotton, and other items attached to plywood, most often painted black. A practice once restricted to paint alone was now expanded to include a number of rather unglamorous materials, in an "aesthetics of junk." Still, like the New York School painters, Follett was interested in the art object as a metaphor for the inner self. The critic Fairfield Porter wrote of her work, "She finds faces everywhere, she animates everything....Her constructions...do not look the way the world looks, though they are put together from the shabbier aspects of city detail. She makes visible equivalents for the invisible contents of her mind."[17]

It should further be noted that Follett's choice of subject matter, which focused on women, is deserving of much further study, as is the role that women painters in general played throughout the fifties and especially during the sixties. Artists like Martha Edelheit, Lettie Eisenhower, Roslyn Drexler, Niki de Saint-Phalle, and Marjorie Strider have been omitted from most studies of the period. Roslyn Drexler's work, in particular, demonstrates the different uses to which images derived from mass culture could be put. Rather than depict women as pinups, as so many male painters did, Drexler subverted these same images to produce paintings that tell of another reality, that of domestic violence.

Follett approached her objects with an anthropomorphic eye, creating mythological creatures such as *Lady with the Open Door Stomach* (1955). While the woman somewhat resembles the ancient fertility symbol, the Venus of Willendorf, her hinged stomach offers a different view of the pregnant female, a robotic look at the fecund. The appearance of this work in the context of a decade dominated by the "machismo" of male painters is all the more surprising.

Jean Follett and Dick Bellamy at Reuben Gallery, New York, 1959
Photo: Fred W. McDarrah

JEAN FOLLETT
Lady with the Open Door Stomach, 1956
Painted wood, gravel, and metal, 46 3/4 x 48 x 3 inches
Whitney Museum of American Art, New York
Purchase, with funds from an anonymous donor

JEAN FOLLETT
Many-Headed Creature, 1958
Assemblage: light switch, cooling coils, window screen, nails,
faucet knob, mirror, twine, cinders, etc., on wood panel
24 x 24 x 4 3/4 inches
The Museum of Modern Art, New York
Larry Aldrich Foundation Fund, 1961

JIM DINE
Five Maroon Rope Pictures, 1961
Oil on canvas with rope, Five panels: 24 x 20 inches each
Private collection

The work that was to emerge in the period after Abstract Expressionism, sometimes labeled proto-Pop, offered a redefinition of the ideas of self to include the context of the artists' daily lives, a context that the Abstract Expressionists had always attempted to transcend. Jim Dine and Claes Oldenburg would make the specifics of the city and the street the source of their art. Like Follett, they would use objects as surrogates for the self. But they would be more literal still: they would search the street for materials, exalting the discard they found in garbage cans.

In an article, "The Legacy of Jackson Pollock," which appeared in 1958, two years after Pollock's death, Allan Kaprow wrote

> The "Act of Painting," the new space, the personal mark that builds its own form and meaning, the endless tangle, the great scale, the new materials, etc. are by now clichés of college art departments. The innovations are accepted. They are becoming part of text books.[18]

In his article, Kaprow attempted to come to terms not only with Pollock's death, but with the ideas introduced in his work.

> You do not enter a painting of Pollock's in any one place (or hundred places). Anywhere is everywhere and you can dip in and out when and where you can.... (Though there is evidence pointing to a probably unknowing slackening of the attack as Pollock came to the edges of his canvas, he compensated for this by tacking much of the painted surface around the back of his stretchers.) The four sides of the painting are thus an abrupt leaving-off of the activity which our imaginations continue outward indefinitely, as though refusing to accept the artificiality of an "ending."... But this type of form allows us just as well an equally strong pleasure in participating in a delirium, a deadening of the reasoning faculties, a loss of "self" in the Western sense of the term. It is this strange combination of extreme individuality and selflessness which makes the work not only remarkably potent, but also indicative of a probably larger frame of psychological reference.[19]

And in a final comment that could stand as a manifesto for the Pop generation, he continued:

> Pollock, as I see him, left us at the point where we must become preoccupied with and even dazzled by the space and objects of our everyday life, either our bodies, clothes, rooms, or, if need be, the vastness of Forty-Second Street. Not satisfied with the suggestion through paint of our other senses, we shall utilize the specific substances of sight, sound, movements, people, odors, touch. Objects of every sort are materials for the new art: paint, chairs, food, electric and neon lights, smoke, water, old socks, a dog, movies, a thousand other things which will be discovered by the present generation of artists.... The young artist of today need no longer say "I am a painter" or "a poet" or "a dancer." He is simply an "artist."[20]

73

This desire to find specific references can still be sensed in a recent comment by Claes Oldenburg. "I also had this theory that Abstract Expressionism is related to the surfaces of the city and it's kind of a thin line between what you see on the streets and what you see in the paintings."[21] And Jim Dine similarly remarked, "The city is so painterly. Everything is pentimento, every ...wall."[22]

Clearly, with the accomplishments of artists like Rivers, Johns, and Rauschenberg, this new generation had even greater freedom for experimentation. In fact, their works reflect a nearly microscopic examination conducted on a giant scale. Whether in a close-up of *Hair* (1960), or a *Red Bandana* (1961), Jim Dine produced works that were characterized by their unabashed directness, yet expressed in the formal language of the painterly field. Like Follett, he too used real objects to make paintings, in his quest to return painting from its previous ethereal heights. A more conceptual work than some of the artist's others demonstrates how important this was to Dine: in *Five Maroon Rope Pictures* (1961), five canvases each are depicted with a color chart at the bottom (a motif that appears elsewhere in the artist's work), but he has also attached ropes to each one, as if they were balloons that required tethering so as to not float away. Like Follett, Dine posited his "objects" as metaphors for the self. He produced, as Oldenburg had before him, a series of introspective self-portraits. Dark and brooding, they bear the influence of European models. These early works are revealing in their evolution from conventional self-portraiture to a combination of portrait and object (see *Checkerboard*, 1959), to object alone (see *Green Suit*, 1959, and *Flesh Tie*, 1960).

First Kaprow with Robert Whitman, then later Dine and Oldenburg, were to engage in the practice of "Happenings," many taking place at the Reuben Gallery. These events were to serve as a kind of testing ground for their ideas. Staged in makeshift rooms, with handmade props, these performances brought the spectator directly into the work of art. Using elements important to later developments, (such as the willingness to deliberately abstract information from its narrative contexts), these artists experimented with different ways of organizing information. Rather than relying on the structures of information found in traditional theater, in which a series of contiguous events create an overall narrative, they allowed a series of seemingly unrelated events to happen one after another.

JIM DINE
The Red Bandana, 1961
Oil on canvas, 62 x 54 inches
Private collection, New York

JIM DINE
Green Suit, 1959
Oil and cloth, 62 x 24 inches
Private collection, New York

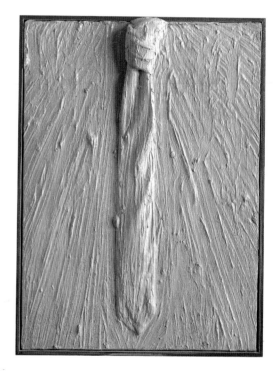

JIM DINE
The Checkerboard, 1959
Oil and collage on checkerboard, 18 1/4 x 18 1/4 inches
Private collection, New York

JIM DINE
Flesh Tie, 1961
Oil on canvas, 16 x 22 inches
Collection of Jasper Johns, New York

JIM DINE
The Blonde Girls, 1960
Oil, charcoal, and rope, 2 panels: 78 x 50 inches each
Collection of Sarah Goodwin Austin, New York

JIM DINE
Black Zipper, 1962
Oil and mixed media on canvas, 96 x 72 inches
The Sonnabend Collection, New York

JIM DINE
The Valiant Red Car, 1960
Oil on canvas, 53 x 132 inches
National Museum of American Art, Smithsonian Institution, Washington, D.C.
Gift of Mr. and Mrs. David K. Anderson, Martha Jackson
Memorial Collection

78

Jim Dine, "Car Crash" performance
at Reuben Gallery, New York, 1960
Photos: Fred W. McDarrah

Dine's 1960 performance, "Car Crash," raised questions about the difference between real and imagined experience. The performance had been preceded by a series of actual events. In the summer of 1959, he and his family had experienced a car crash, and a close friend had died in one. Dine produced a series of drawings, both before and after the performance. The environment at the Reuben Gallery in early November 1960 has been described as follows:

> ...the visitor found himself in a small room, the walls of which were solidly lined with drawings and paintings by Dine. All of the works contained crosses — usually the blocky symbol of the Red Cross — and some had tirelike circles. The white, freshly painted display room was simple, neat and clean.... Several large cardboard crosses hung from the ceiling.... Everything else in the room was white. Paint had been splashed and splattered on the walls, and sections which were not solid white were covered by a fine white grid of vertical drips.[23]

 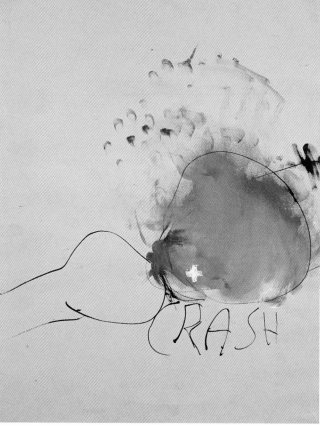

The artist claims that the Happening and the real life events were not related. The drawings exist as some kind of evidence, but who knows of what? Dine was also to produce a painting, *The Valiant Red Car* (1960), a work that signaled future works that would extend the notion of environment. A field of crosses and the words "The Valiant Red Car" make this work read as a billboard, one which memorializes this particular car. (This is a theme Warhol would explore further in his 1963 *Disaster* series).

JIM DINE
Crash Drawing with White Cross #2, 1959
Ink and gouache on paper, 25 1/2 x 19 1/2 inches
Private collection, New York

JIM DINE
Crash Drawing with White Cross #1, 1959
Ink and gouache on paper, 25 1/2 x 19 1/2 inches
Private collection, New York

The Happening was also an important experience for Claes Oldenburg, who arrived in New York in 1956, fresh from a stint in Chicago as a reporter. This first-hand experience covering the streets of Chicago offered a foundation for his aesthetic experimentation in New York. His strong interest in realism attracted him to the work of Chicago writers Nelson Algren and James Farrell, as well as the painter Reginald Marsh. He produced a series of realistic illustrations for *Chicago* magazine, including an untitled illustration (1955) and *Skid Row Figure* (1957).

Oldenburg would find another form to pursue his direct observations of the street. Through the mythic persona of Ray Gun, he offered startling dictums of his stated intent to "make hostile objects human." Oldenburg claims to have had little interest in the purely formal. Allying himself instead with the work of the French artist, Jean Dubuffet, he investigated the primitive. As Barbara Rose writes:

> *Feeling himself drawn by conflicting urges, he decided not to avoid the issue of the contradictions within his personality but to make an art based on oppositions — an art of inherent paradox.... Rather than ignoring his personal conflicts, he determined to "revel" in contradiction.*[24]

Speaking through Ray Gun again, Oldenburg declared his impatience with the limitations of painting: "We are just a little tired of four sides and a flat surface....Painting calms man down and soothes him," whereas

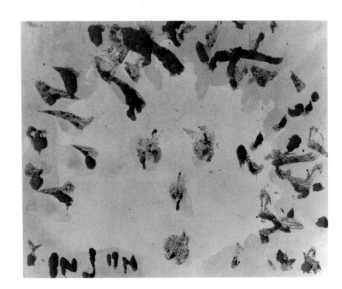

Ray Gun saw man as "only alive when he is...solving situations."[25]

Therefore, not only did notions of past and of everyday experience become usable as subject matter, these artists also exploited work itself — the sign painting, illustration, and drafting that some of them did to get by. By so doing, they drew the visual language of commercial culture into the realm of high art. James Rosenquist, for example, incorporated the lessons of scale he learned from his job as a commercial sign painter. (Before he began his Pop paintings, he produced a body of abstract work, including drawings based on Indian symbols;[26] that he, as well as Lichtenstein and even Warhol, felt the need to make abstract paintings as late as 1959 reflects the continuing dominance of Abstract Expressionism.) And if commercial art was a valid avenue to explore, where would the process end?

CLAES OLDENBURG
"Ray Gun Poster"—U.S. Death Heart #2, 1960
Monoprint, 17 3/4 x 11 7/8 inches
Collection of Claes Oldenburg and Coosje van Bruggen, New York

CLAES OLDENBURG
INJUN Poster, 1961
Monoprint, 13 15/16 x 17 inches
Collection of Claes Oldenburg and Coosje van Bruggen, New York

CLAES OLDENBURG
Untitled (Illustration for *Chicago* Magazine), 1955
Charcoal on paper, mounted on cardboard with masking tape
6 3/8 x 7 inches
Collection of Claes Oldenburg and Coosje van Bruggen, New York

81

CLAES OLDENBURG
Skid Row Figure, 1957
Ink on paper, mounted on cardboard, 10 3/4 x 5 1/2 inches
Collection of Claes Oldenburg and Coosje van Bruggen, New York

CLAES OLDENBURG
Study for an Homage to Céline and Dubuffet, 1959
Pencil on paper, 11 x 8 1/2 inches
Collection of Claes Oldenburg and Coosje van Bruggen, New York

Thus, Roy Lichtenstein could make the leap from paintings of American history to drawings of Mickey Mouse and Bugs Bunny. Lichtenstein also produced a series of paintings based on these themes, although he later destroyed them.[27] Experimenting with a variety of styles and subjects throughout the late 1940s and into the 1950s, Lichtenstein's work reveals the distinct influence of European modernism, and particularly of Paul Klee, Joan Miró, Pablo Picasso and Paul Cézanne; in fact he would literally trace themes from some of these artists' works. In many of them, he articulated "types" of individuals, such as *The Angel, The Cook, The Musician* and *The Street Workers.* By 1948, however, he had produced the first of many works to quote American history paintings.

Like Rivers, he had tackled Leutze's *Washington Crossing the Delaware.* Painted some two years earlier than Rivers's version it showed none of that work's formal sophistication, but quoted instead all the influences of European modernism. A 1954 review of an exhibition featuring some of these history paintings, written by the critic and painter Fairfield Porter and called, "Lichtenstein's Adult Primer: There's Fantasy in the Abstract," said of them,

> *His subject is whatever part of civilization it may be that once was or now is prominently presented to him as significant. He paints a version of an American historical painting as reproduced in a grammar school text book; Indians; Hell's Angels; and, lately, versions of engineers, blueprints of machine*

> *details, assemblies and sub-assemblies, from his experience as a mechanical draftsman. His life as a schoolboy, soldier, teacher of art and machine designer are all in his paintings.*[28]

Although it is one of his earliest "history" paintings, his version of Charles Willson Peale's 1802 work, *Exhuming the Mastodon,* might be considered in a similar light to Peale's original. Peale used this event as a metaphor for the discovery of an American history. The concept of an American past has always been problematic, and in many ways this was no less the case for Lichtenstein than it was for Peale. Lichtenstein would continue to use sources from the American past, searching through the *Album of American History* to make paintings of Captain Stephen Decatur and Isaac Hull and *The Last of the Buffalo.*

It was not until 1960, after his acquaintanceship with Kaprow, Dine, George Segal, and Robert Watts, that Lichtenstein began the comic strip paintings that came to be known as Pop. For them, he could freely draw on his experience as a former draftsman and designer.

82

ROY LICHTENSTEIN
Washington Crossing the Delaware II, ca. 1951
Oil on canvas, 26 x 32 inches
Private collection

ROY LICHTENSTEIN
Indian in Canoe, 1958
Oil on canvas, 30 x 40 inches
Private collection

Much has been written about the formal aspects of Lichtenstein's work, particularly the move, after 1960, toward a cooler, more mechanistic surface. In the late 1940s, he had experimented with many approaches, reflecting interests in Cubism, Surrealism, Expressionism, and finally abstraction. As late as 1958, he had felt compelled to make abstract paintings, but ones which have a look of premeditation, reflecting the mannered, self-conscious state of painting.

Although his 1958 drawings of Bugs Bunny and Mickey Mouse possess the agitated marks of expressionist paintings, they would soon give way to the flat, mechanical surfaces seen in *The Grip* (1962). However, Lichtenstein would never abandon the language of the painter. At a recent lecture, he referred to his painting of a golf ball as "a collection of marks."

Just as Lichtenstein had approached history paintings, in which a moment crystallizes, he went on to seek modern day equivalents. Thus, a ringing phone is translated into a diagram (*Ring-Ring*, 1961), and food is simplified into series of lines and circles, such as *Turkey* (1961), *Swiss Cheese* (1962), and later

Standing Rib (1962). All these paintings have in common a language of visual symbols that is easily understandable, as in advertisements. *Curtains* (1962), for instance, is recognizable without any descriptive text, much like the international symbol which indicates "stop." More complicated images, such as *Woman With Refrigerator*, reveal Lichtenstein's understanding of the manipulative aspects of advertising and the systems of myths on which it functions. In *Woman With Refrigerator*, a broadly smiling woman, who supposedly should stand for all women, is cheerily cleaning the refrigerator, demonstrating that such an activity can surely be fun.

ROY LICHTENSTEIN
Ring-Ring, 1961
Oil on canvas, 24 x 16 inches
Courtesy of James Goodman Gallery, New York

ROY LICHTENSTEIN
Curtains, 1962
Oil and magna on canvas, 68 3/4 x 58 1/2 inches
The Saint Louis Art Museum
Gift of Mr. and Mrs. Joseph Pulitzer, Jr.

It is in the work of Andy Warhol, though, where subject matter is manipulated to achieve the greatest number of meanings. This is due in large part to Warhol's intimate understanding of the mechanics of advertising and the language of commercial art. For throughout the 1950s Andy Warhol held what might be seen as two careers—a fashion illustrator by day and a painter by night. Warhol arrived in New York City from his native Pittsburgh in 1949, the same summer in which Jackson Pollock was featured in *Life* magazine. As a student at the Carnegie Institute of Technology in the late 1940s, Warhol, like Lichtenstein, became acquainted with the languages of painter and designer.[29] His studies in pictorial design, where he excelled at illustration, led him to his first job after graduation, doing fashion illustrations in New York.

During the 1950s, Warhol became well acquainted with the goings on in the New York art world through his frequent visits to the Martha Jackson, Tibor de Nagy, Sidney Janis, and Kootz galleries. Although stories are legendary about his 1958 purchase of a light bulb drawing by Jasper Johns, it was his interest in the work of Larry Rivers that would have the greatest early influence on his art.[30] Asked how he began making his first Pop paintings, Warhol was typically disarming:

> Well, I was just doing advertising and stuff like that and then, how did it all happen? I just loved Larry Rivers's stuff and I used to go and try to buy some of it and it was always too expensive.... Larry had a lot to do with it.[31]

Warhol's preference for narrative over the abstract would naturally have led him to an artist like Rivers. Like Rivers, he also admired drawing, and Warhol's love of this can be seen in the thousands of line drawings completed during the 1950s. In spite of this interest, however, he would increasingly turn to commercial techniques, producing a painting using photostatic machines as early as 1951.

For a 1955 painting, *Girls and Boys*, Warhol traced images from magazines and superimposed them over a background of broad and consolidated gestures. Neither the palette used, nor the subject matter, had anything to do with the New York School. It is in a reading of the painting's content that we can begin to see the results of Warhol's intuitive juxtaposition of ready-made images. Two groups of children, one each of girls and boys, are placed at either end of the canvas. The distance created between the subjects becomes as much a part of the content as the subjects themselves. *Two Heads* (ca. 1957) is constructed in the same way. In this painting, Warhol has already begun to translate some of the stylistic attributes of Abstract Expressionism into pattern, a pattern used to slightly obscure or camouflage his subjects. Perhaps as a gay man in the 1950s, Warhol grew adept at constructing a language of signs and symbols which could live two simultaneous lives, one public, the other private.

Already in his early work, the use of a mythological structure is evident, but rather than the Abstract Expressionists' search for the timeless and universal, Warhol began to use a highly personal and specific mythology drawn from his everyday experience in the world. In one of his commercial efforts, for instance, a

86

ANDY WARHOL
Girls and Boys, ca. 1955
Oil and ink on canvas, 39 3/4 x 48 inches
Dia Center for the Arts, New York

ANDY WARHOL
Dick Tracy, 1960
Casein and crayon on canvas, 48 x 33 7/8 inches
Private collection

series of window displays for the Bonwit Teller department store in New York, Warhol focused on perfumes for a Spring 1959 promotional. Although each of the fragrances had an individual aroma, he chose a pattern to unite the windows—a heraldic crest, ancient symbol of aristocracy and quality. For the perfume Carnet de Bal (Dancecard) he drew within the crest, on a white background, several groups of dancers. As a store window must catch the eye of as many passersby as possible, Warhol selected images that would reach a range of customers. For the well-heeled Bonwit's shopper, he included a group of dancers that quoted Matisse's *The Dance* (hanging just a few blocks away at the Museum of Modern Art). To others who did not know the reference, they still read as dancers. He also included a mock page labeled "My Diary," in which was written, "Dear Diary, I danced with 26 boys named sam and one blue edgar." This caption opened the drawing up to yet other interpretations, with the gender and sexuality of the viewer determining the meaning. Warhol often created images that read as encoded messages for his friends in the fashion community, many of whom were gay. (Just as for his shoe clientele he had created gold shoes dedicated to Kate Smith, Judy Garland, and Diana Vreeland.)[32]

That Warhol understood the language of commercial symbols so well is no longer surprising, now that there is better understanding of his career in the advertising world.[33] However, unlike the illustrations that appeared in *Vogue* and *Harpers Bazaar*, upscale publications that featured illustrations artistically labeled "line art," the graphics of mass consumerism were anonymous.[34] Recognizing the implicit power held by this subject matter, Warhol ultimately rejected the fashion world in favor of images taken from advertisements for Coca-Cola, Campbell's Soup, Del Monte Peaches, wigs, makeup, and corn pads. Instead of haute couture, this was an off-the-rack world, where the democratic dream of cars in every garage and chickens in every pot found expression in the symbols of consumer culture. This was the language of the masses. In a frequently quoted statement, Warhol reminds us that no matter how rich or poor we are, we can never get a better Coke than the one available to everyone else.

> *What's great about this country is that America started the tradition where the richest consumers buy essentially the same things as the poorest. You can be watching TV and see Coca-Cola, and you can know that the President drinks Coke, Liz Taylor drinks Coke, and you just think, you can drink Coke too. A Coke is a Coke and no amount of money can get you a better Coke than the one the bum around the corner is drinking.*[35]

That Warhol would paint several versions of the Coke bottle underscores his understanding of the power this symbol held in American society. In this series of paintings, he takes a crystal-clear look at America. Warhol first painted a brushy version (with all the requisite drips that signified "painting"). In these paintings, the drips and splatters appear as relics of a distant past. Warhol was eventually to reject this approach in favor of one which more closely approximated the "real thing," so much so that it led Emile de Antonio to remark, "It's naked, it's brutal, it's who we are."

Warhol also knew that it was becoming increasingly possible to be who you were not. His 1961 painting *Before and After*, for instance, depicts a nose both before and after it has been altered through plastic surgery, a practice that, as we know today, is no longer limited to the very wealthy. That Warhol found

ANDY WARHOL
"Carnet de Bal by Revillon"
Window installation for Bonwit Teller, 1959

it in newspaper advertisements in 1960 shows that such services were already being advertised on a mass scale. As in *Strong Arms and Broads* (1960), another veiled reference to male beauty, *Before and After* expresses something about Warhol's personal desires. It is now well known that Warhol's parents were immigrants from Czechoslovakia and that he grew up in a working-class neighborhood in Pittsburgh. This, coupled with his homosexuality, set the stage for Warhol as outsider. Coming to the New York fashion world and participating in the construction of beauty as seen through its eyes, Warhol developed an obsession with what he saw as his overly large nose, so much so that in 1957 he had it surgically altered. Warhol's obsession with his nose can be seen as symbolic of his struggle to belong. Dropping the "a" off Warhola, like slimming his nose, made him less "ethnic." Thus, in Warhol's case, his self-invention existed not only on the flat canvas, but in the real world. It is through an understanding of Warhol as a person, therefore, that *Before and After* gains its greatest power as a metaphor for assimilation.

In spite of the decision to erase the telltale brushwork that characterized his first hand-painted version of *Before and After*, it remained impossible for Warhol to erase the facts of his own life. Thus the work

offers two particularly powerful reminders. First, that the vocabulary of symbols that comprise mythological structures, whether in the realm of the commercial, literary or artistic, are, in fact, designed by us, and as such, remain in a continual state of flux. Second, he reminds us how easily we succumb to their homogenizing influence.

Looking at Warhol's "hand-painted" images reminds us of the lasting influence of the New York School, that the generation that emerged as "Pop" artists were deeply engaged in the act of painting, however reformulated it had become. The possibilities for another kind of painting were ever more real. Even if this new language had evolved from some of the lessons of Abstract Expressionism, its subject matter was

ANDY WARHOL
Before and After II, 1962
Oil on canvas, 54 x 70 inches
Collection of Kimiko and John Powers, Carbondale, Colo.

89

ANDY WARHOL
Storm Door, 1960
Synthetic polymer paint on canvas, 46 x 42 1/8 inches
Courtesy of Thomas Ammann, Zurich

ANDY WARHOL
Storm Door, 1960
Synthetic polymer paint on canvas, 72 x 60 inches
Collection of Robert and Meryl Meltzer, New York

derived from that designed by commercial artists and art directors to have "mass" appeal. These were images people lived with on a daily basis, that were used to construct the mythology of industrial culture. In retrospect, it was the artists who explored this subject matter by removing these images from their everyday context who would bring increased awareness of the power they held.

Clearly, Pop art has been perceived primarily on the level of subject matter, and it has not been the intention of this essay to reinforce a reading that centers only on an interest in the symbols of commercial culture. In fact, it is through an examination of this evolution from Abstract Expressionism to Pop art, a period that could bear the ironic label "hand-painted Pop," that a more complex understanding can be gained of a critical period in American art. Along these lines, it is necessary to look beyond the commonly held notion that these artists assumed the stance of the machine, erasing any personal meaning from their work (an idea actively encouraged by Warhol). Although some of them did turn to commercial processes that mediated human expression, the idea that these artists completely obliterated any notion of the personal from their work can be disproved by looking at the totality of their production. These early works provide evidence of the concerns of the artists, and the ways in which they found form for private expressions in public language.

ANDY WARHOL
Coca-Cola, 1960
Oil and wax crayon on canvas, 69 5/8 x 52 1/4 inches
Dia Center for the Arts, New York

1 Quoted in *Adolph Gottlieb: Pictographs* (Edmonton: Edmonton Art Gallery, 1977), unpag.

2 See Serge Guilbaut, *How New York Stole the Idea of Modern Art*, trans. Arthur Goldhammer (Chicago: University of Chicago Press, 1983), p. 121.

3 Interview with the author, March 1992.

4 As a college student, Warhol produced an unflattering caricature of the professor who taught this course, Robert Lepper, which included the title of Benedict's book.

5 For an extensive discussion of these contradictory aspects of Gottlieb's work, see Maurice Berger, "Pictograph into Burst: Adolph Gottlieb and the Structure of Myth," *Arts Magazine* 55, no. 7 (March 1981): 138.

6 Thomas B. Hess, *Willem de Kooning* (New York: The Museum of Modern Art, 1968), pp. 76, 79.

7 See Sidra Stich, *Made in the U.S.A.: An Americanization in Modern Art, the '50s and '60s* (Berkeley: University Art Museum, University of California, and University of California Press, 1987) for a discussion of this topic as well as the emergence of American subject matter during the 1950s.

8 Sam Hunter, *Larry Rivers* (Waltham, Mass.: Poses Institute of Fine Arts, 1965), p. 17.

9 Ibid.

10 Quoted in Frank O'Hara, *Frank O'Hara: Art Chronicles, 1954-1966* (New York: George Braziller, 1975), p. 112.

11 Rivers quoted in Irving Sandler, *The New York School: Painters of the Fifties and Sixties* (New York: Harper and Row, 1978), p. 105.

12 Interview with the author, March 1992. Hartigan also notes that she was interested primarily in painters and poets as her audience.

13 See Ernst A. Busche, *Roy Lichtenstein: Das Frühwerk 1942-1960* (Berlin: Gebr. Man Verlag, 1988). Busche provides an in-depth analysis of the artist's works, with a particular emphasis on the pre-Pop production. There is a detailed section dealing with Lichtenstein's forays into the American past through history paintings.

14 Robert Saltonstall Mattison, *Grace Hartigan: A Painter's World* (New York: Hudson Hills, 1990).

15 Ibid.

16 Interviews with the author.

17 Fairfield Porter, *Arts Magazine* 30, no. 7 (April 1956): 83.

18 See Allan Kaprow, "The Legacy of Jackson Pollock," *Art News* 57, no. 6 (October 1958): 26. See also his contribution to the exhibition catalogue *New Forms — New Media* (New York: Martha Jackson Gallery, 1960).

19 Ibid., pp. 26, 55.

20 Ibid., pp. 56-57.

21 Conversation with the author, June 1992.

22 Interview with the author, May 1991.

23 Michael Kirby, *Happenings* (New York: E. P. Dutton, 1966), p. 191.

24 Barbara Rose, *Claes Oldenburg* (New York: The Museum of Modern Art, 1970), pp. 30-31.

25 Ibid., p. 46.

26 Conversation with the author, April 1992.

27 Interview with the author, June 1992.

28 Fairfield Porter, "Lichtenstein's Adult Primer: There's Fantasy in the Abstract," *Art News* (March 1954): 18, 63.

29 See David Deitcher, "Unsentimental Education: The Professionalization of the American Artist," in this publication, which analyzes the relationship between the training these postwar artists received in art schools and the development of their mature work.

30 In an interview with the author in October 1986, Warhol credited Rivers with influencing his 1960 painting *Dick Tracy*, particularly for his decision to obliterate the letters. It was not that the language was unimportant in this work, but rather, Warhol claims, that "he was trying to be like Larry Rivers." Throughout the 1950s, Warhol visited the Tibor de Nagy Gallery where Rivers was a frequent exhibitor.

31 Ibid.

32 See Kenneth C. Silver, "Modes of Disclosure: The Construction of Gay Identity and the Rise of Pop Art" in this publication. Silver discusses Warhol's homosexuality and its relationship to his work.

33 See my exhibition catalogue, *"Success is a Job in New York..." The Early Art and Business of Andy Warhol* (New York: Grey Art Gallery, New York University, in association with the Carnegie Museum of Art, Pittsburgh, 1989), which discusses the relationship between Warhol's career as a commercial illustrator and his emerging Pop work.

34 See Ellen Lupton and J. Abbot Miller, "Line Art: Andy Warhol and the Commercial Art World of the 1950s," in ibid.

35 Andy Warhol, *The Philosophy of Andy Warhol (From A to B and Back Again)* (New York: Harcourt Brace Jovanovich, 1975), pp. 100-101.

94

ANDY WARHOL
Telephone, 1961
Acrylic and pencil on canvas, 72 x 54 inches
The Museum of Contemporary Art, Los Angeles
Purchased with funds provided by an anonymous donor

David Deitcher

Unsentimental Education:
The Professionalization of the American Artist

As art critic for *The Nation* at the end of World War II, Clement Greenberg surveyed American art and found it promising but imperiled. At the dawn of the cold war, he saw "serious" art jeopardized much as he had at the outbreak of the war in Europe. In 1939, in his essay "Avant-Garde and Kitsch," Greenberg had indicated the threat to art posed by the ersatz seductions and gross simplifications of mass culture by summoning the twin specters of fascist art and Soviet socialist realism. In 1946, the dangers centered on the seemingly more benign contents of *The New Yorker* and *Harper's Bazaar*, as well as the safe modern art "derived from impressionism and its immediate aftermath" promoted by arbiters of American cultural propriety such as Henry Luce and his magazine *Life*. Greenberg pinpointed the object of his postwar misgivings in a review of the Whitney Annual:

> *The middle class...is now surging toward culture under the pressure of anxiety, high taxes, and a shrinking industrial frontier. All this expresses itself in a market demand for cultural goods that are up to date and yet not too hard to consume...and compels the serious and ambitious artist...to meet this demand by softening, sweetening, and simplifying his product.... This state of affairs constitutes a much greater threat to high art than* Kitsch *itself.*[1]

High culture in the postwar United States was threatened, then, by a vast market for "middlebrow" art, music, and literature, which filled the gap between the challenging innovations of Greenberg's "avant-garde" and the fraudulent appeal of old-fashioned kitsch.[2]

A year later, Greenberg offered further insights into the social preconditions for middlebrow culture in "The Present Prospects for American Painting and Sculpture," an essay he published in *Horizon*.

> *A society as completely capitalized and industrialized as our American one, seeks relentlessly to organize every possible field of activity and consumption in the direction of profit, regardless of whatever immunity from commercialization any particular activity may have once enjoyed.*
>
> *It is this kind of rationalization that has made life more and more boring and tasteless in our country, particularly since 1940, flattening and emptying all those vessels which are supposed to nourish us daily.*[3]

Greenberg's belief that American society was "completely capitalized and industrialized" seems to foreshadow the economist Ernest Mandel's observation, made a quarter of a century later, that the period in which the critic wrote these remarks signaled the onset of the distinctive economic and social forms associated with "late capitalism." For Mandel, late capitalism "constitutes *generalized universal industrialization* for the first time in history. Mechanization, standardization, over-specialization and parcellization of labour, which in the past determined only the realm of commodity production in actual industry, now penetrate into all sectors of social life."[4]

Greenberg's understanding of middlebrow culture was not limited to a vision of inexorable commodification and rationalization; it also encompassed the liberal democratizing goals of American public education. It is as if his ideas about the middlebrow reflected a deeper sense of what Theodor Adorno called the "totalization" of culture — the systematization of culture and its subordination to a condition of total control. This was the context against which the supposedly spontaneous creativity of the Abstract Expressionists stood out in such high relief in the late forties, and was so admired by critics such as Greenberg. This was also the context in which the artists of the fifties and early sixties were raised and educated. A grasp of how it affected the generations of these successive decades is crucial to understanding both how these artists actually differed and also the various continuities among them, which have been camouflaged considerably by their obvious dissimilarities.

If a grain of ambivalence can be detected anywhere in Greenberg's analysis, it is in his understanding that the national ethos of democratization was fueled by the unprecedented industrial productivity that the United States had achieved during World War II. He was impressed that Americans possessed the wealth to "think it possible to cultivate the *masses*." But he was doubtful about that productivity's social and cultural effects:

> *It was to be expected that sooner or later the American "common man" would aspire to self-cultivation as something that belonged as inevitably to a high standard of living as personal hygiene. In any event the bitter status struggle that goes on in a thoroughly democratic country would of itself have served by now to put self-cultivation on the order of the day — once it became clear, to the commonality, as it has by now, that cultivation not only makes one's life more interesting but — even more important in a society that is becoming more and more closed — defines social position.*[5]

The vast middle-class consensus about the desirability of "cultivation" could only have grown from longstanding and complex historical processes. Yet Greenberg focused his analysis on these processes' cultural consequences because his ultimate goal was to suggest a hostile context for the "virile," radically antidomestic and antimiddlebrow art of Jackson Pollock and David Smith, which contrasted with the engulfing "femininity" of its middlebrow counterpart.[6] Given the cultural situation he described, Greenberg considered it necessary to deploy this rigidly gendered rhetorical arsenal to win the turf war on behalf of "his" artists. A decade later this same rhetoric of binary antagonism would help conceal the more complex, truly dialectical relationship that obtained between Abstract Expressionism and the post-Abstract Expressionist and Pop art that followed it.

Greenberg could not have foreseen the impact of the cultural transformations he traced on the younger American artists, many of them returning from war to study with federal support through the G.I. Bill, who would constitute the post-Abstract Expressionist generations. Not that the matter of artistic education lay outside Greenberg's interests; far from it, for he knew that in education lay the future. Thus he concluded "The Present Prospects of American Painting and Sculpture" with high praise for the teachings of Hans Hofmann, the German-born artist and educator whom he had also applauded in 1939 in "Avant-Garde and Kitsch."[7] In the 1947 essay, he gave Hofmann's teachings credit for the artistic enlightenment of that small pocket of aesthetic resistance in America that he entrusted with the future of American art: "Hofmann will in the future, when the accomplishment of American Painting in the last five and the next twenty years is properly evaluated, be considered the most important figure in American art of the period since 1935 and one of the most influential forces in its entire history, not for his own work, but for the influence, enlightening and uncompromising, he exerts."[8]

Hofmann's lectures at his school on West Eighth Street had helped Greenberg to arrive at his conception of modernist art as an essentially positivistic, self-critical endeavor that was rigorously opposed to the instrumentality of everyday life. Hofmann had insisted, for example, that it was "the tragedy of the Bauhaus" to have "confused the concepts of the fine and applied arts."[9] Such statements take on special significance in the context of the changes then taking place in American visual culture, since these changes were informed in a variety of ways by a tendency to erode the boundaries between art and design, or between art and life, that Hofmann and Greenberg were determined to reinforce.

These significant shifts in postwar culture cannot be understood in Greenberg's terms as merely a capitulation to "middlebrow" tastes. They were accompanied, for one thing, by a far more active deconstruction of the ideas that had preceded them than Greenberg's imagery of engulfing banality would appear to imply. Beginning early in the 1950s, Robert Rauschenberg and Jasper Johns began producing works that challenged certain of the myths supporting Greenberg's and Hofmann's position. Among others, these included the belief in the Greenbergian figure of the "most important figure," in the notion of an unproblematically "original" work of art, and in a metaphoric conception of "style" as transparent to the experience of the artist, who alone fixes its meaning and value. Rauschenberg had playfully undermined romantic latterday-modernist conceits since 1953, as when, in a well-known "patricidal" gambit, he erased a Willem de Kooning drawing, unmasking the romantic artist's "presence" as an "absence"; or when he replaced the artist's hand with a machine part—a car tire—by collaborating with John Cage and his Model A Ford in the creation of the gritty Zen/Dada scroll known matter-of-factly as *Automobile Tire Print*.[10] And yet it is noteworthy that the logic of Rauschenberg's antihumanist gesture was already implicit in Pollock's steadfastly humanist art. A good deal of what is most radical in Pollock's radical "poured" paintings is the replacement of the artist's hand with a rudimentary mechanical technique: the use of sticks, cans, and the wrong end of paintbrushes to pour industrial-grade liquid paint and enamel onto unstretched, floor-bound canvases. Moreover, the late-fifties and early-sixties manifestations of an often antimacho performance art by men and women, gay as well as straight, can also be connected with the performative aspect of Pollock's art. This link was suggested by Hans Namuth's film and photographs of the artist painting in 1950, by aspects of Harold Rosenberg's 1952 essay "The American Action Painters," and by the use to which both were put in 1958 by Allan Kaprow in "The Legacy of Jackson Pollock."[11]

Rauschenberg's works from the mid-fifties evidence his process-oriented engagement with the logic of action painting. But they also reveal the extent to which this involvement was iconoclastic, and reflected the concurrent revival of interest in Dada and Duchamp. The return of this repressed avant-gardist legacy accumulated momentum throughout the 1950s, having been signaled as early as 1951 by the publication of the anthology *Dada Painters and Poets* (edited, with Duchamp's assistance, by Robert Motherwell). As the decade advanced, exhibitions of works by Duchamp and other artists associated with Dada appeared in galleries and museums in and around New York City.[12] Cage's influential teachings and compositions disseminated an attitude toward cultural production that was as consistent with Duchamp's aesthetic as it was with the ductility of Zen Buddhism, and that strongly affected the generation of artists who would go on to participate in Fluxus, Happenings, and other performance practices.

The aesthetic shift from action painting to Rauschenberg, Johns, and Pop cannot be understood by taking recourse to the "timeless" oscillations that traditional art history charts between, for example, painterly and linear, romantic and classical, "hot" and "cool," abstract and figurative, or aestheticist and avant-garde impulses. Leo Steinberg, for one, has detected in Johns's and Rauschenberg's art, as well as in Pop, evidence of a new kind of picture surface so distinct from the modernist practice epitomized by Pollock's work that he called it "postmodernist." In place of the modernist picture plane, which he understood as "an analogue of a visual experience of nature," Steinberg noted the introduction of a "flatbed picture plane" that registers instead "operational processes." Rather than the metaphoric, vertical plane of modernism, which corresponds "head-to-toe…with human posture," the flatbed picture plane suggests a horizontal printing surface, a "receptor surface on which objects are scattered, on which data is entered, on which information may be received, printed, impressed—whether coherently or in confusion." More significant in the context of this essay than the fact that such art "let the world in again" is the fact that the supposedly autonomous creation of modernist art was supplanted by "operational processes" that "admit[ted] any experience as a matter of representation."[13]

Art such as this presumed that "lived" experience had itself become codified and two-dimensional—like representation. This situation left some artists with little choice but to sacrifice direct engagement with artistic "creation" and to turn instead to montage and the manipulation of preexisting materials—in short, to "operational processes." Steinberg's observation that such art signals nothing less than a shift to a "postmodernist" visual culture finds support in the "simulationist" theories that originated in the late sixties in the writings of the Situationist Guy Debord, and in their later adaptations by Jean Baudrillard.[14] Furthermore, there is clearly an affinity between the "operational processes" of the postmodernist artist and Mandel's observation that in late capitalism labor moves away from the treatment of raw materials to "preparatory and supervisory functions."

The very real differences between Abstract Expressionism and post-Abstract Expressionist art are discernible in this shift from art that proclaims itself an analogue for natural experience to art that heralds the death of all nature; from art that insists upon being taken as the unprecedented creation of a sovereign subject to art that presumes the codification and cultural contingency both of experience and subjectivity. These different forms of art, however, must be understood as cultural responses to the same mutable postwar reality. As critics like Greenberg never tired of noting, the muscular negations of the Abstract Expressionists presupposed the totalization of culture and society. By appearing to capitulate to that totalization, post-Abstract Expressionist artists actually found ways to highlight the contradictions embedded within it. By acknowledging, and even appropriating, some of the techniques of commercialization, these artists were able, paradoxically, to reveal "difference" among the homogenizing effects of late-capitalist patriarchal culture.

The general transformation of American visual culture that began between 1935 and 1945 and was realized in the fifties and sixties coincided with changes in the education of the artist and designer. The new approaches to art instruction primarily affected students in degree-granting university art departments, rather than those who attended small Beaux-Arts derived art schools like Hofmann's. That is to say, it affected many of the central figures in American Pop: most notably, Roy Lichtenstein and Andy Warhol. The aesthetic education of these artists prepared them, as Hofmann's metaphysics of the picture plane never could, to manipulate and "manage" the terms of American mass culture in the postwar era.

To a greater or lesser extent, fine art and the applied arts have been perceived to be in conflict with each another throughout modern times. From the second third of the nineteenth century through the middle of the twentieth, the history of art and design instruction has consisted of institutional negotiations between aesthetic and utilitarian forms: between handicraft and assembly line; between originals and copies; between imagination and convention; between the cultivation of unified perception or of the resources of involuntary memory and the miseries of rote learning. This is not to deny that there were occasions of synthesis. But even the most utopian "sublations" of art into life—William Morris, or Russian Constructivism and Productivism, or the Bauhaus, or De Stijl—can be understood as historically contingent reconfigurations of these dialectical terms.

These elements came into a peculiar alignment within American art and design instruction between 1935, when the Federal Art Project was launched, and 1945, when the war in Europe ended. It is within the context of this distinctly American rapprochement that the complex social determination of the "flatbed picture plane," of Pop art and the postmodernist art they portended can best be appreciated. The American Pop artists aestheticized commodities at the same time that they commodified aesthetics. That is to say, they could slide back and forth with unprecedented ease along an axis extending between high aesthetic structures and the structures of industrial production. This new facility cannot be explained solely in aesthetic terms — as a side effect of the artists' antiromantic repudiation of Abstract Expressionism, say, or of their putatively "realist" response to the image-saturated life of postwar America. To consider this axis and its implications by examining the way these artists were trained is to consider the social construction of the artist who navigates its path so comfortably.

As conceived by Holger Cahill, the Federal Art Project provided relief for unemployed artists and designers during the Depression and encouraged the production of variously anti-elitist and "public" art forms. It is well known that the project commissioned thousands of murals, graphics, and posters. Less familiar is the fact that it instituted nationwide educational programs to construct a vast and socially diversified American public for art. From Spokane to Harlem, over one hundred community art centers were established across the country.

Cahill based this national art agenda on the model of John Dewey's plan for progressive education, reflexive democracy, and the social integration of aesthetic experience. As such, its ultimate goal was to incorporate art into the everyday lives of Americans and to undermine the hierarchical distinction between fine and applied arts; in short, to overturn the notion of art for art's sake by proposing art as a tool for forging a sense of both national and regional identity and assisting in productive self-fulfillment.[15] The domination of Federal Art Project art by social realist and regionalist styles may denote the failure of a naively populist approach to address the problem of shaping a cohesive national culture, but the program's educational goals were more successful. They helped to confer a sense of cultural entitlement and reverence for art on a whole generation of middle-class and soon-to-be-middle-class Americans who came of age during and after World War II. It was this generation that Greenberg would picture "surging towards culture" in such numbers and with such avidity that he considered it "a greater threat to high art than *Kitsch* itself."

Not until the end of Dewey's book *Art as Experience* (published in 1934, one year before the inauguration of the Federal Art Project) did the author observe that in order to overcome the disparity between art and life it would be necessary first to eliminate, in his words, "the economic system of production for private gain."[16] In the absence of such revolutionary social change, however, the individual work of art might still serve as an aesthetic model of experience to be emulated in other areas of life; and it could maintain its traditional bourgeois function as a symbolic repository of harmony and resolution, providing imaginary shelter for the sovereign subject of humanistic culture in the midst of an ever more discordant and fragmented society. Despite the radical implications of Dewey's metaphysics of experience, then, his theory paradoxically ensured that discrete works of art would retain or actually intensify their exalted status. Given the long-term effects of establishing art teaching more securely within general education, and of the assimilation of art within an increasingly spectacular mass culture, works of art and the people who make them were fated to become objects of veneration and mythification in American society.

By the time the Works Project Administration was liquidated in 1943, the government had helped return American art to a private base of patronage: not to its original patrician base, but to the middle class. A whole new public now wanted to buy "original" works of art with which to furnish their houses, as prescribed by *Life*. This was the purpose of the "Buy American Art Weeks" that were held in 1941 and 1942 to sell off thousands of government-commissioned and government-warehoused works of art.[17]

But this was not the full extent of the private support for art that began to develop between 1935 and 1945. There was corporate support as well: since the mid-1930s, companies had been buying art for their own collections. In addition, many more were employing artists and designers in various ways. It was to fine and commercial artists, in fact, and to the burgeoning group of American artists practicing industrial design, that companies turned during the Depression to try to restore the public's lost confidence in American business, and to lure consumers back to the marketplace.[18]

In 1930, the Westinghouse Electric Company of East Pittsburgh hired Donald Dohner, a graphic artist on the faculty of the College of Fine Arts at Carnegie Tech, Pittsburgh, to redesign their products and develop plans for new ones. Five years later, Carnegie introduced a BFA degree with a major in industrial design—the first such program in the United States. It was Dohner who designed the new course of instruction, and without his experience at Westinghouse, he and his colleague, the artist Alexander Kostellow, could not have conceived it either when or as they did. The industrial-design curriculum devised by Dohner and Kostellow prepared its graduates to understand the material requirements of mass production, to anticipate the desires of consumers, and to employ the logic of aesthetic structure. In a paper commemorating the introduction of this immensely influential program, Robert Lepper—Warhol's most important teacher at Carnegie Tech—coined the hyphenated term "artist-designer" to describe the new breed the faculty had hoped to engineer.[19]

The field of industrial design grew and became more prestigious throughout the 1940s, spawning a variety of institutional and pedagogical manifestations. After the war, the usual competition for students among university art departments—always eager to increase enrollment—was heightened as returning veterans (Lichtenstein among them) armed with federal education funds turned in unprecedented numbers to careers in art. Art department administrators and faculty members refashioned their curricula to suit the widest possible range of students.

At the same time, the increasing correlation of the artist's and the designer's education was furthered by the conception of "organic" curriculum planning, which blossomed in the 1940s. In 1942, the College of Fine Arts at Carnegie Tech implemented a "Fine Arts Academic Program" that required students in all its divisions (painting and design, industrial design, and art education) to take new courses, including "Thought and Expression," "The Arts and Civilization," and "Individual and Social Psychology." This academic program was intended, in the words of Dean Keeble,

> to exploit the capacities...and correct the limitations of the typical art student...to provide a complement
> to his particular kind of professional training...to widen the horizon of our young artists, to reduce
> their prejudices and multiply their enthusiasms, to link intellectual and practical interests with their
> creative endeavors and, finally, to integrate them with society and equip them to take an effective part in
> the difficult world which this generation must face.[20]

As a response to the threat of an overly technical education, organic curriculum planning advanced the erosion of hierarchical distinctions between the education of the artist and that of the designer. In this sense it extended a century old tradition of liberal educational reform. But it also emerged at a historically specific moment, when university administrators, educators, intellectuals, and more than a few entrepreneurs shared a widespread sense that this continent alone was likely to survive the war intact. It was incumbent upon Americans, then, to rescue Western culture. This they attempted to do—by the contradictory means of recasting it in the form of a popular humanism.

Hoyt Sherman on the bridge of the flash lab, ca. 1949
Photos courtesy of Ohio State University

Many of the art and design instructors of the 1940s came of age during the 1930s, and identified themselves as pragmatic modernists. They might have sprung from backgrounds in fine art and illustration, as Lepper did, or in engineering, like Hoyt Sherman, an art professor at Ohio State University whom Lichtenstein has credited with the formation of his aesthetic frame of reference.[21] These enthusiastic if little-known modernists responded to the challenge of increased enrollment, and to the demand for more adaptable forms of practical training, by codifying the principles of what they regarded as a universal aesthetic. To achieve greater efficiency — and authority — they invariably turned to science to guide them and support their ideas. Sociology, anthropology, and psychoanalysis, for example, informed Lepper's two-year course "Pictorial Design," which instilled juniors and seniors in the Carnegie design program — Warhol among them (1947-48) — with an awareness of what Lepper called the "social flux"; that is, of their ever changing relationship to the community in which they lived and worked.

Students in the "Pictorial Design" course were asked to scrutinize the Oakland community around Carnegie Tech "with the general viewpoint of a cultural anthropologist." They were to study "people, shelter, exchange of goods and services, means of communication, ceremonial observances, the nature of governmental activity and public services, and community spectacle (i.e. topography, weather, light, movement of people in groups)." This focus recalls the overall outlook of Thomas Hart Benton who, as an instructor at the Art Students League early in the 1930s, had encouraged the young Jackson Pollock to sketch from life. In this way Pollock could distill the essence of the American scene into carefully observed, yet largely imaginary, compositions based on cross-country travels. Lepper clearly intended a more scientific attitude than this. As a combination of social concern and commercial interest, his course stopped at the threshold of market research.

As a final assignment, Lepper's students were to employ the knowledge they had acquired in their field work and the organizational skills they had developed in foundation and studio courses to create "pictorial interpretations" of a novel that Lepper selected for them (in Warhol's class it was Robert Penn Warren's *All the King's Men*).[22] Perhaps the fulfillment of Lepper's course would only be achieved fifteen years later, however, in the anthropologist's blend of complicity and detachment, indifference and incisiveness, that characterized Warhol's Pop art. Considering how Warhol's work helped reconcile people to the conditions of life in an advanced consumer culture, it is not difficult to understand how Lepper could have supported him. Lepper and his colleagues had hoped that the new breed of artist-designer would help to bring about what he, echoing Kostellow, called "stability" or "equilibrium" within the "social organism."[23]

It was experimental psychology, particularly Gestalt, that inspired Lichtenstein's mentor, Sherman, to want to create an innovative — not to say eccentric — introductory course in drawing and pictorial structure at the beginning of the 1940s. Sharing with the founders of Gestalt their belief that "good form" was suited to the psychic and social "task of integration," Sherman sought not just the preservation of high aesthetic experience but the improvement of virtually all processes of production through their assimilation to aesthetic structures.[24] It had long been part of the modernist agenda to reshape consumer products according to modernist aesthetics. Sherman went farther, arguing that his course would benefit not just students of art and design but people in any walk of life, be they factory workers, football quarterbacks, dentists, or soldiers.[25]

Hardly your run-of-the-mill drawing instruction, Sherman's was actually a course in perceptual training. Like many proto-modernists and modernists before him, Sherman imagined the persistence of "fundamental structures" as the transhistorical constant of all aesthetic experience. But he supplemented to this belief his own theory that the artist's approximation of such structures was the result of an "organized perception," and that this "organized perception" could be taught. Artists were not necessarily born, but

101

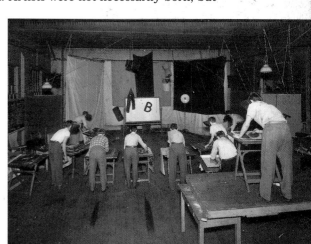

First flash lab, ca. 1942-44

could be made: Sherman could educate them to perceive, organize, and register materially the hitherto disordered data of sense perception, in a continuous, undifferentiated process. As if to fulfill Dewey's belief that all productive processes are potentially aesthetic, and that aesthetic structure should therefore inform all productive processes, Sherman determined to find a way to teach organized perception and to make it as widely available as possible through the standardization and publication of his method.[26]

How does one impart the fluent patterns of organized perception? The course took place in a specially equipped studio, a former artillery shed that stood beside Ohio State's fine arts building, Hayes Hall, and that was remodeled in 1945 to Sherman's detailed designs. Perhaps its most striking aspect was its lack of light. Not only were all the windows in the seventy-foot-long building sealed, but every other form of illumination was tightly controlled. So, for that matter, were the entire host of scientifically freighted and orchestrated variables that together constituted the course. Sherman hinted at the baroque scientificity of his program, and at its central device as well, by referring to his black box of a studio as the "flash lab."[27]

The students met six times a week for six weeks, never for more than twenty-five minutes a session. They spent the first ten minutes of each session getting used to the gloom. As recorded music (often jazz) filled the studio, they were encouraged to relax — to whistle and tap pencils — but also to feel for the limits of the drawing table in front of them, and for the outer edges of the newsprint on which they would soon draw with thick crayons or charcoal. These tables were arranged on four terraces facing projection screens far away at the studio's opposite end. As the course progressed, the tables were moved closer to the screens, to challenge the students' perceptual abilities. Above and slightly behind the terraced section of the space was a "bridge" containing a massive slide projector. Sherman had fitted this device with a "tachistoscope," a mechanical shutter, first devised by late-nineteenth-century psychologists, that made it possible for him to control the duration of a slide projection to within a fraction of a second. Also on the bridge were assorted strobes and spotlights, a gramophone and record collection, and a slide library containing four hundred mostly "abstract" designs that Sherman conceived especially for his course.

After the ten minutes of relaxation and preparation had passed, Sherman would show the first of the twenty slides he would use in each class; or rather he would "flash" it, since it appeared on screen for a tenth of a second or less. Cast again in darkness for the remainder of a minute, the students would draw the configuration they had barely glimpsed, depending mainly on its afterimage. At the end of the minute, another, slightly more complex configuration would pulse before them, and again they would draw in darkness from the afterimage. Later in the course, Sherman would keep the lights on in the studio for longer intervals until, at the end, students were encouraged to test their skills against the ambient light of landscape study.

Much of this program Sherman based on the theory — expounded by experimental psychologists — that when an object is visible for a tenth of a second or less, the human eye cannot perform the saccadic movements that enable perception in depth. By "flashing" slides as he did, Sherman was trying to promote a mode of visual perception that he interchangeably called "monocular" or "aesthetic" vision, in which, he believed, images and objects are likely to be grasped in terms of the relative position, size, and brightness of their constituent parts. For Sherman, "monocular" vision was "aesthetic" because it facilitated the apprehension of images or objects as "wholes"; intensified the student's appreciation for the constitutive role that negative space plays in forming an image; and assisted in the process of transposing objects seen in three-dimensional space into the two-dimensional terms of a picture surface.

Sherman designed and classified his slides according to "optical cues" (relative position, size, and brightness) that he learned about in psychology texts such as Max Wertheimer's "Laws of Organization in Perceptual Forms."[28] He further organized each category of slides in a progression from simple to complex.

Flash lab, ca. 1949

ROY LICHTENSTEIN
Untitled, ca. 1959
Oil on canvas, 68 3/4 x 47 3/4 inches
Private collection

ROY LICHTENSTEIN
Untitled, 1958
Oil on canvas, 24 x 34 inches
Private collection

There is a link here—implausibly enough—between Sherman's proto-high-tech course and the old and tradition-bound drawing instruction of the Beaux-Arts academies. This linkage is established more securely by the sequence that Sherman adopted for his course in its entirety.

According to that venerable Beaux-Arts sequence, one begins to draw "from the flat"; just as, in Sherman's course, one began with slides projected onto a single screen, effectively substituting for the aspiring academician's slavish studies after engravings. Next, where plaster casts of geometrical figures and organic forms introduced the nineteenth-century art student to the problem of transcribing three-dimensional objects into the two dimensions of the drawing surface, Sherman flashed specially devised slides onto three screens, two of which flanked the third, which was set slightly deeper in the space. Finally, with the transition to three-dimensional studies completed, the nineteenth-century student might turn to the classical statue, the live model, or the traditional still life. Sherman gave his students unconventional arrangements of studio props, trash bins, and cutout letters and numbers that he inverted to prevent recognition. In the early part of the course, he illuminated these studies only momentarily, using a strobe, except for a pinpoint of light that would isolate part of one object in order to establish a planar point of reference. As he replaced simple images with more complex ones, and as the course progressed from two to three dimensions, his goal remained the same: "to establish conditions which foster and, in so far as possible, require an organic type of integration…unity in seeing, unity in the process of seeing-and-drawing, unity in the total creative act."[29]

There could be no room in such a course for reflection or conceptualization. Sherman argued that "any self-conscious effort that separates the aesthetic into its verbal components, such as composition, perspective, and tonality, is a sure way of destroying the desired end." Insofar as the flash lab was conceived to promote an explicitly undivided experience ("seeing-and-drawing") that would determine, and be inscribed within, the resulting work of art, any incursion into this protected zone of indivisibility from the inherently differentiating field of language had to be kept at bay. In this sense, training in the flash lab must be understood as a pedagogical formula for preserving the transcendental essence of modernist aesthetic experience.

This transcendentalism was defined with ever greater precision in the phenomenologically oriented critical discourse on Minimalist art in the mid-to-late 1960s, and nowhere more lucidly than in Michael Fried's essay "Art and Objecthood." Fried distinguished modernist art from Minimalism (or "literalism"), which he found alarming in its "theatricality": its promotion of a sense of duration, of the gradual unfolding of the meaning of a work of art, and its promotion as well of a heightened sense of the art object's dependence upon the circumstances of display to determine its meaning and value. When, at the end of his essay, Fried rhapsodized over the modernist art that he considered at war with "theater," he might just as well have been describing the conditions of the flash lab:

> It is this continuous and entire presentness, amounting, as it were, to the perpetual creation of itself, that one experiences as a kind of instantaneousness: as though if only one were infinitely more acute, a single infinitely brief instant would be long enough to see everything, to experience the work in all its depth and fullness, to be forever convinced by it.[30] (Emphasis added.)

Each and every variable in Sherman's course was determined scientifically to secure the availability of transcendent artworks that could bear witness to, and supply temporary experiences of, a subjective indivisibility and perceptual fullness of being. But at a simpler, more patently instrumental level, the program was intended to increase the student's perceptual and organizational power. In an account of his course that he published in 1947, Sherman used charts and graphs to support his claim that his instruction enhanced his students' abilities: to see in the dark, to discern a wider range of tonalities from light to dark, to survey a more extensive visual field—all the while efficiently organizing the teeming disorder of this

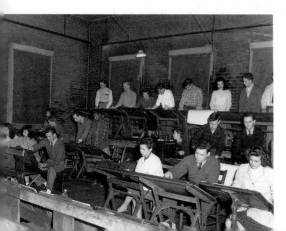

The flash lab, ca. 1942

imposing perceptual array; to respond, in other words, with grace under pressure.[31]

At the same time, then, that Sherman followed the transcendentalist impulse familiar from the discourse of Abstract Expressionist and other modernist art, he was also determined to supply his students with the means to function more efficiently, and with a greater sense of "integration." In short, his course acknowledged the productive imperative that dominated American life more than ever at the dawn of the late-capitalist consumer culture. Further, it presumed that the world had become a more challenging, not to say hostile, and subjectively shattering place; likewise the conditions in which men and women were expected to work. In this context, it may come as less than a surprise to learn that soon after America entered World War II, Sherman offered to train naval cadets in "organized perception" in order to help them more efficiently blast the enemy from seas and skies, by day or night. Sherman himself observed that his discovery of a method to teach drawing and pictorial structure coincided with the Japanese attack on Pearl Harbor.[32] But the birth of his project during wartime cannot explain the curious combination of aggression and defensiveness, technologism and conservatism, that characterizes his approach to art and its instruction, and that found its artistic complement in the work of Roy Lichtenstein.

In its presumption of an environment in which one is likely to be bombarded with perceptual stimuli to the point of abuse, Sherman's method recalls the conditions of industrialized urban life that Walter Benjamin evoked in his study "On Some Motifs in Baudelaire." For Benjamin, the bustling metropolis had become the site of countless minor shocks and potentially major traumas, which, he suggested, had worked with other historical processes to splinter subjective experience.[33] The context of modernity outlined by Benjamin is suggestive in understanding the transcendentalist underpinnings of Sherman's program, and of so much modernist art. But to understand why drawing for Sherman had become an explicitly "*aggressive* seeing-and-drawing act" (emphasis added), it is necessary to look at the more recent past: at Mandel's account of the conditions that emerged — like Sherman's course — in the United States in the midst of World War II, given the forms of production introduced under late capitalism and the "third technological revolution."[34] One would be hard pressed to imagine a form of instruction more directly geared to prepare individuals for life and work under these greatly accelerated conditions than Sherman's.

That this course could indeed help its students to create aesthetic unities while performing "supervisory and preparatory functions" is evident not just in Lichtenstein's mature Pop designs but in the work he created as a graduate student and instructor at Ohio State between 1946 and 1949. Though he could not have used the flash lab when he first attended the school as an undergraduate, between 1940 and 1942 (an early version of the lab was only constructed later in 1942, after he had left), Lichtenstein did learn Sherman's method when he returned to Ohio after the war, and he used it and its suppositions both to create his own art and to teach his younger pupils. His art from the late 1940s had already had a re-presentational structure, though he was not aggressively unifying the mass-cultural image according to the tenets of a virtually classical aesthetic, as he would later on. Instead, during the late 1940s he revised images of medieval damsels and knights from such familiar sources as the Bayeux Tapestry; and, beginning around 1950, he refurbished nineteenth-century potboilers, including Emanuel Leutze's *Washington Crossing the Delaware* and William Ranney's *Emigrant Train*. On all this imagery, and on an imagery of machine parts, he imposed a gently comic modernist style derived from Picasso, Klee, and Miró.

Implicit in Lichtenstein's longstanding will-to-form is an abiding belief in the positive effect of such transcendentalist pictorial organization. This faith in the virtue, if not in the sanctity, of modernist aesthetics suggests an important link between his art and that of Abstract Expressionists. Indeed, the students of Hans Hofmann were joined by the students of teachers like Lepper and Sherman in their common understanding that the modernist picture surface accommodates a symbolic "pictorial space" in which the tensions and contradictions of late-capitalist social life can be resolved. Despite the metaphysical rhetoric and masculinist negational conceits that framed Abstract Expressionism, this art also incorporated structural features of late-capitalist social life. Pop artists may have taken to these structures more willingly, not to say ostentatiously; but not without subjecting them to aesthetic (and in Warhol's case to anti-aesthetic) processes that concealed evidence of formal and ontological differences within these signs of commercial equivalence. If Warhol's anti-aesthetics isolate his art within Pop, this should be taken not just as proof of his early success within the field of commercial design, but as evidence of the more deeply felt cultural antagonism of this working-class artist who was also, not incidentally, the only "out" gay man among his post-Abstract Expressionist peers.

By the late 1940s, when Lichtenstein was creating his variations on previous images, re-presentational tactics were not his exclusive domain. Shortly after the death of Franz Kline, in 1962, the painter Elaine de Kooning wrote a catalogue essay for a memorial exhibition of his work. In it she told of a day, late in 1948, when Kline visited her and Willem de Kooning, her husband, at the latter's Fourth Avenue studio. Kline was anxious to

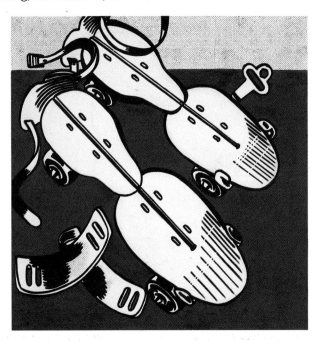

find a way out of an impasse in his work. Two years had passed since Pollock had created the first of his epochal "poured" paintings, and Willem had attracted critical acclaim for the black-and-white enamel abstractions he had exhibited in April 1948 at Charles Egan's gallery. In this climate of expansive innovation, Kline was still creating sensitive drawings and modest easel paintings, some figurative and others in an abstract style that was somewhat too reminiscent of Willem's own. De Kooning suggested to his friend that he put one of the ink sketches he had brought along into the studio's Bell-Opticon opaque projector, which de Kooning himself had borrowed to enlarge his own diminutive sketches onto large canvas supports. Kline's epiphany occurred when he saw the image of his little India ink drawing projected onto the studio wall: "A 4 by 5-inch brush drawing of the rocking chair…loomed in gigantic black strokes which eradicated the image, the strokes expanding as entities in themselves, unrelated to any reality but that of their own existence."[35] From this

ROY LICHTENSTEIN
Roller Skates, 1961
Oil on canvas, 42 x 40 inches
Collection of Pontus Bonnier, Stockholm

procedure, which Kline would continue to use for the rest of his life, there evolved the monumental paintings that he exhibited at Egan's gallery in 1950, and that established his international reputation as a significant Abstract Expressionist.

It was two years after Kline's show that Rosenberg published his essay "The American Action Painters," in which he described this art as a "revolution against the given in the self and the world."[36] Rosenberg followed the artists' own order of priorities in underscoring the importance of their negation—their "constant No"—in determining the meaning of their improvisational method. Yet he admitted that some of the action painters made what amounted to preliminary sketches—"skirmishes," he called them, for the main event that would take place in the larger canvas arena. And in light of such sketches, and particularly of the reproductive procedures that Kline and de Kooning are known to have used, to what extent can their work be described in Rosenberg's terms? Motivated by and actually reproducing something already in the world, such paintings constitute a "revolution against the given" in only the most qualified sense.

That no one has allowed knowledge of this reproductive procedure to interfere in any way with the conventional interpretation of the action painters' art as abstract and expressionist attests to the enduring appeal of these spectacularly staged manifestations of an embattled American postwar humanism. Similarly, the success of Pop art had to take place before the Abstract Expressionists' affection for American

mass culture—for cartoons, comic strips, and movies—could be considered important to works such as de Kooning's "Women."[37] A greater openness to the significance of Abstract Expressionist re-presentation would lead to a more complex understanding of art from the late 1940s through the early 1960s, and would provoke a healthy skepticism toward the commonplaces of both the Abstract Expressionist and the Pop ideologies. For example, art critics and historians ordinarily describe the relationship between Abstract Expressionist practice and everyday American life as one of more or less rigorous antagonism. Yet keeping in mind the totality of Kline and de Kooning's method, would it not be more accurate to say that these artists internalized the mechanical, repetitive structures that dominate postwar American life in order all the more dramatically to stage their resistance to them? The idea that action painters might resort to mechanical reproduction to assist in transcriptions that they then disguised beneath the painterly ciphers of an emphatic originality makes it possible to describe such works not just as "originals" but as *dissimulated copies* as well.

ROY LICHTENSTEIN
Turkey, 1961
Oil on canvas, 26 x 30 inches
Collection of Mitchell Lichtenstein, New York

ROY LICHTENSTEIN
Man with Folded Arms, 1962
Oil on canvas, 70 x 48 1/2 inches
The Museum of Contemporary Art, Los Angeles
The Panza Collection

This less familiar — indeed repressed — aspect of the action painter's method also suggests that the relationship between Abstract Expressionism and the Pop art that followed it is more complex and ambiguous — more truly dialectical — than the familiar binary that critics and art historians have devised and reinforced to keep them apart. When Elaine de Kooning described Kline's revelation on seeing his figurative drawing transformed through gigantism into heroic abstraction, she might just as well have been describing a similar epiphany experienced by the young James Rosenquist. An unmistakable New York School swagger informs Rosenquist's tale of how he learned to see "abstraction everywhere" while employed as a commercial sign painter. Working on a scaffold high above Times Square, he was so close to the image that it was transformed — again through gigantism — into abstraction. Rosenquist was able to endow his montagelike Pop compositions with the push-pull spatial hydraulics that Hofmann had prescribed as a means of establishing maximum pictorial tension in nonillusionistic painting. However, this skill was due less to Rosenquist's experience as a commercial sign painter than to his having studied with Cameron Booth (1952-54) at the University of Minnesota. Booth had studied with Andre Lhote for a year in Paris (1927) before studying with Hofmann for two years in Munich (1928-30).[38]

If Kline and de Kooning dissimulated by producing copies that looked like originals, the Pop artists dissimulated by producing originals that masqueraded as copies. Where the Abstract Expressionist dissimulation was almost wholly overlooked, the Pop equivalent was picked up in the first critical responses to the new art. The contradictory character of the Pop object was central to an unusually lively and revealing debate late in 1963. It was Lichtenstein's earliest Pop paintings that provoked this controversy, which led

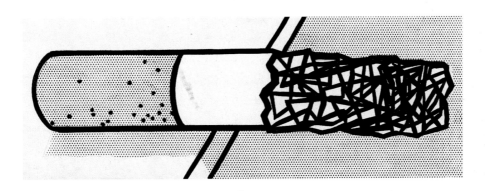

109

critic Brian O'Doherty (also an artist, under the name Patrick Ireland) to identify a completely new class of object: the "handmade readymade." Reviewing the artist's second Pop show in the *New York Times*, O'Doherty labeled him "one of the worst artists in America." Nonetheless, he also credited him with creating paintings that "raised some of the most difficult problems in art."[39]

O'Doherty took note of an argument that had just erupted in the art press: the September issues both of *Art News* and *Artforum* had run angry features about Pop art in general and Lichtenstein's work in particular. Both were written by an esteemed California art teacher, Erle Loran, who had targeted two paintings by Lichtenstein, *Portrait of Mme. Cézanne* and *Man with Folded Arms* (both 1962), in order to excoriate some of the salient features of the new art.[40] Each painting was a characteristically brazen blowup of a diagram from Loran's book *Cézanne's Composition*, then twenty years old. As a manifestation of the far-reaching attempt before and after World War II to extend the benefits of cultural activity and modernist art to larger and more socially diverse numbers of Americans, Loran's diagrammatic analysis of Cézanne's art was something of a vintage forties object. Lichtenstein's pedagogical pastiches join Warhol's "Do It Yourself" and "Dance

ROY LICHTENSTEIN
Cigarette, 1962
Oil on canvas, 12 x 34 inches
Private collection, New York

Diagram" paintings, also from 1962, to form a distinct Pop genre, one that suggests these artists' ambivalent awareness of the middlebrow culture that Greenberg had considered so threatening to art when Loran published his book.[41]

Both Loran and O'Doherty thought it absurd that so many supporters of Pop were defending Lichtenstein by insisting that he "transformed" rather than "copied" his sources. Claiming that only an expert could discern the difference, O'Doherty found this hairsplitting quite beside the point. After all, it had been possible to classify *direct* appropriation as art since 1913, when that "old master of innovation," Duchamp, had "started it all by setting up his readymades...and calling them art, leaving on us the burden of proof that they were not." Both Loran and O'Doherty found the transformation alibi doubly annoying since it clinched the matter of Pop's high-cultural status by resorting to an altogether academic and contradictory dual defense. On the one hand, Pop was art because it "put a frame of consciousness around a major part of American life...we take for granted." On the other, Pop was art because an artist like Lichtenstein transformed his sources "like a good artist should" — a cliched view of fine-art production. Dismissing both defenses, O'Doherty despaired of this "triumph of the banal" and demurred, "Mr. Lichtenstein's art is in the category, I suppose, of the handmade readymade."

Loran wrote his two articles after Lichtenstein's first Pop exhibition in Los Angeles, which included the artist's life-sized versions of images from Loran's book. These articles may well have marked a historical first: there is reason to believe that they supplanted Loran's intention to sue the artist and his dealer for copyright infringement. Such litigious impulses have peppered the history of American art ever since. The angrier of the two tracts appeared in *Art News*, where Loran openly expressed his contempt for Lichtenstein's work and hinted at his desire to sue.

> In a recent sell-out exhibition at the Ferus Gallery, Los Angeles, he [Lichtenstein] *gave the title of* Portrait of Mme. Cézanne *to the black and white line drawing on bare canvas reproduced here. Sale price: $2,000, or more. I suppose I should be flattered that a diagrammatic sketch of mine should be worth so much. But then, no one has paid me anything — so far.*[42]

One does not have to read past the rhetorical question that served as Loran's title ("Pop Artists or Copycats?") to detect what was most provocative about Pop. Like many others, Loran saw Abstract Expressionism as the quintessentially American humanist art: a "monument to the human spirit," an emblem of the "depth and richness of human experience and intuition," and a demonstration of the "true meaning of free democracy...in America." The Abstract Expressionists had opened up new and unprecedented avenues for aesthetic exploration that Loran considered on a par with the "most advanced products of the human mind, comparable in some ways to achievements in physics and chemistry."[43] As an art educator, he was incensed that any self-respecting artist would want to undermine so precious a cultural resource. That such an artist would then be remunerated handsomely for advancing a culture of copies over one of originals was simply more than he could endure in silence.

For Loran, the "transformation" or "copy" debate was spurious: since the Abstract Expressionists had ventured "far beyond the process of transforming nature" to produce paintings that presupposed "no conscious source but have an identity and imagery that is autonomous," transformation — even *were* it detectable in Lichtenstein's art — could only constitute aesthetic regression.[44] For different reasons, Lichtenstein himself shunned the transformation defense. During the first year of Pop's reception, critics so insistently and so often said that the artist transformed his sources that he was compelled to offer his own characteristically laconic corrective. Shortly after the publication of Loran's two articles (the second of which was entitled, significantly, "Cézanne and Lichtenstein: Problems of Transformation"), Lichtenstein remarked in an interview with Gene Swenson that "transformation is a strange word to use. It implies that art transforms. It doesn't, it just plain forms."[45]

Among the critics who joined Loran's assault was Max Kozloff, who worried in *The Nation* that art like Lichtenstein's might signal "a rejection of the deepest values of modern art." When Kozloff noted that for six or seven years in New York "we have been witnessing an attack upon the notion of originality in painting," he pinpointed the central feature of the Loran controversy, and the crucial normative term within the modernist system of aesthetic evaluation that Pop had placed in jeopardy.[46]

Kozloff was concerned about the implications of Pop's attack on artistic invention for "the ethic of most twentieth-century art." He condemned art like Lichtenstein's and Warhol's for depending on the high art "context" for its effect; without that context, he argued, their works would revert back to their status as non-art. Pop, in Kozloff's words, was "as contextual as it is conceptual," an observation that would seem to situate this art within the tradition of what has been called the "historical avant-garde" to the extent that it exposes the institutional framework of art. Kozloff's observation, however, fails to take into account the singularly contradictory character of the "handmade readymade," without which the entire debate about transformation could not have taken place.[47]

The handmade readymade may well have been limited in its critique of earlier aesthetic practices, but it did enable Pop artists to deflate Abstract Expressionist solemnity. Warhol, for example, indirectly addressed the abstract designs of Barnett Newman in paintings of greatly enlarged commercial illustrations (*Telephone*, 1961) and banal everyday objects (*Close Cover Before Striking*, 1962); and Lichtenstein, in 1964, was sufficiently inspired by the sight of a single romance-comic panel (in which a hand in tight closeup slathers paint on a garden fence) to inaugurate a career-long series of paintings and sculptures that show Abstract Expressionist art as neither abstract nor expressionist.[48] The sensational appearance in galleries, museums, and the popular press of Pop's monumental hand-painted and silkscreened ads, headlines, and comic book images forced observers to reflect upon the erosion of Abstract Expressionist belief systems.

ROY LICHTENSTEIN
The Grip, 1962
Oil on canvas, 30 x 30 1/4 inches
The Museum of Contemporary Art, Los Angeles
The Panza Collection

Actually, as Kozloff observed, this erosion dated from a full decade earlier. The viability of Abstract Expressionism depended upon the interrelated concepts of stylistic authenticity, metaphoric structure, and the mythic notion of autonomous creativity. That these preconditions had become at best contestable and at worst discredited by the early fifties is suggested by Kozloff's observation that in that period "there grew a cleavage between the motivating idea and its embodiment, the fusion of which had been the guiding premise of Abstract Expressionism."[49] This is another way of saying that a fissure had opened up between artistic form and content. And Abstract Expressionism had depended upon a supposed fusion of the two, not just for its metaphoric conception of style as transparent to the artist who creates it, but for its claim to descend from an aesthetic tradition that arguably could be traced to the birth of humanism.

In a related observation, Kozloff asserted that the once crucial distinction between abstraction and representation was "no longer relevant." In a sense this was true at the height of Abstract Expressionism, for when Kline and de Kooning used slide projectors to transfer images from one medium and scale to another, they transformed abstraction into representation. Kozloff's point, however, is that even for action painters who had never resorted to the devices of mechanical reproduction, abstract imagery had become encoded, recognizable. "It is quite as possible to put comic strips through their mechanistic paces as it is concentric circles. In fact, as conventionalized icons they ultimately have about equivalent non-meanings."[50] One cannot very well sustain a view of a modernist-vanguard artwork as the last resolutely unique object in the midst of a commodity culture once such a work has joined all others in its failure to establish the illusory union between form and content that would testify to its transcendent status. In this sense, all images have acquired an equivalence with one another in their capacity to yield "non-meaning."

Kozloff's reference to "concentric circles" and "conventionalized icons" recalls Johns's paintings of targets, stenciled numbers, flags, and other "things the mind already knows." These painterly adaptations of the readymade contradicted the humanistic and Abstract Expressionist conception of the artistic image as the unforeseen and therefore authentic result of an organic painting process in which every brushstroke testified (seismographically, as it were) to the presence of the artist-creator. That conception was nowhere more suggestively and concisely contested than in Robert Rauschenberg's two paintings *Factum I* and *Factum II* (both 1957): *Factum II* is an exacting replica of *Factum I*, right down to the vivid pseudo-expressionist drips and slashes of red, gold, black, and white paint. In each work these signifiers of spontaneity are juxtaposed with printed matter that includes a calendar of the year 1956, doubled headshots of President Eisenhower, newspaper clippings containing paired pictures of a burning tenement, and color photos of a lakeside landscape. The casual coexistence on the same pictorial surfaces of the hand- and the machine-made, the "unique" and the reproducible, establishes the terms of an equation in which the painterly rhetorics of existentialism and abstraction are given parity with other, less highly regarded forms of representation.

Factum I and *Factum II* crystallized the emergent logic of the handmade readymade. It only remained for the Pop artists to find their own ways of exploiting the gulf that had opened up between pictorial form and content during the 1950s. Concerning style's increasing dislocation from authorship, Warhol could exult, "I think that would be so great, to be able to change styles. And I think that's what's going to happen, that's going to be the whole new scene."[51] Neither metaphoric nor metonymic, the handmade readymade depleted painting of its symbolic function. It had no "depth." As Roland Barthes observed, no artist can be found "behind" this obdurate object. Confronted by it, the French critic was moved to recall a "true revolution of language."[52]

To the extent that Pop (and earlier works by Rauschenberg and Johns) can be described in terms of such a dissolution of metaphor, it is not surprising that it heralded the corresponding return to prominence of "allegory" — a term in this case referring to the appropriation of preexisting images (or objects) in a seemingly arbitrary fashion that resituates them within a new chain of signifying relations. The signifier, its original

ROY LICHTENSTEIN
Large Jewels, 1963
Magna on canvas, 68 x 36 inches
Museum Ludwig, Cologne

signified now bracketed, generates new meanings potentially antithetical to the old. As Benjamin wrote, "This meaning with that image, that image with this meaning."[53] This structural feature of allegory enabled Pop artists to deploy images that function on the one hand at the level of the most commonplace mass-cultural signs (the comic strip referent) while on the other registering the more rarefied concerns of high art (the comic strip panel of a jet plane exploding, for example, functions—to some—as a critical reference to Abstract Expressionism). It was precisely this allegorical structure that led Barthes to describe Pop as follows: "There are two voices, as in a fugue—one says, 'This is not Art'; the other says, at the same time: 'I am Art.'"[54]

Yet the handmade readymade—perfect vehicle for the contradictory social messages of Pop—also resulted in oddly conciliatory cultural effects. For the Pop artists suspended the normative pairs of terms—unique/reproduced, original/copy, high culture/mass culture—that had until then been maintained in antagonism so as to preserve the integrity of modernist high culture. As early as 1962, when Donald Judd reviewed Lichtenstein's first Pop show, critics recognized that what they most disliked about Lichtenstein's work—its proximity to the stylistic codes and contents of mass culture—was tempered by the "traditional" and "quite expert" composition of paintings like *The Kiss* (1962). Judd wrote, "Respectability comes quickly, is strong and can be shrewd. Lichtenstein's comics and advertisements *destroy the necessity to which the usual definitions pretend*."[55] (Emphasis added.) He was referring to Lichtenstein's ability to navigate his way

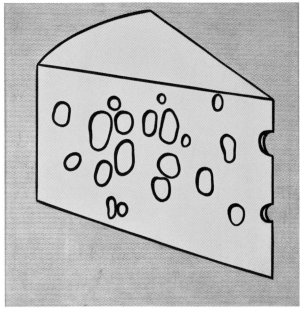

successfully through the "high and low" minefield of normative terms in modernist visual culture. By representing the mass-cultural artifact while re-forming it in such a way as to suggest an abundance of traditional aesthetic rewards, Lichtenstein eliminated the "necessity" of enforcing the boundaries between "high" art and "low" culture.

Pop art could also expose the arbitrariness with which this exclusionary cultural hierarchy had been maintained. Testing the categorical limits of modern art and culture was a self-professed goal of the Pop artists. In 1964, Claes Oldenburg noted that he had always been "bothered by distinctions—that this is good and this is bad and this is better. I am especially bothered by the distinction between commercial and fine art, or between fine painting and accidental effects. I think we have made a deliberate attempt to explore this area."[56] Parody, dissimulation, and the defamiliarizing effect of enlargement enabled Oldenburg to stage his

ROY LICHTENSTEIN
Swiss Cheese, 1962
Oil on canvas, 40 x 40 inches
Collection of David Lichtenstein, New York

aesthetic investigation into the similarities and differences between (to cite his example) a sculpture by Arp and the gravity-induced biomorphism of spilled ketchup. By summoning at once the most exalted and the most debased cultural registers, he foregrounded his "art and the arbitrary act of the artist." Lichtenstein was just as interested in the flip side of this problematic. Responding to a comment about the "impersonality" of his and Warhol's art, he criticized the widespread tendency — born of the numbing effects of life in an advanced consumer culture — to assume that "similar things are identical."[57]

By attracting the spectator's attention to familiar imagery, the handmade readymade taps into the resources of what Benjamin, in the same essay on Baudelaire, calls "voluntary" memory, after Proust — the most commonplace form of recognition, essential to functioning in everyday life, and instrumental throughout the history of capitalism. However, this art exploits voluntary or instrumental memory only to expose its inadequacies. Direct examination of the Pop object prompts awareness not just of the institutional circumstances that separate high art from mass culture, but of ontological differences between a Lichtenstein painting of a comic strip panel and the original image, or between piles of Warhol Brillo boxes and Brillo's own. The Pop artists turned Abstract Expressionist logic on its head when they gave up "invention" (in the traditional sense of that term); but by fashioning objects that also insisted that similar things are, indeed, not identical, they salvaged a vestige of the action painter's resistance to "the given in the self and in the world."[58]

115

Science and technology, the ethos of aggressive productivity, and a romantic belief in art's conciliatory power combined to inform the university art department pedagogies that produced the Pop generation. Clearly, in much of this there are echoes of the Bauhaus. But the transformation of art, design, and their instruction in America was not simply an extension of the lessons of European immigrants such as Josef Albers, Laszlo Moholy-Nagy, Walter Gropius, or, for that matter, Hofmann. Institutions such as the New Bauhaus in Chicago and Black Mountain College in rural North Carolina were certainly influential wellsprings of high modernist pedagogical theory and of avant-gardist experimentation. But the professionalization, and rationalization, of American art instruction was a less celebrated yet significant late modern response to conditions endemic in the U.S. throughout the 1930s and 1940s.

High modernism, as exemplified by Bauhaus teaching, aimed at a practically Hegelian transformation of art and design. Late modernism, as it surfaced in American university art departments

ROY LICHTENSTEIN
Cherry Pie, 1962
Oil on canvas, 20 x 24 inches
The Sydney and Frances Lewis Collection, Richmond, Virginia

—and in transactions among businessmen, artists, and designers—delineated an altogether more instrumental combination of aesthetic and industrial economies. That combination was prompted by historical and economic circumstances so distinct from European conditions between the world wars that it compelled high modernists such as Moholy-Nagy to reconsider and adjust their methods. Moholy's two books *The New Vision* and *Vision in Motion* are separated by more than the seventeen years of their respective publication dates (1930 and 1947); a theoretical gulf divides them. This rift is symptomatic of the contradiction between the Bauhaus design standard, which presides over, and is itself the product of, a painstaking, virtually ecological investigation, and an American economy fueled by what Moholy variously condemned as waste or "forced obsolescence."[59]

The American art instructors of the 1940s introduced many of the artists we associate with Pop to the technical skills and belief systems that they considered indispensable to modern art and design. Of Pop artists it can truly be said that they were among the first generation of American artists to be professionally educated in university art departments, or in fully accredited, degree-granting art schools. They experienced a unique, transitory moment in the history of American art instruction, when a singularly rational approach to teaching unprecedented numbers of students the skills of pictorial organization and commercial design was united with a still romantic belief in the inherent beneficence of art and science. The efficient, now remote, pedagogical methods by which Warhol and Lichtenstein were taught endowed both artists with the mastery of form and contradiction that so completely characterizes their work. This odd conjunction of a demystifying, often positivistic approach to art training with an ongoing, romantic belief in art's conciliatory, restorative powers constitutes an important historical precedent—and structural analogue—for the Pop artist's contradictory aesthetic procedure, and for its ultimate product, the "handmade readymade."

116

1 Clement Greenberg, "Review of the Water-Color, Drawing, and Sculpture Sections of the Whitney Annual," 1946, in John O'Brian, ed., *Clement Greenberg: The Collected Essays and Criticism*, vol. 2 (Chicago: University of Chicago Press, 1986), pp. 57-58.

2 "As Kurt List, the music critic, says, we may be witnessing the emergence of a new, middlebrow form of popular art that, while it exploits many of the innovations of avant-garde art, lowers their intensity and dilutes their seriousness in order to convert them into something calendars and magazines can digest—as if in answer to a public that is making new and higher demands on the art offered to it." Ibid., p. 57.

3 Greenberg, "The Present Prospects of American Painting and Sculpture," 1947, *Collected Essays*, p. 163.

4 Mandel divides the history of capitalism into a sequence of "long waves" in which rates of profit rise and fall, and along with them rates of capital accumulation. One such long wave—the "long wave of the third technological revolution"—begins in 1940-45, as the rate of profit increases due to the "weakening (and partial atomization) of the working class by fascism and the Second World War." This prompts a "massive rise in the rate of profit, which promotes the accumulation of capital. This is first thrown into armaments production, then into the innovations of the third technological revolution," which is marked by "generalized control of machines by means of electronic apparatuses (as well as by the gradual introduction of nuclear energy)." This, in turn, promotes a long-term rise in the rate of profit, which Mandel sees extending through 1966. Ernest Mandel, *Late Capitalism*, trans. Joris De Bres (London: Verso Edition, 1978), pp. 121, 131, 387.

5 Greenberg, "Present Prospects," p. 163.

6 Even when Greenberg is not excoriating middlebrow art per se, the terms of his critique remained rigidly gendered: "[David] Smith's art is more enlightened, optimistic and broader than Pollock's, and makes up for its lesser force by a virile elegance that is without example in a country where elegance is otherwise obtained only by femininity or by [a] wistful, playful, derivative kind of decorativeness."

Turning to writing in the art magazines of the day, his use of disparaging gendered terms gives way to openly ridiculing sexual—or rather homosexual—ones: "The discussion of American art, even in the most exalted circles, is a kind of travelogue patter—this is what fills the three or four art magazines that live an endowed existence in New York and whose copy is supplied by permanent college girls, male and female."

"Present Prospects," pp. 167, 162.

7 After claiming that "Picasso, Braque, Mondrian, Miró, Kandinsky, Brancusi, even Klee, Matisse and Cézanne derive their chief inspiration from the medium they work in," Greenberg adds the following footnote: "I owe this formulation to a remark made by Hans Hofmann, the art teacher, in one of his lectures. From the point of view of this formulation, Surrealism in plastic art is a reactionary tendency which is attempting to restore 'outside' subject matter. The chief concern of a painter like Dali is to represent the processes and concepts of his consciousness, not the processes of his medium." It is no exaggeration to state that Hofmann's "remark" remained central to Greenberg's criticism through the 1960s, informing such later, yet central, formulations as "Modernist Painting" (1965). See "Avant-Garde and Kitsch," *Collected Essays*, vol. 1, p. 9.

8 "Present Prospects," pp. 169-70.

9 Hans Hofmann, "Search for the Real," in Sara T. Weeks and Bartlett H. Hayes, Jr., eds., *Search for the Real and Other Essays* (Cambridge, Mass.: MIT Press, 1967), p. 47.

10 It is not insignificant that these artists and their colleagues were all acquainted with each other throughout the crucial period of the early 1950s. Willem de Kooning, Franz Kline, Robert Rauschenberg, Cy Twombly, John Cage, and Merce Cunningham, among others, summered together at Black Mountain College in 1952. Willem and Elaine de Kooning were also present at Black Mountain during the summer of 1947—Rauschenberg's first there—having been invited by Cage. See Calvin Tompkins, *Off The Wall: Robert Rauschenberg and the Art World of Our Time* (Harmondsworth, Middlesex: Penguin Books, 1980), pp. 31, 96-97. Also, Walter Hopps, *Robert Rauschenberg: The Early 1950s* (Houston: Menil Foundation, 1991).

11 See Harold Rosenberg, "The American Action Painters," reprinted in *The Tradition of the New* (Chicago: University of Chicago Press, 1959), pp. 23-39; and Allan Kaprow, "The Legacy of Jackson Pollock," *Art News* 57, no. 6 (October 1958): 24-26.

12 The Rose Fried Gallery and Sidney Janis Gallery mounted exhibitions devoted to Marcel Duchamp and Dada in 1952 and 1953; Duchamp assisted in organizing the Janis show, and mounted a memorial exhibition of Katherine Dreier's collection at the Yale University Art Gallery; the Philadelphia Museum of Art installed the Louise and Walter Arensberg Collection, including forty-three works by Duchamp in 1954; and finally, at Duchamp's suggestion, James Johnson Sweeney organized "Jacques Villon, Raymond Duchamp-Villon, Marcel Duchamp" at the Solomon R. Guggenheim Museum, New York, in 1957. See "Chronology," in Anne d'Harnoncourt and Kynaston McShine, *Marcel Duchamp* (New York: The Museum of Modern Art, 1973), pp. 26-27.

13 Leo Steinberg, "Other Criteria," in *Other Criteria: Confrontations in Twentieth-Century Art* (New York: Oxford University Press, 1972), pp. 82-91.

14 "In societies where modern conditions of production prevail, all of life presents itself as an immense accumulation of spectacles. Everything that was directly lived has moved away into a representation." See Guy Debord, *Society of the Spectacle* (first published in French, 1967); English trans. (Detroit: Red & Black, 1983), unpag. See also Jean Baudrillard, *Simulations*, trans. Paul Foss, Paul Patton, and Philip Beitchman (New York: Semiotext(e), 1983).

15 See Francis V. O'Connor, ed., *Art For the Millions* (Boston: New York Graphic Society, 1973), pp. 13ff.

16 John Dewey, *Art As Experience* (New York: Paragon Books, 1979), pp. 326-27.

17 See Serge Guilbaut, *How New York Stole the Idea of Modern Art*, trans. Arthur Goldhammer (Chicago: University of Chicago Press, 1983), pp. 55-59.

18 See James Sloan Allen, *The Romance of Commerce and Culture* (Chicago: University of Chicago Press, 1983). In 1946, Greenberg noted "the increasing practice on the part of commercial firms of having what in popular estimation are high-art artists illustrate their advertisements." "Review of the Whitney Annual," *Collected Essays*, p. 57.

19 On the development of the industrial-design program at the Carnegie Institute of Technology, see Arthur J. Pulos, *The American Design Adventure* (Cambridge, Mass.: MIT Press, 1988), p. 165. For Robert Lepper's paper commemorating the introduction of this program, see an untitled manuscript in Lepper materials, Carnegie Mellon University Archives.

20 Dean Keeble, quoted in Glen U. Cleeton, *The Story of Carnegie Tech: The Doherty Administration (1936-1950)*, vol. 2 (Pittsburgh: The Carnegie Press, 1965), pp. 136-37.

21 "Gene Swenson: Where did your ideas about art begin?
Roy Lichtenstein: The ideas of Professor Hoyt Sherman on perception were my earliest important influence and still affect my ideas of visual unity." Gene Swenson, "Interviews with Eight Painters, Part I, What is Pop Art?" *Art News* 62, no. 7 (November 1963); reprinted in John Coplans, ed., *Roy Lichtenstein* (New York: Praeger Publishers, 1972), p. 53.

22 See Robert Lepper, "Processes in Professor Lepper's Courses in Pictorial Design, August 1948," Lepper materials, Carnegie Mellon University Archives, pp. 1-6.

23 In a symposium about Pop that Peter Selz organized at the Museum of Modern Art in 1963, Hilton Kramer—never a fan—made the following statement: "Pop art does not tell us what it feels like to be living through the present moment of civilization; it is merely part of the evidence of that civilization. Its social effect is simply *to reconcile us to a world of commodities, banalities and vulgarities, which is to say, an effect indistinguishable from advertising art.*"(emphasis added.) See Peter Selz, "Symposium on Pop Art," *Arts Magazine* 37, no. 7 (April 1963): 38-39.

24 "The writer was pursued by the notion that underlying pictorial organization there was a key idea which had not yet been fully clarified, and that if this idea could be clarified, great improvements in teaching art might be possible, and perhaps the relation of art to other phases of modern life might be more clearly apparent." See Hoyt L. Sherman, *Perceptualism: The Artist's Vision*

(Columbus: Ohio State University, 1944), p. 1. "Could we then claim that psychology is particularly fitted for the task of integration? I think we can, for in psychology we are at the point where the three great provinces of our world intersect, the provinces which we call inanimate nature, life, and mind." See Kurt Koffka, *Principles of Gestalt Psychology* (New York: Harcourt, Brace, 1935), p. 10.

25 Sherman recommended the "flash drawing course" for "reading, athletics, architecture, engineering design, landscape architecture, floriculture, photography, interior decorating, window trimming, advertising, music, optometry, dentistry, newspaper and scientific reporting . . ." and for waging war. He trained the perceptual and kinesthetic capacities of the Ohio State football team quarterback in 1948, claiming to have improved his performance. See Sherman, *Perceptualism*, pp. 69-75, and Sherman, *Drawing by Seeing* (New York: Hinds, Hayden & Eldredge, 1947), p. 51.

26 "I have leaned heavily, and naively probably, on John Dewey's *Art in Experience* [sic]. I've never forgotten it." Sherman, quoted in David Ecker and Stanley S. Medeja, *Pioneers in Perception: A Study of Aesthetic Perception. Conversations with Rudolf Arnheim, James L. Gibson, Nelson Goodman, Henry Schaefer-Simmern, and Hoyt Sherman* (St. Louis: Cemrel, Inc., 1979), p. 309.

27 The "flash lab" was in fact the second of two studios that were built in the shed adjacent to Hayes Hall. The first, altogether more provisional, dates from 1942. This description of Sherman's studio and his course derives from Sherman's *Drawing by Seeing*.

28 "I became acquainted with Gestalt theory and figure-ground about 1939 and knew that ground was a critical factor over the figure, aesthetically. The ground always influences the figure. That was Helmholtz's demonstration; and I used the other cues of Wertheimer...." Sherman, quoted in Ecker and Medeja, pp. 259, 267.

29 Sherman, *Drawing by Seeing*, p. 3.

The tachistoscope had been used to remarkably similar effect at Ohio State University since the mid-1930s in the long-term investigations of Samuel Renshaw, Professor of Psychology, into "the effects of practice on the development of superior methods to yield enhancement of performance, or to discover the means of making effective use of such methods in training people to see more accurately and more rapidly." Though Sherman admitted to no such influence, it is hard to say how much he relied on Renshaw's work to formulate his own ideas. Renshaw's study, which was published in 1945, includes statements closely parallel to Sherman's own. In relation to Sherman's comments quoted above, consider Renshaw's statement: "Seeing, to be effective, must be unitary, coherent, and fluent. Perceptual training by tachistoscopic methods enforces from the first this theoretically sound procedure." The fact that a patently instrumental study by a university psychologist should be indistinguishable from the methods of an art instructor underscore yet again the strange confluence of utility and aesthetics that informed the education of the artist on American university campuses during this period. See Samuel Renshaw, "The Visual Perception and Reproduction of Forms by Tachistoscopic Methods," *Journal of Psychology* 20 (October 1945): 218.

30 Michael Fried, "Art and Objecthood," in Gregory Battcock, ed., *Minimal Art: A Critical Anthology* (New York: E. P. Dutton & Co., 1968), p. 146.

31 Sherman, *Drawing by Seeing*, pp. 18-19.

32 Sherman claims that he and an unnamed colleague from the psychology department "sold" the idea of a flash-based "aircraft identification program" to the United States Navy early in the American involvement in World War II. See Ecker and Medeja, p. 251.

33 See Walter Benjamin, "On Some Motifs in Baudelaire," in Hannah Arendt, ed., *Illuminations*, trans. Harry Zohn (New York: Schocken Books, 1969), pp. 155-201.

34 "The inception of the use of electronic data-processing machines in the private sector of the American economy in 1954 finally opened up, for numerous if not all branches of production, the field of accelerated technological innovation and the hunt for technological surplus-profits which characterizes late capitalism. Incidentally, we can thus date the end of the reconstruction period after the Second World War and the start of the boom unleashed by the third technological revolution from that year." Mandel, *Late Capitalism*, pp. 194-95.

117

35 Elaine de Kooning, "Franz Kline: Painter of His Own Life," *Art News* 61, no. 7 (November 1962): 67-68. Reprinted from *Franz Kline* (Washington, D.C.: Gallery of Modern Art, 1962).

36 Rosenberg, "The American Action Painters," p. 32.

37 For an example of the increased receptivity of critics after Pop to the importance of mass-cultural interests among Abstract Expressionists, see Thomas B. Hess's text in the exhibition catalogue *Willem de Kooning* (New York: The Museum of Modern Art, 1968), especially pp. 76ff. There Hess noted the artist's complaint that nobody had ever noticed how funny the "Women" really were. Resorting to a traditional art-historical reflex, Hess then claimed these and other paintings (*Attic*, 1949, *Gotham News*, 1955-56) as a "direct influence" on Pop artists. For an analysis of Kline's involvement with popular culture, see Albert Boime, "Franz Kline and the Figurative Tradition," in *Franz Kline: The Early Work as Signals* (Binghamton: State University of New York, 1977). There he cites Elaine de Kooning's story of Kline's self-discovery through opaque projection, and continues as follows (p. 17): "The process of magnification had a double meaning for Kline: it monumentalized his work and simultaneously legitimized it in his eyes through its analogy with the movies' primitive ancestor, the comic strip." In keeping with the image of the Abstract Expressionists as cultural descendants of Prometheus, Boime understood this to "foreshadow Lichtenstein's and the photorealists' more mechanical amplification of images."

38 See Marcia Tucker, "James Rosenquist," in *James Rosenquist* (New York: Whitney Museum of American Art, 1972), especially pp. 14-15.

39 Brian O'Doherty, "Doubtful but Definite Triumph of the Banal," *New York Times*, 27 October 1963, sec. 2, p. 21.

40 Erle Loran, "Cézanne and Lichtenstein: Problems of Transformation," *Artforum* 2, no. 3 (September 1963): 34-35; "Pop Artists or Copycats?," *Art News* 62, no. 5 (September 1963): 48-49, 61.

41 Be that as it may, Loran's book managed to unite Alfred Barr, Thomas Craven, and Clement Greenberg in their regard for what the last described as a "more essential" understanding of Cézanne's art than any other he had encountered in print. See Greenberg, "Cézanne's Composition by Earle (sic) Loran," *The Nation*, 29 December 1945, reprinted in *Collected Essays*, vol. 2, p. 47.

42 Loran, "Pop Artists or Copycats?," p. 49. Lichtenstein remembers that the Castelli Gallery was approached by the publishers of Loran's book. A new edition, printed in 1963, would have been in preparation at the time the controversy took place. Unpublished interview with this author dated 27 June 1983.

43 Loran, "Cézanne and Lichtenstein," p. 35.

44 Ibid.

45 Swenson, "Interview with Eight Painters," p. 53.

46 Max Kozloff, "Art," *The Nation*, 2 November 1963, p. 284.

47 Ibid., p. 285. On the concept of the historical avant-garde, and the "neoavant-garde" into which Pop may fit more comfortably, see Peter Bürger, *Theory of the Avant-Garde*, trans. Michael Shaw (Minneapolis: University of Minnesota Press, 1984), esp. pp. 57-58.

48 See David Deitcher, "Lichtenstein's Expressionist Takes," *Art in America* 71, no. 1 (January 1983): 84-89.

49 Kozloff, "Art," p. 285.

50 Ibid.

51 Andy Warhol, quoted in Swenson, "What is Pop Art?," reprinted in John Russell and Suzi Gablik, eds., *Pop Art Redefined* (London: Thames and Hudson, 1969), p. 117.

52 Roland Barthes, "That Old Thing, Art...," in *The Responsibility of Forms*, trans. Richard Howard (New York: Hill and Wang, 1985), p. 205. The manifesto of the "true revolution in language" that Barthes refers to in this essay was Barthes's own "The Death of the Author" (1968). See Barthes, *Image-Music-Text*, ed. and trans. Stephen Heath (New York: Hill and Wang, 1977), pp. 142ff.

53 Benjamin, quoted in Benjamin H. D. Buchloh, "Allegorical Procedures: Appropriation and Montage in Contemporary Art," *Artforum* 21, no. 1 (September 1982): 46.

54 Roland Barthes, "That Old Thing, Art...," p. 198.

55 Donald Judd, "Roy Lichtenstein," *Arts Magazine* 36, no.7 (April 1962): 52. Reprinted in Kaspar Koenig, ed., *Donald Judd: Complete Writings 1959-1975* (Halifax: The Press of the Nova Scotia College of Art and Design, 1975), pp. 48-49.

56 Bruce Glaser, "Oldenburg, Lichtenstein, Warhol: A Discussion," *Artforum* 4, no. 6 (February 1966); reprinted in Coplans, *Roy Lichtenstein*, pp. 62-63.

57 Ibid.

58 Warhol's work is usually described as if it were the fulfillment of his frequently quoted observation that "everybody should be a machine." Yet there is a considerable difference between a Warhol image (or object) and the thing it represents, and that difference is aesthetic. The difference between Warhol's aesthetic (trans)formations and Lichtenstein's is that the latter's are consistent with a conventional modernist understanding of "fundamental structure." Warhol's art can be considered "anti-aesthetic" insofar as his repertory of expressive devices — his deliberately off-register silkscreen method, garish color, and employment of seriality in place of more traditional methods of composition — are distillations of the aesthetic logic of advertising and other forms of commercial design.

59 "Design in this country is basically different from that in Europe. A country like the United States, rich in resources, raw materials and human ingenuity, can afford to be wasteful. Thus the economy in the United States has incorporated into its structure the frequent change of models and quick turn-over, by declaring older models obsolete long before their technical usefulness has ceased.... The theory and practice of forced obsolescence leads — in the long run — to cultural and moral disintegration because it destroys the feeling for quality and security of judgment. Continuity of culture results from a primary concern for quality rather than for novelty." See Laszlo Moholy-Nagy, *Vision in Motion* (Chicago: Paul Theobald, 1947), p. 33.

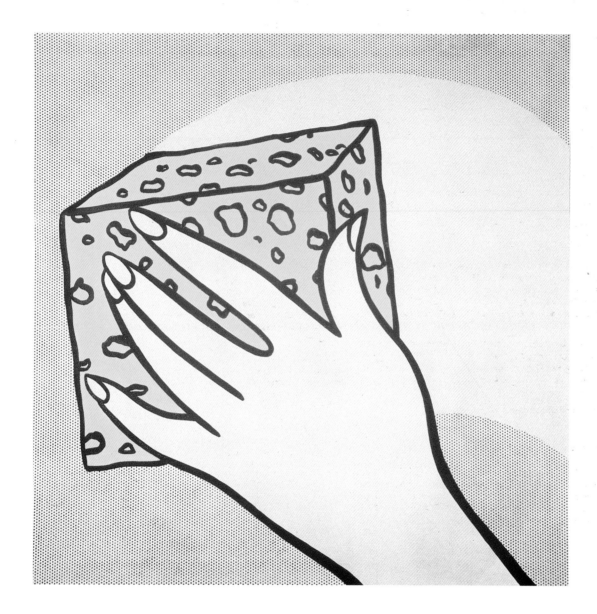

ROY LICHTENSTEIN
Sponge II, 1962
Oil on canvas, 36 x 36 inches
Collection of Peder Bonnier, New York

JASPER JOHNS
Flag, 1954-55
Encaustic, oil, and collage on fabric, mounted on plywood,
42 1/4 x 60 5/8 inches
The Museum of Modern Art, New York
Gift of Philip Johnson in honor of Alfred H. Barr, Jr., 1973

John Yau

Famous Paintings seen and not looked at, not examined

I.

Successive generations of art historians, theoreticians, and critics have characterized Jasper Johns's first solo exhibition, which opened at the Leo Castelli Gallery on January 20 and closed on February 8, 1958, as a pivotal event in their histories of postwar American art. Most have agreed that Johns's paintings of the American flag, targets, numerals, and the alphabet embodied a series of brilliant and unexpected formal resolutions to the crisis which had plagued Abstract Expressionism, and which was particularly evident in the work of one of its foremost practitioners, Willem de Kooning. According to Clement Greenberg and others,[1] this crisis was one that Jackson Pollock, who had died in a car accident in 1956, two years before Johns's show opened, had also been unable to continue resolving in the years preceding his death. For after successfully breaking with art's figurative tradition in the late 1940s, both de Kooning and Pollock were said to have started "retreating" from abstraction to figuration around 1950. As Greenberg saw it, it was as if they found they could go no further, could no longer make art without spatiality and an external reference to the world, and had chosen to go back to something that was less aesthetically pure — the figure within an illusionistic space.

Consequently, during the mid-fifties, both Pollock and de Kooning were seen as artists who had ultimately failed the rigorous, unrelenting demands of abstract painting, and had opted for a safer, easier course. Thus, Pollock's first poured paintings, with their allover compositions, which were done between 1947 and 1950, and de Kooning's more conventionally painted abstractions from around the same time, were seen as major accomplishments; and the figurative works they did subsequently were considered betrayals of abstraction. Because Pollock and de Kooning were unable to sustain their breakthroughs, painting, the critics were suggesting, had reached a dead end, as well as a climax, in Pollock's poured paintings.

It was within this context that Jasper Johns's first show was received; a context which began to be established a decade earlier by the leading formalist theoretician and critic, Clement Greenberg, who, ironically, saw little merit in Johns's work. However, Greenberg's persuasive arguments about the historical importance of abstraction, about art's need to synthesize new techniques and materials, and about the resulting autonomy that occurred in painting when medium and support were fused together, became the basis for younger critics' elaborate codifications of contemporary art. Despite Greenberg's own low opinion of Johns's work, his valorization of process and his formulation of art's inherent goals have formed the bedrock of almost all the arguments that have been developed by subsequent generations of historians and critics in their readings of Johns's early work. Critics and historians such as Roberta Bernstein,[2] Barbara Rose,[3] Max Kozloff,[4] Robert

Rosenblum,[5] and others have argued that Johns's early work was a groundbreaking solution to the formal problems that every modern artist has to address. By developing readings based on Greenberg's codifications of Pollock, readings which have never been fully discredited, these critics used Johns's early work to further establish a seemingly flexible discourse by which art could be measured, and in doing so originated the beginnings of an academic tradition, one which has persisted in one guise or another for more than four decades.

II.

In his highly influential 1948 essay, "The Crisis of the Easel Picture," Clement Greenberg developed the initial codification of Pollock's first poured paintings in his generalization of the basic features of an allover painting:

> ...a surface *knit together of identical or closely similar elements which repeat themselves without marked variation from one edge of the painting to the other. It is a kind of picture that dispenses, apparently, with beginning, middle, end.*[6]

Greenberg's critical framing of Pollock's first poured paintings became the yardstick by which all contemporary paintings were measured. Since the late fifties, it has been the primary source for the valorization of the grid, symmetry, and allover unity.

JASPER JOHNS
Flag Above White, 1954
Encaustic on canvas, 23 1/4 x 20 inches
The Sonnabend Collection, New York

During the fifties and sixties, Greenberg and his adherents were instrumental in the perception that de Kooning's "Women" series betrayed abstraction and that Pollock's black poured paintings (1951-53) marked the beginning of his decline as a major artist. The one exception that Greenberg made about Pollock's paintings was his technique of thinning the viscous enamel into an ink-like liquidity, which allowed it to be absorbed by the canvas. Through his application of a reductive, essentializing approach, Greenberg was able to codify Pollock's accomplishment in terms of two technical advances: allover composition and the fusion of the medium and support. And it was with these formal paradigms in mind that Rose, Rosenblum, and others saw Johns's allover compositions as announcing the demise of Abstract Expressionism. In order to acknowledge Johns's achievement, this generation of younger critics had to depart from Greenberg's conclusions regarding the importance of techniques that explicitly recalled Pollock's methodology. In this regard, they differed from the more orthodox formalist critics, such as Michael Fried, Rosalind Krauss, Kenworth Moffet, and Karen Wilkin, who adhered to Greenberg's conclusions and tended to verify only the work of abstract artists who continued the technique of pouring or, as it came to be called later, staining. In tandem with their emphasis on abstraction's need to be a self-referential "surface knit together" was their insistence on techniques derived from Pollock, rather than ones derived from the medium, whatever it was. This led the orthodox formalists to conclude that Johns's allover compositions were minor, because they contained references to the world and were done in encaustic, a medium that works very differently than enamel. In their eyes, Johns's paintings were neither continuations of Pollock's techniques nor pure abstractions—standards that they felt must be upheld.

For Johns's supporters and advocates, his references to known "things" and his use of encaustic were noteworthy achievements, because his work could still be seen within the context of Greenberg's valorization of allover composition, as well as the historical necessity of fusing medium and support. For these critics, Johns's work embodied both historical continuity and a major avant-garde rupture; it was allover painting which was neither purely self-referential nor the result of being poured. In order to contain these references within Greenberg's formal paradigms, younger critics concluded that Johns's work was literal in its meanings. This allowed them to see his paintings of "flat" things within the same context they saw Pollock's poured paintings. Both were considered exemplary instances of art for art's sake. The difference was that Johns's vocabulary was derived from what they saw as banal "things" rather than from the medium itself, and conveyed a message of detachment, irony, and doubt about art's capability of meaning anything other than literal statements about the inability to mean. The alphabet and numerals, they reasoned, alluded to nothing but themselves as abstract "things" or signs, because they neither spelled anything out nor added up. They were read as self-referential signs which did not resolve into any specific meaning. In this regard, Johns's recontextualization of numerals and the alphabet was seen as an extension of Marcel Duchamp's displacement of a bicycle wheel or bottle rack into an art context.

123

JASPER JOHNS
Target with Four Faces, 1955
Assemblage: encaustic and collage on canvas with objects,
26 x 26 inches, surmounted by four tinted plaster faces in wood
box with hinged front, Box closed: 3 3/4 x 26 x 3 1/2 inches
Overall dimensions with box open: 33 5/8 x 26 x 3 inches
The Museum of Modern Art, New York
Gift of Mr. and Mrs. Robert C. Scull

JASPER JOHNS
Gray Target, 1958
Encaustic and collage on canvas, 42 x 42 inches
The Sonnabend Collection, New York

JASPER JOHNS
Gray Rectangles, 1957
Encaustic on canvas, 60 x 60 inches
From the collection of Barney A. Ebsworth, St. Louis

Johns's first solo exhibition consisted of fourteen paintings and assemblages, and two works on paper, made between 1954 and 1957; it included *Flag* (1954-55), *Flag Above White* (1955), *Gray Alphabets* (1956), *Target with Plaster Casts* (1955), *Target with Four Faces* (1955), *Green Target* (1955), *Canvas* (1956), *Book* (1957), *Flag on Orange Field* (1957), *White Numbers* (1957), and *Drawer* (1957). Although *Green Target* had been included in a group show at the Jewish Museum, and *Flag on Orange Field* and *Small White Flag* had been seen in display windows at Bonwit Teller, Johns was a young, unknown artist whose work was familiar only to a small circle of friends and fellow artists. However, even before the exhibition opened, there were signs of a desire for change swirling in the air.

The most notable sign came from Thomas Hess, the editor of *Art News* and an eloquent supporter of the Abstract Expressionists, who asked Castelli if he could put *Target with Four Faces* on the cover of the January issue when a snowstorm delayed shipment of the intended cover from Europe. While Hess placed *Target with Four Faces* on the magazine's cover, he did not perceive Johns's work as a groundbreaking response to the crisis formalist critics asserted was haunting Abstract Expressionism. On the table of contents page, the description of Johns's painting reads:

> *Jasper Johns, who painted* Target *in encaustic on newsprint, and added a box shelf of plaster heads, is the newest member of a movement among young American artists to turn to a sort of neo-Dada —pyrotechnic or lyric, earnest but slyly unaggressive ideologically but covered with esthetic spikes. Johns's first one-man show places him with such better known colleagues as Rauschenberg, Twombly, Kaprow and Ray Johnson.* [7]

In a short review, which was also included in the January issue, Fairfield Porter, a friend of de Kooning and a figurative painter, wrote:

> *He uses an encaustic medium, which he taught himself, to paint large paintings of some simple visual symbol, like the American flag, a target, the lower case letters, or printed numbers; or else the symbol is almost erased in it. His painting is neither about painting nor the "art symbol": it has to do with looking. Not looking as a sensation, nor about the visual world; nor is there a concern with myth (except indirectly perhaps—is a flag a mythical symbol?). He looks for the first time, like a child, at things that have no meaning to the child, yet, or necessarily. What meaning they may have may be irrelevant to his absorption in looking…Johns' paintings compel your attentiveness: they bring you back to what art is in itself, before its meaning, before its usefulness.* [8]

Both the description of the cover and Porter's review make no large claim for Johns's work, particularly in relationship to Abstract Expressionism. Rather, the description places Johns's work within a contemporary, art historical context ("a sort of neo-Dada"), while Porter proposes that Johns's paintings are connected to a state of looking that is innocent; and that he functions like a child who is not yet aware of the meaning of the "things" he incorporates into his work. In retrospect, the assertion of an art that is "slyly unaggressive ideologically," as well as Porter's recognition of "innocence," helped lay the groundwork for such later claims as Johns's detachment and formally-rooted refusals to evoke meaning.

Porter's framing of Johns's consciousness within a zone of innocence anticipates the way Pop art and Minimalism would be received in the 1960s; it stands behind both Andy Warhol's desire to be like a machine and Frank Stella's statement: "What you see is what you see." Now, more than three decades after Johns's first show opened, it is clear that his work, its use of known "things," set a formal precedent for artists of his and subsequent generations, but in one of the first reviews written of Johns's work, Porter neither proposes that Johns's work heralds a break with Abstract Expressionism nor posits that he has broken new ground.

In another review of the exhibition, Robert Rosenblum wrote:

Of the many things that upset preconceptions in this first one-man show there are the subjects themselves, for Johns is dedicated to images which outside picture galleries evoke nonesthetic reactions. There is the American flag, which one respects or salutes; targets which one aims at and hopes to hit; numbers one counts with; and letters, which one uses to make words to be read. To see these commonplaces faithfully reproduced in sizes from large to small is disconcerting enough, but not so bewildering as the visual and intellectual impact they carry. His theme selected, Johns will then manipulate it in multiple guises, so that the American flag, for example, may appear in its nude red-white-and-blue state; or against an orange field whose color vibrations should give Rothko or Albers pause, or as a monumental canvas entirely in white.[9]

In his conclusion, Rosenblum went further than Porter in his estimation of Johns's work:

To explain the fascination of these works, one might refer to their disarming rearrangements of customary esthetic and practical responses, but one should also mention the commanding sensuous presence of their primer-like imagery, which has the rudimentary, irreducible potency of Abstract Expressionism. And not least, there is Johns' elegant craftsmanship (in general, a finely nuanced encaustic) which lends these pictures the added poignancy of a beloved, handmade transcription of unloved, machine-made images. In short, Johns' work, like all genuinely new art, assaults and enlivens the mind and eye with the exhilaration of discovery.[10]

Like Porter, Rosenblum develops a framework for Johns's work. Paralleling his notion of innocence, but more formally biased in its appeal, is Rosenblum's understanding of Johns's approach to subject matter, which he sees as the displacement of nonaesthetic things into an aesthetic context. The other key phrases in Rosenblum's review are "faithfully reproduced" and "irreducible potency," both of which can be seen as anticipating Pop art and Minimalism. Although they utilize different vocabularies, Porter and Rosenblum are essentially in agreement about Johns's relationship to subject matter, to his recontextualization of "things" that can be used into things that cannot be used for art, into things which exist solely in an aesthetic realm that is prior to use and thus meaning. Within this formalist view of Johns's art, one which presupposes that modern art is essentially hermetic in meaning, Porter and Rosenblum formulate the notion that, like all true abstract art, Johns's art is self-referential.

127

Like these early reviews, the responses to Johns's exhibition suggest that many people in the art world felt that painting was undergoing some kind of crisis, and wanted to see evidence of change. On the first Saturday of the exhibition, Alfred Barr, of the Museum of Modern Art, was so impressed by Johns's work that he called his associate, Dorothy Miller, from the gallery and asked her to come right over. During the next few hours, the two of them chose a number of paintings to present to the museum's Acquisitions Committee. Barr's enthusiasm must be seen in context. At the time he recommended that the Museum of Modern Art obtain works by an unknown artist having his first solo show, the Museum owned relatively few works connected with Abstract Expressionism, particularly examples from the postwar period. For the most part, the Museum's collection consisted of examples of European modernism.

Barr was far more sympathetic to European modernism than he was to the accomplishments of the Abstract Expressionists, and most likely considered the young artist's work to be an extension of the European modernist, high art tradition. This possibility is borne out in a letter to Barr dated January 30, 1958, (ten days after Johns's show opened), in which Frank O'Hara, a poet on the Museum's curatorial staff, wrote in response to Barr's query: "Incidentally, I was intrigued by the flag on orange field which, along with the all-grey painting with drawer, seems to do such a drastic reinterpretation of the Albers convention."[11] In connecting Johns's art to both formal issues and the geometric tradition of European modernism, O'Hara anticipates the historicizing view that the "flags," targets, and numerals were a bridge between the group of Abstract Expressionists with an affinity for geometry (Robert Motherwell, particularly his *Little Spanish Prison*, Barnett Newman, and Mark Rothko) and the Minimalists. It should also be noted that O'Hara connects Johns to a minor European abstract artist who developed his reductive approach in an attempt to deal with the interaction of color. Rather than breaking new ground, Johns's work was thus seen by at least one member of the Museum's curatorial staff as a "reinterpretation," albeit a "drastic" one.

By the time the exhibition closed, all but two of the paintings (*White Flag* and *Target with Plaster Casts*) were sold. The Museum of Modern Art had obtained three (*Green Target, Target with Four Faces,* and *White Numbers*) for its collection, precipitating a heated debate in the art world, particularly among members and advocates of an older generation, while most of the rest had been bought by trustees of the Museum. Castelli ended up buying *Target with Plaster Casts* for his own collection, while Johns kept *White Flag* for himself. The show had catapulted an unknown artist into public view. Nothing like this had ever happened before. Clearly, Johns's work had touched the sensibilities of numerous critics, curators, and collectors, who in turn had cleared a large, unprecedented space for him and his work.

128

Johns was twenty-eight years old when the exhibition opened. Within five years, Frank Stella and Andy Warhol, both of whom had taken strong cues from Johns's work, had embarked upon successful careers. During this same period the art world changed and grew in ways no one could have foreseen. The paintings of the Abstract Expressionists, particularly the "Action" painters, began to be seen as part of a history which had ended with Pollock's untimely death: as the products of an excessive, misguided, introspective subjectivity, which a younger, more rigorous, more objective generation was correcting; or as examples of a serious, high-minded, existential practice, which an emerging generation of fun-loving or detached, ironic individuals had jettisoned in favor of banal images and icons borrowed from popular culture.

JASPER JOHNS
Drawer, 1957
Encaustic and assemblage on canvas, 30 1/2 x 30 1/2 inches
Rose Art Museum, Brandeis University, Waltham, Mass.
Gevirtz-Mnuchin Purchase Fund

The central figure in all these shifts was Johns, who was acknowledged as the first artist to use a familiar icon, namely the American flag, in a way that advanced modernist principles regarding pictorial composition. According to advocates such as Rose and Rosenblum, Johns's *White Numbers* represents a major formal advance in modernist composition, and can be said to exist between Pollock's *Number 1A* (1948) and Warhol's soup cans; it is used to seal Pollock within history, as well as to pave the way for a younger generation.

Not surprisingly, the transformations that occurred in the art world between the late 1950s and the mid-1960s are mirrored in the changes that marked Johns's career. Between 1958 and 1964, when he had his first retrospective at the Jewish Museum, Johns went from being a young unknown to being internationally recognized as an innovative artist whose work was instrumental in the rise of both Pop art and Minimalism. Within this same period, art historians and critics such as Lawrence Alloway, Rosalind Krauss, Kenworth Moffet, Barbara Rose, Robert Rosenblum, William Rubin, Leo Steinberg, and others, developed more particular readings of Johns's paintings in an attempt to embed his project within their narratives of art history, particularly in regard to their definitions of formal developments and pictorial advances. Instead of striving to develop a reading of his work which would echo and clarify its lucidity, they saw his work in terms of

their own academic vocabulary, one which was for the most part derived from Clement Greenberg. As a result, most of their narratives can be read as acrobatic interpretations of the dominant critical rhetoric of the fifties and sixties, which was the formalist paradigm of progress and its anti-humanist notion that art's goal was to purify itself of extraneous information, such as spatiality, image, line, gesture, and handmade marks; it was to eliminate all traces of the subjective in favor of the objective. For these critics, meaning was either purely formal or it was something assigned to art, an unnecessary burden.

Through their emphasis on the importance of the literal and non-metaphorical, which were extensions of formalist paradigms, Johns came to be seen as the master of detachment, the maker of neutral

129

JASPER JOHNS
Canvas, 1956
Encaustic and collage on wood and canvas, 30 x 25 inches
Collection of the artist

moods, the hermetic literalist, the ironic game player. Instead of looking at Johns's work and developing a discursive response based on a close examination of it, what these critics did was demonstrate how Johns's work validated their views of modernism and the avant-garde. In effect, they used Johns to reify their conception of art history as a linear construct. Right from the start, the early formal readings of Johns's work seemed to get at only a very small part of its meaning. Johns's *Flag* seemed to be both about itself and about something else. The problem was — and it continues to be — that the critics championing his work could not figure out how the "flag" was about itself or how it was about something else, or how these two seemingly disparate realms might be connected. Their inability to resolve these issues within their categories, or by their definitions and terms, has led many to conclude that Johns's work is enigmatic, even hermetic, particularly since the artist himself has refused to explain his work to others. Johns's refusal to frame his work has enabled them to some

130

degree to stop looking at his work, and to recognize it only in their terms. Consequently, his work is deemed important because it fulfills previously ratified standards which do not in turn clarify his art. Thus, in the first article on Johns, Rosenblum writes:

> Johns has extended the fundamental principles of Abstract Expressionism to the domain of commonplace objects. Just as Pollock, Kline, or Rothko reduced their art to the most primary sensuous facts — an aesthetic tangle of paint, a jagged black scrawl, a tinted and glowing rectangle — so, too, does Johns

JASPER JOHNS
Green Target, 1955
Encaustic on newspaper and cloth over canvas, 60 x 60 inches
The Museum of Modern Art, New York
Richard S. Zeisler Fund

reduce his art to rockbottom statements of fact. The facts he chooses to paint, however, are derived from a non-esthetic environment and are presented in a manner that is as startlingly original as it is disarmingly simple and logical.[12]

In building upon and refining what he wrote in his first review, Rosenblum uses "reduce" and "fact" to connect Johns to Pollock, as well as to describe what he has come to see as the only viable approach an artist should take; and this vocabulary becomes basic to the reception of Minimalism. In Rosenblum's eyes, Pollock and Johns are exemplary models of what a painter should do because the former reduced his art to "the most primary sensuous facts," while the latter reduced his to "rockbottom" ones.

The primary obstacle critics have had trouble overcoming is that Johns's "flags" implode formalist categories; they eliminate illusionism but retain a recognizable image; they are geometric but the design isn't his; they are physically insistent objects which incorporate manmade, abstract "things" (numerals and the alphabet); they seem to be suspended between abstraction and figuration; the surface is simultaneously a record of nuanced brushstrokes and a natural unavoidable buildup of encaustic, its materiality. While these

131

characteristics distinguish his work from others, critics have persisted in evaluating it according to formalist paradigms by resorting to generalized codifications based on the work of another artist, Jackson Pollock.

It can be said that in the decades since Johns's first exhibition, generations of critics have seen his work in relation to their definitions of art's central formal issues, which are largely based on their circumscribed readings of modernist art, and consequently have failed to comprehend the depths of radical, imaginative thinking behind his decisions. They have been unable to connect the thinking with the doing. Johns's "flag" paintings have been seen as examples of a neo-Dada spirit[13]; literal presentations of flat "things"[14]; restatements of Duchampian principles of displacement[15]; reactions to Abstract Expressionism[16]; conflations of abstraction and representation[17]; evocations of his childhood[18]; a biographical reference to the

JASPER JOHNS
White Target, 1957
Encaustic on canvas, 29 7/8 x 30 inches
Whitney Museum of American Art, New York
Purchase

Revolutionary War and the role Sergeant William Jasper played in raising the flag[19]; both a literal and objective commentary regarding the banality of the world and its symbols[20]; a veiled criticism of McCarthyism and the xenophobia sweeping across America during the 1950s[21]; important stylistic precedents for Pop art and Minimalism.[22] All of these readings of Johns's art are based on encoded readings of art and art history. A determinedly self-interested group, critics and art historians have reduced Johns's work to demonstrations of the validity of their paradigms. What all of these critics fail to address is Johns's observation about his approach to art: "I decided to do only what I meant to do, and not what other people did....I tried to remove that from my work. My work became a constant negation of impulses."[23] To propose that the "flag" paintings have an autobiographical root, are an ironic art game, or are personal, political or social commentary, is to ignore Johns's "negation of impulses," as well as to overlook the source of the idea for painting a flag, which, as he has stated, was a dream he had had. It could be said that the dream enabled Johns to defer his "negation of impulses" long enough for him to begin working on a painting; it gave him a space that was his. And within that space he discovered other possibilities, such as targets, numerals, and the alphabet, or, as he put it, "things seen and not looked at, not examined."[24]

In setting the foundation for subsequent readings of Johns's work, the early readings largely confined themselves to formal issues, with only a few attempting to expand upon their formal base and address psychological and iconographic issues. In his attempt to take the formal, biographical, psychological, and iconographical into account, Leo Steinberg proposed that Johns no longer used paint as a medium of transformation. For Johns, a painting must be what it represents; because the picture is flat, the only things that can be painted without make-believe are those which are flat by nature. He also saw Johns's use of "flags," numerals, and maps as evocative of his childhood, the years he spent in a one-room schoolhouse in South Carolina.[25]

Following Steinberg, Rose, and Rosenblum, most critics have continued to see Johns's early paintings as a reaction against Abstract Expressionism's subjectivity. These early critics defined Johns's work as objectively literal, as well as decidedly non-metaphorical. In doing so, they were connecting his work to their narrow, formally biased reading of Pollock's, which was seen as the apotheosis of art for art's sake. This particular reading of Johns's work, the one that has played the most central role in subsequent readings of his work, as well as art in general, feels narrow-minded in its focus and ungenerous, not to say unventuresome, in its appraisal. It makes Johns into an artist who is more concerned with art history and the right thing to do than with making art. It makes him into a figure who is conscious of the verifying process of art historians and critics, rather than an artist who has always gone his own way. Finally, it makes Johns into a self-conscious artist who had the critics in mind when he painted his first "flag." By establishing this relationship, the critics were able to maintain a certain power; they were the audience the artist had in mind to please when he or she began to paint. And it is through this relationship, one that has prevailed in the art world in one form or another (in the 1980s, for example, one could substitute "collectors" and "gallery owners" for "critics") for more than four decades, that critics and historians were able to formulate a central or academic tradition, which other institutions in the art world would help refine and maintain.

The problem with a formalist reading of Johns's early work is that it reduces it to a reaction against Abstract Expressionism, makes it into a preferable stylistic alternative, while a psychological reading suggests that Johns is encoding a secret message within his work, that he is using art to publicly exhibit something he simultaneously wants to keep hidden from view. Both of these readings connect Johns's work to a social and artistic world in ways that limit its range of possible meanings, and which the artist himself has contradicted. In speaking about his early years in New York, Johns has stated: "It was not a matter of joining a group effort, but of isolating myself from any group."[26] This remark suggests that Johns was thinking of neither the artistic nor social worlds when he made his art, that he was working out of a state of extreme and deliberate isolation, and that this chosen state echoed the one he had no power to change, the one he inhabited from day to day.

The reason both formal and psychological readings fail is that each of them, no matter how acrobatic in its response to Johns's art, approaches it with a set of prejudices which ultimately circumscribe it, make it conform to the terms of the defining vocabulary. Johns's work, however, demands unique and specific readings. Of course, this is the mark of all great art, that it requires a new way of looking and thinking capable of discerning the underlying logic of its proposals rather than maintaining its own set of prejudices.

Given the historical importance and supposed impenetrability of Johns's work, one feels it is time to begin examining the validity of the readings of his work that generations of critics and viewers have learned to take for granted. Did the first generation of critics contribute to more than a superficial understanding of Johns's work? Or did they help obfuscate his paintings in ways that have continued to make his work seem beyond our comprehension? Did the early readings lead to initial insights which subsequent generations could build on? Or did their readings engender further misreadings? Did the initial readings of Johns's work grasp the depths of meaning it embodied? Or did it reduce the work's meaning to a narrow aesthetic realm? I would submit that the latter case is the truest in all of these instances. If, as Johns has said, and there is no reason to disbelieve him, he chose the targets and numerals because they were "things seen and not looked at, not examined," and that in this regard they echoed his dream of painting a flag, then his works of the fifties and early sixties — his *Flag, Flag Above White, Target with Plaster Casts, Drawer, Book, Device Circle, 4 the News, Map*, and *Thermometer*, to name only a few — have suffered the ironic fate of becoming famous paintings that are seen and not looked at, not examined. They have become "things" we have taken for granted.

IV.

In order to begin to understand Johns's art, and the complexity of his development over nearly forty years, we have to go back to the beginning, to *Flag* (1954-55), which was the first time he incorporated the American flag into his work. It may not have been the first time he used encaustic, since *Star* (ca. 1954) is listed as being done in "encaustic on canvas with glass and wood."[27] Johns has said that he got the idea for the painting from a dream he had had in which he saw himself painting a large American flag. He started the painting in enamel, working on a bed sheet. In the list of paintings accompanying his first exhibition, *Flag* is listed as being in "encaustic and collage on fabric."[28] In the catalogue accompanying his retrospective at the Jewish Museum, it is listed simply as "encaustic and collage."[29] In Max Kozloff's monograph, the first on the artist's work, it is listed as "encaustic and collage on canvas."[30] In Michael Crichton's monograph, published in conjunction with Johns's large retrospective at the Whitney Museum of American Art, *Flag* is listed as "encaustic, oil, and collage on fabric."[31] And, finally, in Roberta Bernstein's critical survey, *Jasper Johns' Paintings and Sculptures 1954-1974: "The Changing Focus of the Eye,"* it is listed as "encaustic, oil, and collage on fabric mounted on plywood."[32] The dates of the painting are variously given as 1954, 1955, and 1954-55. These technical discrepancies may seem small, but in this case can also be seen as contributing to a misreading of the work. Among other things, it raises questions about the accuracy of formalist readings which have based their judgments on the synthesis of materials, techniques, and process, because they have not taken into account the full range of materials Johns used to make *Flag*.

Johns's dissatisfaction with the slow drying enamel with which he began may have been due to the difficulty he would have had in seeing what would result from following out an idea he got in a dream. Having already started the painting in one medium, he could have abandoned it and started over again in encaustic. The reasons for not doing so may have been either the lack of materials or the desire to follow through on something he had already started. Johns's choice of a sheet also suggests that it may have either been the largest piece of material close at hand; that he saw the painting as an experiment, something to try; or that it was a way of returning to the dream's site, that he was transforming it into something that existed within his dream, that he was attempting to return to the source by reenacting what had transpired while he was asleep. In doing so, he was making the ineffable, the dream or unreachable source, into a fact. It most likely also occurred to Johns that the painting was an echo of the one in the dream, and that one cannot faithfully reproduce a dream. Thus, we should look at Johns's "flag" paintings as individual facts which have one element in common rather than as variations on a theme.

There is a sense of urgency as well as discovery in all this, a sense of Johns's excitement over a new idea or, in this case, a startling dream. In using a sheet, Johns makes the painting self-referential. It is

about itself, about a dream for which there is no external measure, or for which the only measure is the painting itself. Before switching to encaustic, he applied pieces of newspaper collage, which helped soak up the oil, as well as acting as a buffer between the sticky enamel surface and the encaustic. Finally, he affixed the painting to a plywood backing.

The changes that characterize the making of *Flag*, as well as its unstable combination of materials, contradicts the widely accepted point of view of Johns as a painstaking craftsman and rigorous intellect. It further suggests that at this point in his career he did not have in mind either a fully thought-out rejection of Abstract Expressionism or a resolution to the compositional crisis said to have plagued de Kooning

JASPER JOHNS
Figure 4, 1959
Encaustic and collage on canvas, 20 1/4 x 15 1/8 inches
Collection of Nina and Michael Sundell, New York

JASPER JOHNS
Gray Painting with Ball, 1958
Encaustic on canvas, 31 1/2 x 24 1/2 inches
FAE Musée d'Art Contemporain, Pully/Lausanne

and Pollock during the early fifties. If anything, the scenario suggested by *Flag*'s combination of materials is that Johns was someone who initially learned techniques through an engagement with the demands of his materials. And that when he began working on the sheet, he did not fully understand the dream's implication, how during the course of working on the composition, and solving its technical problems, he would discover a connection between the American flag and the fabric support through the medium of encaustic.

At first the encaustic must have seemed like an efficient way to get around the problem of waiting for enamel to sufficiently dry before applying another layer of paint. Unlike enamel or other oil-based paints, encaustic is a medium which begins hardening once it is removed from the heat; it solidifies rather than dries. It is made of beeswax and comes in a solid form which must be heated before it can absorb any pigment. The heat causes it to liquefy. When it is removed from the heat and applied to a surface, it solidifies or "freezes," functioning as a preservative.[33]

V.

In an interview, part of which focused on his early years in New York, Johns described the foundation of his artistic project:

> I had the wish to determine what I was. I had the feeling that I could do anything.... But if I could do anything I wanted to do, then what I wanted to do was find out what I did that other people didn't, what I was that other people weren't.... It was not a matter of joining a group effort, but of isolating myself from any group. I wanted to know what was helpless in my behavior—how I would behave out of necessity.[34]

For Johns, the dream of painting an American flag was an undeniable instance of "helpless" behavior, and he acknowledged it out of "necessity." If he did not respond to the dream, it would have been something he would never learn more about; it would have been a road not taken, an idea left behind. To ignore the dream would have been to contradict his belief in himself: "I had the feeling I could do anything." If he "could do anything," then why not a painting of the American flag?

In a larger, more general sense, Johns has defined both the basis of his project and the focus of his practice in terms of determining "what" he was, rather than trying to propose "who" he was: "I wanted to find out what I did that other people didn't, what I was that other people weren't." Johns's art establishes contingent equivalents among "him." This sense of himself as a constantly changing object, a complex, decentralized "what," runs completely counter to the historical paradigm of the artist whose work is either a subjective expression of the individual's identity, the construction of his or her fictive "I," or the objective identity or essence of the art medium.

Johns is one of the first artists to recognize that the division of subjective and objective into separate categories is an illusion, and that because of that "pure abstraction" is at best a fiction. He knows that objects and subjects are mutually linked, even dependent upon one another. If his work is an implicit critique of anything, as critics have stated, it is not art, but the philosophical underpinnings by which art is measured and understood; and by extension it is a critique of criticism. It is one of the reasons why Johns would be so receptive to the work and writings of Marcel Duchamp when he was introduced to them late in 1958, and to the philosophical writings of Ludwig Wittgenstein, which he discovered in 1961.[35] In their different ways, each would confirm and clarify something he already understood and articulated in his work, that the categories of subjective and objective were false distinctions.

Thus, instead of choosing to state and restate "who" he was or "what" art was through the mastery of his methods and materials, with the illusion of limitlessness this type of practice conveys, Johns chose to surrender all definitions of the self to the material's demands, its inherent behavior. It is in this surrender that Johns believes he will find the links between subjective and objective, between behavior and necessity; and in the inextricable links between them he will discover "what" he is. It is this focus that enables him to negate his impulses. In stark contrast to the artist who speaks to the world through his or her command of materials, Johns attempts to discover what constitutes a material's identity, its necessary behavior, and through that discovery glimpse evidence of the self's provisional existence.

Johns's approach to art making is fundamentally different than the one in which the artist commands his or her materials to do what he or she wishes; and it goes against the whole notion of mastery and masterpiece. It should also be noted that his approach is significantly different from the models of objectivity and detachment espoused by other artists who have been linked with Pop art and Minimalism. And, while Johns's work has been seen as a refutation of Abstract Expressionism, it does not jettison a concern with the self, as many critics have asserted. Rather, it rejects the notion of an essentialized or unified central self, a fictive "who," in favor of a "what," something more primary and contingent.

Johns's work is no more purely objective and neutral than the work of the Abstract Expressionists is purely subjective and expressionistic. Rather, Johns shifts the site of his practice from the articulation of an essential self through materials to a site where the artist can discover what the materials reveal about the provisional existence of the self. Thus, Johns is neither as detached nor as literal-minded as some critics have made him out to be. Instead of displacing the "flag" from one context to another, which has been characterized as a post-Duchampian gesture, he displaced himself — "what" he was — by allowing his materials to become the measure by which he would make art. He would "live" in his materials rather than through them. By, as he put it, "negating his impulses," by surrendering his feelings and thoughts to the materials' demands, their inherent behavior and specific properties, he would be able to glean some evidence of "what" he was. Defined this way, art becomes an echo or mirror that reveals something intrinsic about what the artist is — his material existence in the world as well as in time.

For critics and historians of postwar American modernism, the critical importance or status of new materials such as enamel and acrylic has been determined by the progress they enable the artist to make in solving pictorial issues. This critical framework, its emphasis on the resolution of formal problems through the combination of accepted technical innovations and appropriately modern materials, links the artist to the paradigm of progress and a materialist utopia; it makes him or her a counterpart of someone like Henry Ford, who introduced the concept of the assembly line into the factory. For formalist critics, the meaning of an artist's materials is largely confined to their technical efficiency in solving pictorial problems. Clearly, Pollock could not have started making his poured paintings in 1947 without enamel, a far more liquid material than traditional oil paint. It was enamel's liquidity that enabled Pollock to forgo a brush for a stick, to begin working on the floor, and to increase the size of his compositions beyond the scale imposed by the easel. However, Clement Greenberg saw enamel solely as a technical means which enabled Pollock successfully to resolve important pictorial issues, and made a bridge between it and acrylic, between Pollock's pouring of diluted enamel and the stain paintings of Morris Louis and Kenneth Noland. He emphasized enamel's technical possibilities rather than its metaphorical and metaphysical ones. It has been Greenberg and his followers who have been literal-minded, rather than Pollock or Johns.

About the meaning of his breakthrough works of the late 1940s and early 1950s, Pollock said:

When I am in my painting, I'm not aware of what I'm doing. It is only after a sort of "get acquainted" period that I see what I've been about. I have no fear of making changes, destroying the image, etc., because the painting has a life of its own. I try to let it come through.[36]

In this remark at least, one senses that for Pollock art was about establishing the autonomy of the self through the

137

JASPER JOHNS
Fool's House, 1962
Oil on canvas with objects, 72 x 36 inches
Collection of Jean-Christophe Castelli, New York

painting and vice versa, rather than about art or art's objectives; and that enamel enabled him to establish a dialogue that could possibly achieve autonomy for both painter and painting. Comparable to Pollock's desire for autonomy is Johns's statement: "I wanted to know what was helpless in my behavior, how I would behave out of necessity." Pollock believes a "painting has a life of its own," a life that must be acknowledged and respected, while Johns wants to discover how he would "behave out of necessity." However, Greenberg and those critics who took cues from him saw the paintings of Pollock and of Johns in terms of their understanding of art history; they subsumed both artists into their narratives, thus denying them the autonomy they had achieved in and through their work.

For many Abstract Expressionists, and this included Pollock, meaning came later; it was something that was assigned to the work, a kind of ex post facto framework. Robert Motherwell summed up the break Pollock and others of his generation made when he stated that "modern artists have no generally accepted subject matter, no inherited iconography."[37] Motherwell believed that what separated the Abstract Expressionists, of which he was one, from the European modernists was that the former were compelled to "re-invent painting, its subject matter and its means."[38] And that this reinvention was often the result of "a very simple concept."[39] If, in the light of Motherwell's observations, it can be said that Pollock's introspective gaze became reductive, a search for the self's irreducible essence through means the artist believed were essential and essentializing, (drawing and the line), then Johns has gone the other way. His introspective gaze is focused on discovering evidence of the provisional self in the world, its flux. The frame of the gaze is determined by his materials. And yet, like Pollock, Johns reinvents painting. The difference is that he shifts his attention from the possibilities inherent in a synthesis of essentializing means and materials to discovering further insight into the provisional nature of his materials. However, and this is what links Pollock and Johns together, the reinvention is not in terms of styles and materials, but how those "things" enabled them to achieve autonomy. And it is this autonomy, this severing of the bonds between modernist art and modernist criticism, which critics have been unable to recognize.

The rupture between means and meaning that characterizes Abstract Expressionism is something that Johns rejected. He did not feel that he could do something, anything, and then discover what it meant; this sense of freedom was really an illusion. For Johns, methodology was one way to clarify an aspect of the material's identity, and this clarification occurred because the artist focused on the inherent behavior of his materials. In this regard, Johns's practice bears comparison to Pollock's: both believe a painting has a life of its own. It suggests that in their drive for autonomy, both made art which critics have been unable to understand; implicit in their desire for autonomy is their declaration of independence from established discourses.

In the case of encaustic, Johns discovered a mediating material which has enabled him to connect one realm to another, the blank canvas in his studio to things in the constantly changing world; his body, the complex, contradictory states of consciousness animating it, to familiar things; his recognition of himself

JASPER JOHNS
Device Circle, 1959
Encaustic and collage on canvas with objects, 40 x 40 inches
Private collection

as a fundamentally isolated being to the isolated states embodied in his art. Encaustic has allowed him to name aspects of himself. Johns not only lives inside his materials, but he is trapped in them, much as he (and each of us for that matter) is trapped inside a body. This is the essential condition all of Johns's art acknowledges.

Although Johns exists in various adjacent and overlapping realms, it is not clear to him what connects him to them or them to each other. To discover these links, Johns decided that his materials (in the beginning, a bed sheet, newspaper collage, enamel, encaustic, and plywood) should dictate how they were to be synthesized, the final form they would take. Johns's practice is one of intervention; he connects one thing to another because he has discovered an inextricable link between them. This intervention shows him something about "what" he is. More than a refutation of subjectivity, Johns's definition of art rejects both subjectivity and objectivity, both interior, personal impulses and exterior, predetermined, objective standards. For him, personal impulses are a false sign of freedom, while a priori objective standards are concerned with conformity and consensus opinion rather than truth. Johns derives his terms from the materials he uses. Someone who tells you who he or she is, or what art is, has accepted that there is a preexisting social or art historical contract connecting the artist to the viewer.

Johns did not acknowledge the existence of this contract, this context in which an exchange of accepted views of art and life could occur. It is one of the reasons why his early work was so disquieting to informed viewers. And, not surprisingly, their response was to attempt to embed the work within a tradition, within the existing social and art historical contracts. His work of the fifties was not solely a record of the act of making a painting; its construction arises out of a larger set of concerns. It was not an objective embodiment of art's drive toward a pure state; it has too many impurities, too many signs of life, to be considered pure. It took no sides in the supposed argument between abstraction and figuration that dominated much of the critical discourse of the fifties and sixties: it is neither abstract nor figurative. Nor has it ever been, as Mark Rosenthal has asserted, "various and devious inclusions and plays on the nature of art for the delectation and confusion of the observer."[40] Johns's art is focused on something more fundamental than art issues or witty games designed to both confuse and amuse the viewer. Through it he attempts to discover "what" he is—his constantly changing form—amidst the shapelessness of time.

VI.

There are a number of links between Johns's choice of materials (encaustic and a sheet) and the American flag. First, in contrast to oil paint, which is generally placed on top of gessoed canvas, forming a kind of "skin," encaustic fuses with the support, making the entire object a unified "thing." (More than anything else, it is this fusion which connects Johns's work to Pollock's poured paintings. For although reached by very different means, the fusion their works embody can be read as proof of the painting's autonomy, which is a state both Pollock and Johns wished to achieve.) Johns initially understood encaustic to be a synthesizing material—it both

JASPER JOHNS
Thermometer, 1959
Oil on canvas with object, 51 3/4 x 38 1/2 inches
Mr. and Mrs. Bagley Wright, Seattle

fuses with the support and absorbs pigment — rather than a depictive one. Typically, a flag is made of canvas, which has been woven together out of dyed threads. Both an encaustic painting and a canvas flag are the result of a fusion of color, composition, and support. This is the underlying logic Johns discovered in reenacting his dream; it is what made his first "flag" painting seem to him to have been the inevitable consequence of his desire to discover "what" he was, to learn what was helpless in his behavior. The conjunction of materials and subject matter made certain responses necessary; they determined his actions rather than the other way around.

In the course of applying encaustic to the canvas, each brushstroke solidifies almost immediately, making the entire procedure an additive one in which each stroke retains to some degree its identity. Woven out of threads, a flag is also the result of an additive process. By using encaustic to mediate between himself and the world, between his desire for evidence of "what" he is and proof of his existence, as well as between the canvas and the world he simultaneously is estranged from and inhabits, Johns is able to have the blank canvas generate its double in the world. In doing so, the blank canvas, which represents his nonexistence in the world as well as in time, is transformed into a single work of art, which represents his provisional existence in the world and in time. It is through art as a generative act, one in which encaustic shows Johns how to mediate between nonexistence and existence, between invisibility and visibility, that he discovers some evidence of "what" he is. This evidence is always incomplete and provisional. Johns knows that encaustic cannot reveal everything about itself all at once, that there is always something more to be learned, that some other aspect of its existence can still be clarified.

Flag underscores the fact that on a material level a painting and a flag are pieces of colored cloth. And yet, both are also something more. The meaning of Johns's *Flag* arises in part out of the synthesis that he has presided over: it decontextualizes the American flag by transforming its basic features into a physical entity which is neither a flag nor a painting of a flag. Johns's *Flag* names only itself, evoking both its extreme isolation and the absence of all links. It asserts its autonomous physical existence in the world, while also implicitly acknowledging its dependency on others for recognition. We may, however, come to it with an agenda of what it could mean or we may try and discover "what" it is; this is the zone the painting inhabits. It makes us question ourselves as we look at it, see ourselves seeing it. What distinguishes Johns's art from others is that he sets the terms of recognition by choosing familiar "things" which break with the critical discourses in which the recognition of art is encouraged to occur. In a very real sense, Johns's work not only made a break with the art that was around him, but also ruptured the framework of discourses holding modern art in place.

141

VII.

If Johns had known from the outset the central role encaustic would play in the formulation of his project, he would have used it to start *Flag*. That he did not suggests that he discovered the implications of his dream during the course of working on the painting, and that it was out of an engagement with his materials and subject matter that he realized the various links between them. Thus, while Pollock became disengaged from his materials so that gravity came to play a larger role in his poured paintings, Johns became increasingly intimate with materials and their inherent processes, which is the opposite of being detached. Encaustic also enabled him to recognize that the flag and canvas are linked in another way; both are "things seen and not looked at, not examined." Both are "things" the viewer or critic comes to with an agenda rather than with an open mind and eyes. In doing so, the viewer establishes a position from which he or she can judge the painting; or, to put it another way, the painting must justify itself, its existence, according to the rules defined by an external source. It is this insight that enabled Johns to go on to targets, numerals, and the alphabet — each of which echoes the encaustic, the process of painting, and the canvas itself in different ways, each of which is also, like the flag, a "thing seen and not looked at, not examined." Each then is a fact that challenges the accepted notion of meaning, of recognizing and knowing.

Flag is a relatively large painting the viewer experiences from two radically different locations, afar and close up. These two seemingly disconnected experiences raise questions about the relationship between recognition and knowing. Flag is something the viewer recognizes but can never know. This is what the viewer finds unsettling about the painting. After recognizing it, what it represents from a distance, the viewer is compelled to move right up to it, to closely examine the semitransparent surface. In doing so, the viewer quickly realizes that there is something, some disturbance, contained behind the stripes and stars, and moves even closer. At this point, the viewer is no longer seeing the painting in its entirety, but is scrutinizing its surface, while remembering what it looks like. Here, seeing and the memory of something seen echo against recognition and not knowing.

Johns's placement of collage elements within the encaustic functions in two ways; it draws further attention to the painting, while underscoring encaustic's identity as a preservative. Flag is not the result of a state of innocent looking, as Fairfield Porter suggested in his review. It is a painting which seamlessly conflates two disparate perceptions — immediate recognition with deferred discovery — in a way that suggests that we do not know the "things" we think we know, the "things" we take for granted, that there is more to being in the world than recognition, that we can name something and still not know what it is. (This experience parallels the phenomena known as black holes, things which astronomers have named without knowing exactly what they are.)

In conflating recognition and knowing, Johns reveals to some degree the state of isolation he inhabits. And yet, looking at the painting, the viewer never feels it to be a purely personal expression. Flag defines a zone bordered by the private and public, as well as by curiosity and wisdom, through the way it fixes a relationship between recognition and knowing. However long we look at the painting, there are parts of it that are impossible to read. We recognize the collage elements but we cannot make out all of the images and words. This very precisely defined experience goes beyond the realm of art about art and echoes the kinds of disjunctive spaces that routinely occur in human relationships, the overlap between the private and public realms, and how these impact on the desire for knowledge. What is striking about Johns's early paintings is that they evoke this complex aspect of human relationships, as well as the desire for knowledge, without being narrative or anecdotal; everything that the viewer experiences in front of the painting is due to its presence.

By framing the painting with discourses derived from accepted terms, critics inserted a vocabulary between the viewer and the painting, and thus appropriated Flag for their own ends. Writing over the painting this way, generations of critics and historians can be said to have erased the painting, placing in its stead a more acceptable and historically correct version. Nowhere is this erasure more apparent than when the viewer closely scrutinizes the painting and finally sees the words "Pipe Dream" in relatively large letters, more or less in the center of the composition.

Johns applied the collage fragments after he started the painting, partly as a way to establish a buffer between the enamel and encaustic he was about to begin applying. He placed "Pipe Dream" as a kind of sign to himself. The phrase alludes to his dream; to his recognition that this painting, and maybe all painting, is nothing more than a fantastic hope; and to René Magritte, whose work Johns saw at the Sidney Janis Gallery in 1954. Titled "Magritte: Word vs. Image," the exhibition included several versions of the "Ceci n'est pas une pipe" ("This is not a pipe") motif.

Johns's reference to Magritte, to his own dream, and to his wish that the painting be something more than a "pipe dream," evokes much about his state of mind at this point in the making of the painting.

Certainly, Duchamp wasn't who he was thinking about—that would come months after his first exhibition closed. When he affixed the collage to the painting's surface, he had no idea that he was about to discover the basis of his project, that encaustic would reveal the terms he would use to continue. For him, there was still something unreal about doing a painting of the American flag.

Johns uses encaustic as a mediating material which simultaneously preserves and transforms the flag. These acts in turn echo specific properties of encaustic. Heat (one might take this as a sign of human presence) transforms encaustic from a solid to a liquid, from an inert material to an active one, capable of absorbing and preserving something from the world. In absorbing the "flag," encaustic also absorbs the canvas; it acknowledges the world it inhabits.

When Johns covered the words "pipe dream" with encaustic, he was preserving his hope, keeping it to himself even as he acknowledged it. His decision not to explain his work, not to surround it with language, was something he had understood about himself long before his art was seen by others. For just as Johns has never wavered from his commitment to have his materials set the terms of his investigation, he has never presumed to tell us what is before our eyes.

VIII.

In *Thermometer* (1959), which was exhibited in Johns's second show at the Leo Castelli Gallery (February 15-March 5, 1960), he placed a thermometer between two panels, so that it is literally inside the painting. Each panel contains a wide range of colors, which have been laid down in open brushstrokes. On the inner edge of both panels a vertically aligned row of stencils has been used to denote an alternating sequence of numbers. Thus, "120" is stenciled at the top of the left panel, and "110" is stenciled a little below it and on the right panel. Done in "correct" sequence and presumably corresponding to the objective measures of either the Fahrenheit or centigrade systems, the numbers validate the external presence of the thermometer rather than the painting's existence.

For while the colors may be seen as warm or cool, hot or cold, the thermometer ruptures this association. Done in oil, the painting seems at odds with itself. And although the thermometer is "inside" the painting, it measures the temperature of the environment, of the place (or context) in which the painting is placed. In *Thermometer*, Johns recognizes that even when a painting, its material existence and thus its meaning, is misunderstood, it does not exist apart from its environment. By using the panels, their colors and numbers, to validate the thermometer as an instrument of measure, as well as to rupture certain associations, Johns proposes a reversal: he shows us how we use a painting to validate something outside itself, and, in doing so, divide it, turn it against itself. If Johns chose the flag because it was thing seen, not looked at, not examined, then he may have chosen the thermometer because it is a thing looked at, examined, but not seen. We look at it not for what it is, but for what we want it to tell us. In *Thermometer*, Johns recognizes the rupturing space

JASPER JOHNS
Water Freezes, 1961
Encaustic on canvas with object, 31 x 25 1/4 inches
Private collection

between a painting's existence, its meanings, and the expectations of meaning brought to it by the viewer. *Thermometer* can be understood as Johns's critique of how *Flag* was looked at by the critics; it tells them that what they want to know of painting can be derived from looking at it, rather than imposing an external standard upon it to discover something. The sequence of numbers evokes a system of measurement, but it may not be aligned correctly.

The relationship between a painting and its environment is further explored in *Water Freezes* (1961), which also contains a thermometer. Unlike *Thermometer*, *Water Freezes* is done in encaustic and the palette is restricted to various shades of gray. In the lower part of the painting, the word "Water" has been placed on the left panel and the word "Freezes" on the right. While the phrase describes something intrinsic to water, it also alludes to a state of transformation that is threatening to the painting's existence, because encaustic is likely to crack when the temperature drops below a certain point; it is a warning. At the same time, the phrase echoes both water's and encaustic's states of being, which are solid and liquid. The juxtaposition of "water," encaustic, and mercury convey the painting's provisional, bounded status; it cannot transcend its material state.

In the beginning of his career, Johns discovered an inextricable link between a blank canvas and the American flag, between an undefined state and a defined one. In *Water Freezes*, Johns uses a thermometer to establish an echo between the essential properties of encaustic (its solid and liquid states) and those of water (its solid and liquid states). This awareness of encaustic as a material which is either solid or liquid also led him to transform a map of the United States into paintings such as *Map* (1962). Surrounded by the Pacific and Atlantic Ocean, as well as divided into states, the map can seen as both a visual and physical representation of encaustic, its solid and liquid states, as well as a recognition of its susceptibility to cracking under certain temperature conditions.

In contrast to most examples of Pop art and Minimalism, *Water Freezes* defines its own provisional status. Neither art nor life are permanent, the painting tells us. However, if one sees and understands a painting, begins grasping its meaning (which is the nature of its existence), perhaps its survival will be guaranteed for some length of time. Perhaps we, the painting's caretakers (and therefore the caretakers of its meaning), will (like the encaustic) preserve it from harm and misunderstanding. And in order to preserve it, we must begin recognizing it in its original form.

1 "Perhaps neither de Kooning nor Gorky has ever reached, in finished and edited oils, the heights they have in fugitive, informal sketches, in drawings and in rapidly done oils on paper.

"(But in 1951 Pollock had turned to the other extreme, as if in violent repentance, and had done a series of paintings, in linear blacks alone, that took back almost everything he had said in the three previous years.)" Clement Greenberg, "'American Type' Painting," in *Art and Culture* (Boston: Beacon Press, 1961), pp. 214, 228.

2 "Johns' most obvious reaction against Abstract Expressionism was in his use of recognizable subject matter in a radically new way." Roberta Bernstein, *Jasper Johns' Paintings and Sculptures 1954-1974: "The Changing Focus of the Eye"* (Ann Arbor, Mich.: UMI Research Press, 1975), p. 6.

3 "Mainly this shift toward a new sensibility came, as I've suggested, in the fifties, a time of convulsive transition not only for the art world, but for society at large as well. In these years, for reasons I've touched on, many young artists found action painting unconvincing. Instead, they turned to the static emptiness of Barnett Newman's eloquent chromatic abstractions or to the sharp visual punning of Jasper Johns's objectlike flags and targets." Barbara Rose, "ABC Art," in *Minimal Art: A Critical Anthology*, ed. Gregory Battcock (New York: Dutton, 1968), p. 281.

4 "None of this would have much interest as a situation, however, were it not that Johns, almost single-handed, deflected the course of Abstract Expressionism." Max Kozloff, "Jasper Johns," in *Renderings: Critical Essays on a Century of Modern Art* (New York: Simon and Schuster, 1968), p. 206.

5 "Instead, Johns has extended the fundamental premises rather than the superficial techniques of Abstract Expressionism to the domain of commonplace objects." Robert Rosenblum, "Jasper Johns," *Art International* 4, no. 7 (September 1960): 74-77.

6 Clement Greenberg, "The Crisis of the Easel Picture," *Art and Culture*, p. 155.

7 (unsigned) "Cover," *Art News* 58, no. 9 (January 1958): 1.

8 Fairfield Porter, "Jasper Johns," ibid., p. 20.

9 Robert Rosenblum, "Jasper Johns," *Arts Magazine* 32, no. 4 (January 1958): 54.

10 Ibid., p. 55.

11 Museum of Modern Art Archives.

12 See Rosenblum, "Jasper Johns."

13 See "Cover," *Art News*.

14 Leo Steinberg, "Jasper Johns: The First Seven Years of His Art," in *Other Criteria: Confrontations with Twentieth-Century Art* (New York: Oxford University Press, 1972).

15 See Rosenblum, "Jasper Johns."

16 See Kozloff, "Jasper Johns."

17 Clement Greenberg, "After Abstract Expressionism," *Art International* 6 no. 8 (October 25, 1962): 25-27.

18 See Steinberg, "Jasper Johns: The First Seven Years of His Art."

19 Charles F. Stuckey, "Letters: Johns: Yet Waving?'" *Art in America* 64, no. 3 (May-June 1976): 5; and Barbara Rose, "To Know Jasper Johns," *Vogue* 167 (November 1977), p. 323.

20 Joseph E. Young, "Jasper Johns: An Appraisal," *Art International* 13, no. 7 (September 1969): 50-56.

21 Nan Rosenthal, "Drawing As Rereading" in *The Drawings of Jasper Johns* (Washington, D.C.: National Gallery of Art, and New York and London: Thames and Hudson, 1990), p. 19.

22 See Kozloff, "Jasper Johns," and Rose, "ABC Art."

23 Michael Crichton, *Jasper Johns* (New York: Abrams, in association with the Whitney Museum of American Art, 1977), p. 27.

24 Ibid., p. 28.

25 See Steinberg, "Jasper Johns: The First Seven Years of His Art."

26 Crichton, *Jasper Johns*, p. 27.

27 Ibid.

28 Leo Castelli Gallery Archives.

29 Alan R. Solomon, *Jasper Johns* (New York: The Jewish Museum, 1964), p. 27.

30 Max Kozloff, *Jasper Johns*, (New York: Abrams, 1969), p. 64.

31 See Crichton, *Jasper Johns*, p. 103.

32 Bernstein, *Jasper Johns' Paintings and Sculptures*, p. ix.

33 Frances Pratt and Becca Fizell, *Encaustic: Materials and Methods* (New York: Lear Publishers, 1949).

34 See Crichton, *Jasper Johns*, p. 27.

35 Rosalind Krauss, "Jasper Johns," *The Lugano Review* I/2, no. 2 (1965): 84-113.

It should be pointed out that in an earlier incarnation, Krauss agreed with Michael Fried, who she quotes: "(It is, I think, significant that Duchamp was a failed modernist — in particular, a failed Cubist — before he turned his hand to the amusing inventions by which he is best known.)," p. 86.

A Greenbergian formalist, Krauss concludes her critical dismissal of Johns with "Color used as a vehicle for optical resonance and color used as a coat hook can indeed be synthesized only by playful verbal manipulation, by pun, by intellectual irony, by everything, in short, except painting," p. 96.

36 Francis V. O'Connor and Eugene V. Thaw, *Jackson Pollock: A Catalogue Raisonné of Paintings, Drawings, and Other Works* (New Haven, Conn. and London: Yale University Press, 1978), vol. 4, p. 241.

37 Maurice Tuchman, *The New York School: The First Generation* (Los Angeles: Los Angeles County Museum, 1965), p. 37.

38 Ibid.

39 Ibid.

40 Mark Rosenthal, "Dancers on a Plane and other Stratagems for Inclusion in the Work of Jasper Johns," in *Cage Cunningham Johns: Dancers on a Plane* (New York: Alfred Knopf, and Anthony d'Offay Gallery, 1990), p. 119.

A version of this essay will appear in John Yau's forthcoming book, *Jasper Johns' Early Work, 1954-1962: Famous Paintings and Sculptures Not Looked At, Not Examined* (Houston: Houston Fine Art Press).

146

CY TWOMBLY
Untitled (Panorama), 1959
Oil, crayon, and pencil on paper, 58 1/4 x 95 1/4 inches
Courtesy of Galerie Karsten Greve, Cologne

Linda Norden

Not Necessarily Pop:
Cy Twombly and America

I.

"Structures, not subjects," John Cage once said of Jasper Johns's pictorial preoccupations:

> ...*if only that will make us pause in our headlong rush through history to realize that Pop art, if deduced from his art, represents a misunderstanding, if embarked upon as the next step after his, represents a non-sequitur. He is engaged with the endlessly changing ancient task: the imitation of nature in her manner of operation.*[1]

Cy Twombly, whose permanent departure for Rome in 1957 — just as American painting veered from its "high" art, expressive mode into the messy domains of material and popular culture — exempted him from this headlong rush, has nevertheless suffered judgment at the level of subject. Because Twombly almost single-handedly pursued the tradition of the American in Rome, opting for the mantle of expatriate and the "Mediterranean effect," his "Americanness" has rarely been discussed.[2]

He has remained an elegant odd-man-out, virtually silent on the facts of his life and work; an artists', writers', and rich collectors' artist, far more familiar in his adopted homeland than here in the United States. And his intensely personal, almost effete painting — the alternately nervous and restrained "written" mode of drawing, the scatological smears of paint, the esoteric echoes of poets past that he pencils onto his surfaces and which have meant so much to the European audiences he attracted from the late fifties on — would seem as remote from the commercial objects and images implied by the word "Pop," as Rome is from New York.

So why is this expatriate artist included in an exhibition titled "Hand-Painted Pop?"

The subtitle of the exhibition — "American Art in Transition, 1955-1962" — offers one possible clue. Certain events demarcate periods irrevocably. For Americans, World War II and our role in its outcome would have to be counted as one such event. And for those artists just beginning their careers during the heady postwar years, the tremendous critical success of Abstract Expressionism at that time — which almost immediately transformed its key players into a generation of heroes, a cultural equivalent for our "boys" overseas — would also have to be counted as pivotal. Chronologically, at least, this is Twombly's generation: his closest contemporaries are the American artists who came of age in the early fifties, artists who might well be described as the first true "second generation" of American painters.

Like most powerful myths, the story of the New York School is less a fabrication than an amplification of a great deal of genuine discovery. But the story of the generation that came of age in its wake has been less frequently or fully explored. Or rather, it has been collapsed into a beginning and an end — with Pop art as its only outcome, and popular culture as its only subject.

A decade that witnessed the hearings of Joseph McCarthy; the launching of Sputnik; the inaugurations of both Dwight D. Eisenhower and John F. Kennedy; the creation of Jack Kerouac's *On the Road* and Allen Ginsburg's *Howl*; Larry Rivers's *Washington Crossing the Delaware*, Robert Rauschenberg's *Monogram*, and Louise Bourgeois's fetishistic sculptures; Dick Clark's "American Bandstand," Aaron Copland, Motown, and Elvis Presley, can hardly be described as politically, socially, or culturally monolithic. What all of these figures have in common, however, is an unabashed engagement with what it means to be American.

Yet, as the story of the decade's art gets told, in revision after revision, the route from Abstract Expressionism to Pop seems to remain fixed. Even as the focus shifts from the contributions of individual artists to the context of media, publicity, process, and reception, the conclusion always seems foregone: between the early fifties and early sixties, American art — or the prevailing notion of what constituted American art — moved from the excluding, high art domain of expressive gesture to the popular arena of commercial imagery and icons. But any story that ends only by equating American culture with mass culture is itself an excluding story — and one that ironically fails to account for the messiness of the masses.

Suppose instead, we start with the simple facts of time and place, and agree that the decade in question can be characterized as one in which America and Americans become unusually preoccupied with what it means to be American. Suppose we agree, too, that the unprecedented success of Abstract Expressionism, and the variety of its manifestations, made way for a truly new generation, at once faced with "the anxiety of influence" and blessed with the precedent of a legitimated American avant-garde.

If we also allow that the quest for signs of an authentic American culture took place on more than one front, then Twombly's eschewal of commercial imagery and his move to Rome need not be reason enough to divorce his art from that of his American contemporaries. There are, as Leo Steinberg has said, "other criteria": an American in Rome is still an American.

II.

In the gesture we don't see the real shadow of fulfillment, the unambiguous shadow that admits of no further interpretation. "The gesture tries to prefigure," one wants to say, "but it can't."

Ludwig Wittgenstein, *Philosophical Grammar*[3]

Rauschenberg has said that before he and Twombly met — in 1950, at the Art Students League in New York — Twombly had already begun to explore a mode of drawing that fused and *confused* drawing with writing.[4] By 1955, when he painted *The Geeks*, Twombly's mastery of this "confused" written mode of drawing reveals just how well he had succeeded in this effort — and how far he had moved from Pollock's gestural drips.

Twombly, like Pollock, uses the surface on which he paints as a field, a repository for rapid traces of movement. Both cover the field with seemingly abstract, gestural marks which overlap and interpenetrate — the gestural quality in each case determined by the speed with which they appear to have been made. But here the similarities end.

Pollock painted on the neutral, light ground of unprimed canvas. Its uniform, uninflected surface prevents any mistaking this surface for a thing: it is, resolutely, a surface for painting. Even when the splattered paint seeps into the canvas fibers, penetrating the otherwise reflective off-white, these stained areas serve to underscore the flat ground instead of creating patches of recessional depth. The visual declaration of surface is further reinforced by Pollock's treatment of the edges of the canvas, where the tangle of swirled and splashed paint shrinks back on itself, creating a kind of interior frame for his painterly activity.[5] (Pollock is still, as Twombly might have said, "making a good picture.") Pollock also provides a reassuring sense of increment and decision, by applying at least five different colors of paint in what appear to be distinct layers. Despite the complex interlace of painterly whorls, the image looks to have been created in separable "acts" of color. The combined effect of the interior frame and distinct color episodes leads to the visual conclusion that his painting is indeed finished, complete.

Twombly, on the other hand, paints on a thick and sullied, almost viscous ground into which his thinly traced lines seem to be scratched and buried. The sheer number of marks gives the surface an object quality — a notepad by the phone, a public wall, a piece of unexposed film. The surface itself appears to have a history even as it remains open to more. Instead of serving as unobtrusive support for the artist's invented imagery, Twombly's support counters the marks he submits it to, making the act of painting or drawing an act of aggression, in ways that parallel a graffitist's appropriation of a subway car wall. Though it is less open to inflection than Rauschenberg's series of "White Paintings" — less radical a statement — Twombly's surface functions similarly, as a repository for random jottings, or accumulations of private references, rather than the base for a choreographed set of performed actions.[6] And, as with Rauschenberg's reuse of his quilt and pillow in his *Bed* (1955), it becomes difficult to discern when or where the art-making begins and whether it has, in fact, been completed.[7]

This opening up of the art-making process may well have been catalyzed by Pollock's willingness to drip and throw paint, or de Kooning's willingness to smear it.[8] But the opening up that the generation beginning with Rauschenberg makes possible extends beyond paint. These are, in a sense, the first American artists since the American Romantics of the nineteenth century to acknowledge what our postmodern generation now sings as its refrain. To be American (or post-industrial) is to begin again and to begin with the "always-already," to begin, that is, with the premise that Johns later transcribed as aphorism: "Not mine, but taken."

Twombly's willingness to open the field of painting took a less literal and material form than Rauschenberg's, occurring as it did through the "fusion and confusion" he pursued through drawing as writing as drawing. Interestingly, where Rauschenberg's early paintings infuriated numerous older artists — witness Barnett Newman's famous retort after seeing Rauschenberg's White Paintings: "What, does he think it's easy?" — Twombly's tend to infuriate a more general audience. The written quality of his marks makes us persist in trying to read his surfaces.

Unlike Pollock's consistent, cumulative arabesques, Twombly's scrawls vary in density and configuration in ways that subvert any pictorial unity. In *The Geeks*, for example, in addition to numerous circular and spiraling scribbles, we see the letters "A" and "C" written in varying degrees of legibility, but in no apparent order or composition. There is an awkwardness to the line quality that differs from the bravura confidence of Pollock's splashes and drips. And in this painting — though not always — the title reinforces this

ROBERT RAUSCHENBERG
Bed, 1955
Combine painting: oil and pencil on pillow,
quilt, and sheet on wood supports, 75 1/4 x 31 1/2 x 8 inches
Fractional gift of Leo Castelli in honor of Alfred H. Barr, Jr.
to The Museum of Modern Art, New York

CY TWOMBLY
The Geeks, 1955
Oil, crayon, and pencil on canvas, 42 1/2 x 50 inches
Courtesy of Thomas Ammann, Zurich

sense of awkwardness. "Geek," Webster's *New World Dictionary* tells us,

originates in the echoic of unintelligible cries. 1. A performer of depraved or grotesque acts in a carnival,
etc. such as biting off the head of a live chicken 2. any person considered to be different from others
in a negative or bizarre way, as a teenager seen as being awkward, tall, or gangling, stupid or anti-social.

Yet this painting is hardly an illustration or evocation of a particular pathology. *The Geeks* has about it, instead,
the feel of a place, in this case New York. The vertical, spindly quality of the lines, the anger and anxiety
perceptible in the rapid overlays, the density and dirty feel of the surface do not differ significantly from three
other paintings shown with *The Geeks* at the Stable Gallery in 1956 whose titles carry very different
associations — *Free Wheeler, Criticism, The Academy* — yet all of which have also been labeled, "(New York
City)." This sense of place is equally apparent — and clearly different — in the 1957 and 1958 paintings Twombly
labels "(Roma)." In *Blue Room (To Betty di Robilant)* (1957) (Roma), for example, Twombly uses the same
oil, crayon, and pencil on canvas and the same mode of linear marking that he used in the New York City

151

paintings mentioned above, but to very different effect. There is more open space, the lines are less agitated,
there is a sense of drift rather than digging. Though the edges of the canvas still seem arbitrary — it still
reads, that is, as a random receptor for random marks, not a composed image — the emptier field allows us to
discern a few more coherent graphic marks. But the subtitle, "To Betty di Robilant" — an American friend of
Twombly's who also settled in Rome during 1957 — renders the painting more personal and less accessible
than those discussed above.[9]

Twombly's marks, in other words, project an aura of specificity that remains undisclosed,
subverted by their palpable sensation of touch and their maddening approximation to writing. Maddening,

CY TWOMBLY
The Blue Room, 1957
Oil and crayon on canvas, 56 1/4 x 71 5/8 inches
The Sonnabend Collection, New York

because we want to *read* these images and can't. As with Rauschenberg's combine paintings of the same year, the parts don't add up to any whole. Pollock's fluid, rhythmic lines, on the other hand, never come close enough to writing to provoke a desire to read. We sense them instead as abstract forms, bodily gestures, material objective-correlatives for a mood, organized into a unified image-field. As Lawrence Alloway has observed, Pollock's gestures of this period are connected with calligraphy, "but a non-referential calligraphy, in which art's connection with a kind of instinctive gestural message-making is retained and no acts of translation are required of us (you don't have to know the language)."[10]

       There is a scene in one of Luigi Pirandello's Sicilian short stories — "Conversing with Mother" — which, as filmed by the Taviani brothers for their 1985 movie, *Kaos*, uncannily conjures the quality of Twombly's distinct graphic marks. In the scene, the camera focuses on an anguished widow — the mother — prematurely weathered by the harsh facts of her life and by the equally harsh terrain visible through the open

door behind her. She is standing by a table, speaking rapidly and gesticulating wildly. We gather that she is dictating a letter — an impassioned plea — to her two sons in Santa Fe, New Mexico, who abandoned their mother some fourteen years earlier and have not been heard from since.

       Across the table, her back turned to us, a younger woman dips a pen repeatedly into an inkpot and scrawls on sheet after sheet of yellow paper as the widow's words pour out. We sense a discrepancy between the leisurely pace of the young woman's writing and the accelerating urgency of the widow's speech.

CY TWOMBLY
Untitled, 1960
Oil, crayon, and pencil on canvas, 38 1/4 x 55 1/8 inches
Collection of Ralph and Helyn Goldenberg, Chicago

But the full impact of the scene occurs in an image: as the camera shifts abruptly to the paper on which the widow's thoughts have been recorded, we see not words but chaotic, uneven lines of scribble—lines the widow believes will carry her thoughts and feelings across the Atlantic to her sons. As she cannot read or write herself, the pages of scribbles have momentarily satisfied her need to act and to express herself, even though they will fail to provide the solace of a response. The central image—of visible, even expressive, marks "unfaithful" to the words we hear—gains its impact by making explicit the inadequacy of *any* articulation to the thoughts and feelings we hope to communicate; by placing us, as it were, in the gap between experience and expression. This is the gap in which Twombly paints, the gap between one body and another.

"Most painting *defines* the image," Twombly said some thirty-five years ago, in the only statement he has ever published. "It is therefore to a great extent illustrating the idea or feeling or content. It is in this area that I break with the more general processes of painting...." For Twombly, instead, "each line is the actual experience with its own innate history. It does not illustrate—the imagery is one of private indulgences rather than an abstract totality."[11] It is this admission, I think—to an imagery of "private indulgences," as much as the marks themselves—that differentiates Twombly's disjunctive and fetishistic marks from the gestural objective-correlatives so carefully pursued by a Pollock or a Kline and from the moral expectations of painting still harbored by a Rothko or a Newman.

III.

To Imagine Painting a Language ...

By 1960, when he painted *Sunset Series III* and the *Untitled* painting owned by Ralph and Helyn Goldenberg, Twombly's "private indulgences" have metamorphosed from lines and proto-letters into an even more baffling and inscrutable array of cryptic configurations. In all three of the "Sunset Series" paintings a loosely vertical column comprised of discrete, penciled, doodle-like figures rises to a larger circle over which Twombly uses crayon in broad swathes of red, blue, some purple, and white. In *Sunset Series I*, this circular form surmounts a vertical one, giving it a phallic presence; in *Sunset Series III* the circle is fringed with a scalloped line and feels more feminine; in *Sunset Series II*, the colored strokes cover the circle, rather than hover above it, and the circle just reads as a circle.

The white space surrounding this "column" is populated, in turn, by a disparate array of penciled shapes and markings—another phallic form, this time like a cigar with propellers; a rainbow-like doodle of concentric half-circles; an isolated letter "A"; tiny drifts of a pinkish-white paint, sometimes outlined in pencil, sometimes not, sometimes numbered, sometimes not—which compete with often illegible inscriptions, stray strokes of colored and graphite pencil, and a boxed-off area filled with more organized notations. The penciled shapes here read less like writing on a surface than animated personae in a non-dimensional mind-space: forms appear to be in flux. In *Sunset III*, for example, the left canvas edge bisects a winged form so that it appears to be moving out of, or into, the field. And in this airy medium, the stray accumulations of paint are like drops of water on closed eyes—a startle that instantaneously brings interior thoughts into collision with the external world at the threshold of the skin.

Twombly's use of his paint as "stuff," rather than as a medium for color, parallels Rauschenberg's "creative palette," in which all materials—objects, images, paint—are used straightforwardly, as if to declare their independent histories.[12] One of Twombly's achievements has been his ability to give paint its corporeal dimension, a feat only de Kooning had managed as well. Unlike de Kooning, however, Twombly accomplishes this transformation directly, without need of any figural support: de Kooning's pink paint became

153

154

CY TWOMBLY
(Study for) Sunset, 1960
Oil and crayon on canvas, 49 1/4 x 65 inches
Courtesy of Galerie Karsten Greve, Cologne

CY TWOMBLY
Sunset Series Part III (Bay of Naples), 1960
Oil and graphite on canvas, 75 x 79 inches
Collection of Dieter Hauert, Berlin

"flesh" on his women; Twombly's does so just by dint of his smearing it onto his canvas.

An unusual series of paintings from 1961-62 asserts this willful transformation more ironically. Over a penciled line, Twombly fills five circles with pink, red, brown, silverish, and white paint, and labels them, respectively, with the words "Flesh," "Blood," "Earth," "Mirror," "Clouds." It is so, because it says so. Below the line, Twombly draws a palette-shaped rectangle and, treating the shape as the palette it refers to, squeezes on more dabs of the same colors. The captions here amplify those above and are even more ironic —for example, to the right of a white smear, labelled "white," Twombly scribbles, "For diluting dreams"; next to some brown, "Browns for earth"; next to a row of reds and pink, "Reds for flesh + blood." And at the of the canvas, almost illegibly crossed over, Twombly copies out a passage from Sappho: "But their hearts turned cold and they dropped their wings" and signs and dates his work, "Cy Twombly/Roma 1962." By overtly declaring the artist's touch and presence (through his direct use of paint and handwritten notations) even as he alludes to effects conventionally achieved via the erasure of the artist's touch, Twombly pays homage to the idea of metamorphosis so central to Western art, while simultaneously undermining its mimetic basis. This is not too different from what Rauschenberg achieved in his *Rebus* (1955), by juxtaposing a facsimile of Botticelli's *Birth of Venus* with his own "art-marks," contemporary comic strips, scientific illustrations, newspaper photos of current events, and even some scribbling by Twombly.[13] But, as always, Twombly's appropriations are more subtle, more highbrow, and perhaps, more audacious.

Twombly's attention to the mark as the smallest signifying particle of an image, as well as his efforts to create an equivalence between corporeal and non-material phenomena, then, have their parallels in the concurrent experiments of Johns and Rauschenberg. At the same time, his development of a kind of private language of repeated, recognizable signs links him not just to Johns and Rauschenberg, but to Warhol and Dine and many of the American artists most often discussed under the umbrella of Pop. These artists push the painting itself to the "condition of gesture" by repeating a recognizable repertoire of images or signs, and repeating them whole.[14] In Twombly's painting, however, this repetition may be more difficult to discern.

To look at any one isolated Twombly painting from this period is to be dumbfounded. Since none of the individual configurations read as painterly abstractions—even without any knowledge of the broad scope of Twombly's work, these "figures" come off as cartoony ideograms—there is no possibility of simply submitting to the "beauty" of the painting. In fact, the isolated signs and invocations which Twombly deploys over his surfaces here convey not illegible writing, but rather some incomprehensible patois, one that is both hieroglyphic and verbal. Twombly's occasional inclusion of legible English phrases, like his clear writing of "Queen for a Day"—a multiple entendre that alludes specifically to the daytime American TV show of the fifties and more generally to a "sometime" homosexuality—in the upper left corner of *Sunset Series II*, only makes matters worse. Even more than Twombly's mid-fifties "written" paintings, these simultaneously beg and frustrate "deciphering." It becomes quickly apparent that there is no one meaning offered up by any individual sign or painting. Twombly's images are not symbolic.

But as we become familiar with a broader range of his paintings, we begin to grow conversant with Twombly's vocabulary. It becomes tempting to treat the paintings like Rosetta stones, picking out recognizable forms, playing with possible readings by relating their use in one painting to their use in another. Certain patterns emerge: Twombly often plays abstract, referential configurations—such as the grid in the lower right corner of the Goldenbergs' *Untitled*, or the ruled box containing numbered geometric pieces in *Sunset III*—against his more fetishistic shapes, which often collide, in turn, with massings of pure paint, the artist's signature, the date, and the place where the work was painted.

Some of Twombly's forms are almost self-identifying, if only at the level of allusion. For example, an elliptical pencil shape with the word "Pool" scribbled inside it, sometimes colored blue and surrounded with a fringe of green and/or accompanied by the dedication "To Poussin," conjures that most famous expatriate artist in Rome and his prior exploration of the Ovidian myths that occupied Twombly during this period. This association becomes more apparent if we know Twombly's *Woodland Glade (To Poussin)* (1960) (Roma), in which the penciled ellipse — filled with a few blue strokes and the word "pool," and surrounded by a few arcs of wispy green pencil and pale pink and white paint — is the entire image, save for the penciled inscriptions. When we see this "complete" sign, we more quickly recognize its variations as they occur in more complex paintings.

Of course, it helps to know something about Poussin and Ovid, as well. When Twombly paints Poussin's pool, and juxtaposes his signature and the current date to a title he has also borrowed from the artist, he is appropriating that association in much the same way that Johns does when he puts the American flag to his own painterly ends, or that Warhol does when he co-opts the Coke bottle. "Not mine, but taken" describes a mindset common to all three. What remains so impressive about each of these artists' very different appropriations, and what distinguishes their work qualitatively from the postmodern generation of the eighties, is their ability to give new life to symbols "exhausted" by general use, by making their "private indulgences" public. It is precisely because their appropriation is so personal that it is so compelling.[15]

IV.

To begin again,
not to win
but sing.   Charles Olson[16]

Since at least the early seventies, when his close friend Heiner Bastian began writing about him, Twombly's commitment to Rome and the larger context of the Mediterranean and its attendant mythology have dominated discussions of his art.[17] It is, of course, impossible to ignore all that Twombly's move to Rome made possible in his art. In the fables of Ovid and the spirit of the Mediterranean Twombly found the magic of myth and its capacity to enlarge the scope of one's "private indulgences" through identification and metamorphosis, much as Warhol did — and at much the same time — through his identification with a more contemporary galaxy of gods and goddesses.[18] Not surprisingly, Bastian's claim for the importance of Ovidian mythology to Twombly's art coincides with much of the revisionist treatment of Pop. In both cases, the meaning of an individual artist's production is magnified by a mythological context which can easily be allowed to eclipse the private experience that generates the work.

The cover photo Bastian selected for his book on Twombly is telling. Twombly, as shepherd, sits pensively at the base of a tree, legs apart, hands on knees, innocent among the surrounding sheep. So

157

CY TWOMBLY
Untitled, 1961
Oil on canvas, 31 1/2 x 39 inches
Private collection

comfortable does he look in this Arcadian surround that it is only belatedly that we ask: "Who is this person?" "How did he get there?" "Does he have a name?" Even as he endows Twombly with a context, or milieu, Bastian generalizes Twombly's experience and erases his personal history and Americanness. While Twombly differs from those of his American contemporaries who were beginning to identify themselves with their immediate environment, his project does connect with an earlier American quest for self and history, or self in history. It was in an American place — Black Mountain College — that Twombly first began to fuse myth and history with the personal and the erotic. It was at Black Mountain College that Twombly established his relationship with Robert Rauschenberg, and where he was exposed to the seductive bombast of the poet Charles Olson, rector of the college during Twombly's years there. It is not possible here to do justice to Olson's meandering poetics and the expository "post-modern" or "post-logical" propositions he was developing during the very years Twombly attended Black Mountain, but they remain, I think, central to Twombly's preoccupations.

Olson's devotion to the reinsertion of breath in poetry, and his approach to history and mythology, are echoed in Twombly's emphasis on the vocative and aural capacities of words and his insistence on touch in the formation of his image. These concerns, of course, are hardly new to twentieth-century art or literature, but Olson's (and, I believe, Twombly's) stance has to be read as a resistance to the dictates of the then-dominant New Criticism and as diametrically opposed to the existential outlook that permeated Abstract Expressionism.

For Olson, a "post-modern" poetic was one that worked against the self-imposed restraints he associated with modernism. He rejects the notion of history as "something you're stuck with in some inexorable manner and it grinds you out, you're always too late because it all happened last year. It's an awfully sad way to think," and argues instead for an understanding of history as "what a person *does*," the vector of his various acts. "Too long it has been only what he *has* done, thus a bore." By defining history as "the practice of space in time," Olson worked to bring literary thinking up to the level of earlier twentieth-century mathematics and criticism.[19]

"Art," Olson says in "Projective Verse,"

does not seek to describe but to enact ...it is the equal of its cause only when it proceeds unbroken from the threshold of a man through him and back out again, without loss of quality, to the external world from which it came, whether the external world would take the shape of another human being, or of the several human beings hidden by the generalization "society" or of things themselves.[20]

Olson's thinking on an American preoccupation with origins is also key. The first lines of Olson's first and most famous book, *Call Me Ishmael*, announce his self-consciously "post-modern" writing, his recognition that "the poet is merely the second time" and that, as he said of Melville, "to go back to come forward is to seize the beginning as already begun."[21]

All of these concerns are apparent in a series of images Twombly began in 1960-61, which he titled *Birth of Venus*. I often think of these images as serving for Twombly in the way Johns's flags served for him, though the nature of the "origins" or "birth" Twombly explores has a longer history than Johns's appropriated flag can carry. Though Twombly's title refers overtly to a mythical episode, it is not specifically Ovidian: Ovid gives only a few lines of the *Metamorphoses* to Venus's birth, and then only by way of recollection. Twombly's image nevertheless conveys Ovid's mythic method: ambiguities between writing and the material allusions to "water" or "body parts" read as metamorphoses between these abstract and palpable phenomena.

Cover of *Cy Twombly: Bilder/1952-76* by Heiner Bastian
Photo: *Plinio de Martiis*

CY TWOMBLY
(Study for) School of Athens, 1960
Oil and crayon on canvas, 49 1/4 x 65 inches
Courtesy of Galerie Karsten Greve, Cologne

Formally, Twombly's *Birth of Venus* represents a consolidation and isolation of a single sign — much like the "Woodland Glade" described above. He returned to the theme, and image, repeatedly during the early sixties.

The similarities and differences between Rauschenberg's inclusion of a reproduced image of Botticelli's *Birth of Venus* in his *Rebus* come to mind again: both appropriate the historical legacy of the image and myth, but where Rauschenberg appropriates literally by incorporating a reproduction of the hard-edged Botticellian version, Twombly appropriates the name and makes it his own by reenacting the myth with his own fingers. This introduction of touch — fingerprint — into the act of appropriation is one of Twombly's most distinct characteristics.

Twombly's art, in this sense, summons not just Olson's belief that "what happens at the skin is more like than different from what happens within," but the broad phenomenological precept that man's reintegration in the present lies chiefly in recovering consciousness of the body's part in thinking. Olson's conception of "projective verse" aimed less at a reintegration of body and mind than at a recognition of the body as membrane and orifice, container and conduit, as "gate" between public and private, present sensation and projected past — the appropriate metaphor for language.

There is, however, a significant difference between the tenor of Twombly's and of Olson's sexuality, a difference that sets off many of Twombly's contemporaries from the competitive machismo with which so many Abstract Expressionist artists were identified. Where Olson insisted on a phallic trope as "simply man's most immediate way of knowing nature's power," Twombly conjures androgynous forms that suggest a less monolithic history. His sexuality is never didactic, and all the more convincing for it.

"Mine is the need to be where it will always never be the same again," Rauschenberg said some thirty years after his and Twombly's time at Black Mountain College, "a kind of archaeology in time only, forcing one to see whatever the light of darkness touches, and care."[22] Twombly, whose retreat from this American preoccupation with forward trajectory has dominated the same thirty years, has found in the literature and legends most Americans perceive as "Not theirs," a way to make them his own — and ours. If Warhol's luck, and genius, lay in the coincidence of his "private indulgences" with those of a broad American public — his love of things and spectacle seems more conspicuously American than Twombly's invocations of private loves lost — Twombly's willingness to begin again — "not to win/but sing" — is also American.

160

1 John Cage, "Stories and Ideas," in *Jasper Johns* (New York: The Jewish Museum, 1964), p. 22.

2 "Mediterranean effect" is the evocative phrase Roland Barthes coined with reference to Twombly's art in what may be the most popular essay written on the artist, "Sagesse de l'Art," ("The Wisdom of Art"). The essay serves as the catalogue introduction to the Whitney Museum of American Art's 1979 retrospective, "Cy Twombly: Paintings and Drawings 1954-1977." It should be added, however, that Barthes, not untypically, simply made poetic what had first been observed by the German critic and personal friend of Twombly, Heiner Bastian. Twombly's first American retrospective, in fact, had been held four years earlier at the Institute for Contemporary Art in Philadelphia. That exhibition included extensive essays by both Bastian and curator Suzanne Delehanty which focused extensively on Twombly's engagement with mythology and the Mediterranean arena, providing a context for Twombly's art much indebted to his European reception.

3 Ludwig Wittgenstein, *Philosophical Grammar*, trans. Anthony Kenny (Berkeley: University of California Press, 1974), p. 150.

4 See Calvin Tomkins, *Off the Wall: Robert Rauschenberg and the Art World of Our Time* (New York: Doubleday, 1980), chapter nine.

5 The notion of an "interior frame" in many of Pollock's paintings was suggested by Robert Pincus-Witten in his article "Cy Twombly," *Artforum* 12, no. 8 (April 1974): 62.

6 Of course, what was unique about Rauschenberg's "White Paintings" was their blankness: they made room for inflections of light (the environment) and for projections of the viewers' — and not just the artist's — projections. This was not, however, true of most of Rauschenberg's early work, which tended to give equal billing to a wide range of conventional, unconventional, and personally charged materials.

7 Two anecdotes seem appropriate here:

1. Several people attending Black Mountain College during the summer of 1951, when Rauschenberg painted his first series of Black Paintings, have commented that Twombly assisted him. I mention this not to give Twombly "credit" in their conception, but to point up another form of the "openness" that I see as so central to this period. It is hard to imagine Pollock working collaboratively.

2. I have also been told by numerous people, including Twombly, that many of the canvases he used during the first few years of the fifties — at Black Mountain and in his Fulton Street studio in New York — got recycled. Just before he painted *The Geeks*, for example, Twombly did a series of paintings with white markings on a sooty, gray ground. All but one of these — the 1955 painting *Panorama* — have been "lost." But Twombly himself mentioned the possibility of their simply having been recycled; and Paul Schimmel recently told me that Robert Indiana claims to have paintings of his (from this period) that cover some of Twombly's and, possibly, Rauschenberg's.

8 As Rauschenberg has said, "I'm sure that the freedoms that the abstract expressionists indulged in changed the possibilities and limitations of every artist. Pollock particularly. Pollock's early paintings were very tight and came out of false fantasy. When he started dripping, I think his whole body was engaged in the process. It became very personal then. And if he could *drip* paint, de Kooning could *smear* it. That really had to change the scene." Quoted in Barbara Rose, *Rauschenberg* (New York: Elizabeth Avedon Editions, Vintage Contemporary Artists, 1987), p. 50.

9 Already, in the mid-fifties, Twombly incorporated dedications to friends into some of his untitled paintings or works on paper — e.g., a 1956 untitled work on paper with the written inscription "To Eleanor Ward." (Eleanor Ward was owner and director of the Stable Gallery where Rauschenberg and Twombly showed between 1953 and 1956.) By 1959, however, Twombly's "dedicated" paintings and drawings evolve into a series of homages or entreaties to more public personae drawn from literature and painting — e.g., *To Sappho* (1959); *To Leonardo* (1960); *Woodland Glade (To Poussin)* (1960); *To Virgil* (1964). Not only do these homages serve to collapse history through private dialogue (see below on this subject); they add an oral and aural dimension to the painting which continues to characterize virtually all the writing that Twombly incorporates into his work. When he later began to copy lines of poetry onto his surfaces, Twombly generally chose passages that asked questions, expressed feelings, or produced richly phonic rhythms, as opposed to those that described visual phenomena. Twombly's quotations do more than provoke distinctions between reading and viewing, or image and text. As with Rauschenberg's use of recorded sound effects in his early Happenings, Twombly's written speech engages the viewer sensually in the artist's own pursuit of how things mean.

10 Lawrence Alloway, "American Drawing," catalogue introduction for the Solomon R. Guggenheim Museum exhibition, September 17 - October 27, 1965.

11 Cy Twombly, "Signs," in *Esperienza Moderna*, no. 2 (1957): 32.

12 I am alluding, here, to the way Rauschenberg has described his "palette" as consisting of any materials he chose to incorporate into his paintings — light bulbs; dirt; stuffed dead animals; the equipment of technology, even paint — and to his assertion that "All material has its own history built into it. There's no such thing as 'better' material." An anecdote underscores the point: "I remember in the Navy I painted a picture of someone and I didn't know much about painting. I used blood for the red — *my blood*." Rose, *Rauschenberg*, pp. 57-58.

13 Rauschenberg's *Rebus* includes several colored-crayon drawings that had been given to him by Twombly. I believe that some of the penciled scribbling is Twombly's too.

14 I am thinking here of R. P. Blackmur's discussion of "Language as Gesture": "In a sense," says Blackmur, "any word or congeries of words can be pushed to the condition of gesture either by simple repetition or by a combination of repetition and variation. . . . It is not at all the meaning that the words *had* that counts, but the meaning that repetition, in a given situation, makes them take on." In *Language as Gesture: Essays in Poetry* (New York: Harcourt, Brace, 1952), p. 13.

15 Twombly often makes the private nature of his appropriations apparent to the viewer by treating his canvases as both homage and personal letter. When he summons Leonardo, or Poussin, or Sappho, he addresses them in the same way he does his personal friends: "To Leonardo," "To Poussin," "To Betty di Robilant. . . ." There is both humility and conceit in these entreaties.

Twombly's use of private allusions and sexually charged signs also induce a sense of voyeurism that parallels Rauschenberg's use of his *Bed* or Johns's use of body parts in *Target with Plaster Casts* (1955). And this sense of voyeurism, which Warhol, too, knew how to exploit so well, only intensifies our desire to "know what's going on," even as we feel excluded.

16 From a draft for "A Lion Upon the Floor," quoted in Tom Clark, *Charles Olson: The Allegory of a Poet's Life* (New York: Norton, 1991), p. 49.

17 See Heiner Bastian, *Cy Twombly: Bilder/Paintings, 1952-1976* vol. 1 (Frankfurt, Berlin, and Vienna: Propylaen-Verlag, 1978), pp. 38-39.

18 Twombly's method, however, could be described as "metamorphic" from the start: his linear marks may not have entailed reference, but in their motility and approximation to writing they also appear to be undergoing endless transformations.

19 Charles Olson, *The Special View of History* (Berkeley: University of California Press, 1970), p. 15.

20 Charles Olson, *Selected Writings*, edited and with an introduction by Robert Creeley (New York: New Directions, 1966), p. 64.

21 Charles Olson, *Call Me Ishmael* (San Francisco: City Lights, 1947), p. 1.

22 Quoted in Andy Grundberg, "Another Side of Rauschenberg," *New York Times Magazine*, October 18, 1981, pp. 43ff.

MEL RAMOS
The Joker, 1962
Oil on canvas, 50 x 44 inches
Guess, Inc., Marciano Collection, Los Angeles

Stephen C. Foster

Early Pop
and the Consumptive Critic

Abstract Expressionism created a crisis in criticism through its withdrawal from articulated social purpose. Pop art's apparent social significance, however, only compounded this crisis by prompting a reenactment of the mass culture critique. For the first time the perennial recipients of a traditionally one-way critique — the masses — finally began returning critical fire, or at least appeared to be in a position to do so. Out of a deep sense of insecurity over the role of the critic, and the "creating culture"[1] that criticism conventionally advocated, Abstract Expressionism was rewritten according to a normative aesthetic that Pop was alleged to debase and abandon. As a result, recent critics of both a liberal and conservative persuasion have felt confident in proclaiming that Pop announced "the dawn of post-modernism."[2] In the process the two movements have been deprived of an important dimension of historical continuity.

Contrary to conventional wisdom, the mid-1940s to the mid-1950s witnessed the failure of modernism in America. Clement Greenberg and Harold Rosenberg had both recognized the tenuousness of modernism and sought by radically different means to deal with it: the former by rejecting the crisis out of his own obsessive modernism; the latter in exploiting it out of disillusionment with modernism's exhaustion. For Greenberg, there was no question of abandoning modernism. Indeed, his investment in the concept clouded his ability to perceive challenges to modernism as anything but threats and aberrations. Greenberg's critical "revolution" had been, and continued to be, a revolution of the right.

> *All values are human values, relative values, in art as well as elsewhere. Yet there does seem to have been more or less of a general agreement among the cultivated of mankind over the ages as to what is good art and what bad....There has been an agreement then, and this agreement rests, I believe, on a fairly constant distinction made between those values only to be found in art and the values which can be found elsewhere. Kitsch, by virtue of a rationalized technique that draws on science and industry, has erased this distinction in practice.*[3]

Committed above all to warranting modernism and the historical motion it implied, Greenberg dug down deeply into the philosophy of history for a model that would make the success of modernism and modernists inevitable.[4] Ironically enough, it was offered as a rationale of modernism at precisely the time that an analytical philosophy of history was emerging strongly and when idealistic aesthetics were being mercilessly dismantled and discarded. In 1966, Morse Peckham declared with a sober finality that

...in spite of divergences of opinion, we are all in agreement that traditional philosophical aesthetics is hopelessly bankrupt....Indeed, aesthetics seems to provide no directions even for the simple observation of human behavior when it can be categorized as artistic behavior....Happily, we are not alone. In recent years a number of philosophers have subjected traditional aesthetics to the most penetrating analysis and have arrived at uniformly negative results.[5]

In the prevailing intellectual world of the late fifties and sixties, Greenberg's determinism was as improbable as his historically driven process of art's "self-criticism." Nevertheless, conservative responses seemed, at least in the short run, to prevail.

Greenberg had invested his entire concept of culture in art, from which all further (descending) cases of culture were extrapolated. The moral imperative of his and like positions and their relationship to mass culture critique is well described by Herbert Gans.

The so-called mass culture critique is important because it is concerned with far more than media fare and consumer goods. It is really about the nature of the good life, and thus about the purpose of life in general.... It is also about which culture and whose culture should dominate in society, and represent it as the societal or national culture in the competition between contemporary societies and in the historical record of cultures or civilizations.[6]

The implications of this for Greenberg's subsequent power within the art world developed as one might have expected. It was his criticism that most bolstered art's sense of its own importance at a time when American cultural business had reached fever pitch. And it was Greenberg's scheme that permitted the remythification and popular success of modernism.

Although Greenberg's positions were given added force by the illusion that once again the art world occupied a central, privileged place in the life of modern culture, this was a "popular" idea embraced by the very mass cultures Greenberg was nominally educating. Jean Duvignaud rightly notes that,

For a long time this theory belonged exclusively to very narrow artistic groups and creative élites, but in the last century it changed its social sphere and spread to the middle classes whose basic education through school and art galleries, popular books and more recently radio, films and television, has been dominated by the idea of "beauty" or the "possibility of beauty's existence."... And those who suddenly feel for reasons of social prestige that they ought to discuss art, but who out of ignorance have to rely on popularizers, also further extend the strange notion that there is an absolute beauty from which everyone can receive grace.[7]

Long committed to the notion that the United States inherited modernism, advanced its historical course, and extended its inevitable course to conclusion, the critical and historical worlds responsible for this perspective lost sight of the fact that they "won" based on their assimilation by popular culture. It seems to have occurred to few that the forces responsible for the victory were basically conservative and that in plotting their short-term victory they may have been ensuring their long-term defeat.

Heir as well as opponent to the fifties and Abstract Expressionism, Pop inherited the deterioration of believability in these modernist myths, until nothing was left but sentiment. Jacques Barzun's remarks in 1960 that Abstract Expressionism's abolition could not be sustained ("Their work is all denial."[8]) had proven to be true. The result, as he saw it, was a frame of mind essential for understanding Pop: "... like experiencing the relief that Henry James found even in the death of those best loved; it is license to practice a serene and silent atheism."[9]

Scarcely new, the crisis of criticism (and the crisis of modernism of which it was a part) had already emerged clearly by the onset of World War I. In its most acute form, the crisis transformed itself into a frank anti-modernism. By 1945, it already constituted a thirty-year-old tradition in its own right. The very concept "criticism," understood historically, is a modernist phenomenon; that is, the upshot of modernism's operational understanding of culture and its presumed ability or intention to ramify culture's operations. Above all, as a means of keeping culture working through its prescription of remedies for existing problems, criticism was preeminently culture's means for maintaining, restoring, or establishing an effective social and cultural equilibrium. Criticism and art acted, in these terms, as tangible correlatives of a larger social agenda and assumed responsibility for meaningful relationships with larger culture, their capacity to compete for social influence, and their ability to change social consciousness. But in the late fifties and early sixties the "modernist culture" of traditional critical purpose was in decay, and, for lack of persuasive theory to turn to, progressive critics embraced criticism as a cultural process rather than a moral text. To salvage their independence and integrity, conservative art critics were forced to seek nothing less than the rehabilitation of modernism; they were forced into remythification.

That Max Kozloff experienced difficulty in establishing the Pop artists' intentions is clear:

> The elaborate sarcasm of these projections confuses and mystifies their total handling of the problem of disgust—for no one knows whether there are essentially pictorial reasons for the new form, whether it is, perhaps, a dialogue with Pirandello (or Ionesco) now transposed to the realm of visual art, or whether, finally, they are in subversive collusion with Americana, while pleading the cause of loyalty to high art and a new beauty.[10]

Not knowing what side to take, or whether or from what position to launch the attack, he also seems unsure of what exactly he is attacking. I would propose it is neither the art, which, as many critics had pointed out, posed no "special" problems, nor the fact that the art performed badly within the parameters of normative aesthetics. What Kozloff was responding to was the unstated counterposition to the elitist culture he represented. That is, what worried Kozloff was the articulation of a latent criticism by an art that provided the occasion for a culturally visible critical dialogue that had so far existed as a hidden and largely unwritten text.

Recognizing this throws significant light on Greenberg, who concentrates on demonstrating the inferiority of the work by faulting it on formal grounds, for its conservatism and for its failure to move the style history of art to new horizons of significance.

> Whatever novel objects they represent or insert in their works, not one of them has taken a chance with color or design that the cubists or abstract expressionists did not take before them....Nor has any one of them...yet dared to arrange these things outside the directional lines of the "allover" cubist grid.[11]

Unheedful of the "other side," and unwilling to admit the philosophy of criticism into the debate, Greenberg ignored the possibility that there was a countercriticism, or at least one that deserved a response. By moving the basis of his criticism to an aesthetics accessible to the masses, Greenberg established a position from which he could continue to assert his superiority.

Other critics found less problems in the form than in the content.

> The reason these works leave us thoroughly dissatisfied lies not in their means but in their end: most of them have nothing at all to say....The interpretation or transformation of reality achieved by the pop artists, insofar as it exists at all, is limp and unconvincing.[12]

In claiming that Pop has nothing to say, Peter Selz really means that Pop has nothing of importance to say, or has nothing of importance to say to those who are looking for transformations of reality that communicate special messages. This is a good illustration of criticism misunderstood as a product rather than a process (conservative critics failed to see the irony in this). Selz expresses anger with Pop artists—too cowardly to face the times they live in and too lazy to apply themselves seriously to art (or the right kind of art, requiring dedication)—who no longer care about "caring about."

165

166

PETER SAUL
Bathroom Sex Murder, 1961
Oil on canvas, 69 x 59 1/2 inches
Courtesy of Frumkin/Adams Gallery, New York

Herbert Read, in a tone bordering on desperation, goes even further: "Until we can halt these processes of destruction and standardization, of materialism and mass communication, art will always be subject to the threat of disintegration."[13] In part or in whole, these texts clearly illustrate the thesis of Edward Shils, who wrote the following in 1961, when early Pop criticism was just emerging.

> The contention has been made frequently that mass culture is bad because it serves as a narcotic, because it affects our political democracy, because it corrupts our high culture…the real fact is that from an esthetic and moral standpoint, the objects of mass culture are repulsive to us. This ought to be admitted. To do so would help us to select an esthetic viewpoint, a system of moral judgements which would be applicable to the products of mass culture; but I think it would also relieve our minds from the necessity of making up fictions about the empirical consequences of mass culture.[14]

The variations are endless. Erle Loran takes the peculiar tack of attaching value to Pop as a

negative means of encouraging man's idealism. Apparently, its badness will guarantee a successful "search for the myths of the soul."

> Serious, ennobling art means too much to man in this automated world. He needs the look and the feel of something sensitively made, by hand. Pop art will have a healthy effect in making these simple things apparent….It may encourage man's eternal search for the myths of the soul.[15]

It is only with Thomas Hess that the possibility of a new criticism is openly admitted and even

PETER SAUL
Valda Sherman, 1961
Oil on canvas, 51 x 59 inches
Courtesy of Frumkin/Adams Gallery, New York

assumptions of the artistic elite are, if not invalidated, at least perceived as inadequate.

eat many artists today seem dissatisfied with the basic limits of Art, not for esthetic reasons, but for
so l ones. There is a kind of protest in many of these works, but it is not against the values of
middle-class society as were the dada manifestations. Rather the new protest is in favor of society
—or for People in general.... [16]

In dismissing aesthetic for social misgivings, Hess expresses concern about art's relationship to society and its structural basis in the lives of what he calls "people in general." With Hess, the mass culture critique is evoked, if not as a critical debate, at least as a "new protest" impossible to appreciate without the concept of "critique."

In what is basically a conservatively stated article, Alan Solomon implies, nevertheless, that it may be the conventional artworld that has lost the beat.

Yet in retrospect the way in which the present group emerged has not only an air of undeniable
consistency but also a distinct flavor of historical inevitability. This new style could neither have been
encouraged nor prevented, nor could it have been contrived; it has followed an organic course which
makes it an absolute product of its time. [17]

Subject to its time, and historically inevitable, Pop not only questioned but obviated the basic assumptions of traditional criticism. Solomon's point is interesting because it is an early dismissal of the question, "How should things be?" Although stated in the language of historical determinism, it more importantly reflects a concept of art as a function (as opposed to product) of culture. Hardly a startling position, it nevertheless rarely found its way into Pop's critical literature.

On a more aggressive note, Allan Kaprow throws the challenge in the face of high art in a way that is clearly designed to put it on the defensive. In this passage, Kaprow proclaims not only the ascendency of the popular arts and the questionable relevance or authority of the high arts, but the critical project that, for him, it clearly promises to achieve.

...the commercial artists, I dare say, are not yet accustomed to serious reflections on their role, and in any
event, they will blithely soar ahead on the strength of their traditions and enviable confidence. I do not
worry about the commercial for very likely, before the rats, they will inherit the world and deserve it
to boot. I say this with more anticipation than bitterness, because if the fine arts have given us greatness
in the best sense of that word, we have also inherited from their history monstrously funny pieties. [18]

Conservative critics continued to limit their definition of criticism to writings "about" art. Little attention was paid to criticism as a process, historically or sociologically defined; a criticism which might or might not involve the writing of criticism (criticism as a written, and read, thing); might or might not involve analysis of works of art.

Others began to address what increasingly seemed to become a prerequisite consideration; that is, the fundamentally altered effectiveness of late fifties and early sixties criticism based on redrawn relationships between criticism, art, and larger culture, of which the writings become only specific illustrations. Stated in its simplest form, the thesis of this argument asserts that "art criticism" was deprived of "criticism" by Pop art itself, and was, for the most part, left with a genre of writing better suited to consumption than to critical process. The institutional basis of Pop art, established from outside the art world, could find no effective counterpart in its art criticism. That is, the institutional theory of art tacitly stated in Pop could, with few exceptions, be neither understood nor adequately defined by the existing languages of normative criticism. Alloway was aware of this when he stated:

Aesthetics, instead of being the result of operations of a special sense, as Fry believed—one separated
from other human functions—can be identified with the passing scene. It is a move away from

*normative aesthetics, which exist as a set of rules to be tested by a comparatively few objects. In a sense it is the conversion of aesthetics from language (*langue*) to speech (*parole*), in F. de Saussure's sense. That is to say, an aesthetic of uses, of actualization, rather than of a theoretical system.*[19]

George Dickie has rightly noted that art involves institutional roles in an essential and defining way. This is especially so of any art incorporating true critical purpose. To be critical implies, in some important sense, belonging to the culture and its institutions. That is, the concept of art criticism makes no sense cut loose from institutional roles and the role of art as a cultural institution. In addition to being "of" a culture, criticism, be it expressed in art or art criticism, must contribute to the definition of that culture (or must conceive of itself in those terms). Unlike the traditional conception of criticism as an "art derivative" activity, "criticism" or "art as criticism" must be constitutive of the culture.

The problem of idealistic art criticism has resided in what Dickie identifies as its failure to address art's non-exhibited characteristics;[20] in the case of Pop, its "operational" basis in culture and "transactional" value in addressing and readdressing culture. As a product of a theory of art that was never stated as theory, Pop's relationship to the conventional art world became predictably tenuous. Indeed, it was more serious than that. Pop underscored the fact that all art was involved in institutional roles "in essential and defining ways," but further clarified that most art (and criticism) was incapable of responding to the culture of which it was a function and of which it was an authored text. This was perhaps most true of the very

art that most claimed its justification through the "tradition" of benevolent cultural critique; the tradition of telling what is right or wrong, good or bad, deep or superficial…true or untrue. For an art no longer accepting an idealistically conceived sender/receiver model, the concept of how to receive receded in importance. The relief experienced with Pop involved the promotion of the spectator to participant; a participant liberated from earning the right to participate formerly withheld for the privileged.

The question of reception was reversed; the critic became the receiver and the receiver became the critic. The plight of the critic required the re-creation of a subject that would submit to art criticism; that is, the re-creation of an art that required the mediating critic, and an art that required a traditional audience needing art criticism. For the consumption of art by culture, the critic seeking art world empowerment attempted to substitute art understood through criticism.

The mass culture critique is an attack by one element in society against another; by the cultured against the uncultured, the educated against the uneducated, the sophisticated against the unsophisticated,

JOHN WESLEY
Stamp, 1961
Oil on canvas, 24 x 24 inches
Collection of the artist

JOHN WESLEY
Coat of Arms, 1962
Oil on canvas, 48 x 48 inches
Collection of the artist

170

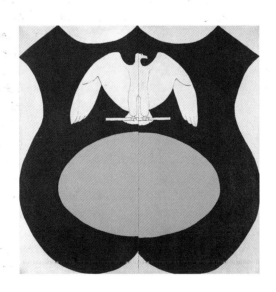

JOHN WESLEY
American Eagle Badge, 1962
Oil on canvas, 24 x 24 inches
Collection of the artist

the more affluent against the less affluent, and the cultural experts against the laity.[21]

In the process, the art critic undermined the project of authentic criticism. An instrumental criticism was replaced by a product of consumption. The ironies of the situation are endless. Herbert Read condemned the ignorant mass of consumers:

> *...it is not the artists who provoke the critic, but the public that has lost its sense of values. It is they who, because they are bored and alienated, accept instead of the work of art (which always demands concentration and effort on the part of the spectator) a sensational stimulus as brief and banal as any side-show in an amusement park....And so in the end we arrive at the social problem — not so much the question of the role of the artist in society or the proper use of leisure in an affluent society, but the general problem of the decadence of our civilization.*[22]

Even in the hands of friendlier critics, the trite, banal, stereotypical, truistic, self-explanatory, and self-apparent so relished by the "masses," were dismissed as "mere" content, subservient to a supposedly larger formalist Pop agenda; were reduced from their enormous complexity to the status of "tricks." Given all this, the traditional critic, whether acting for or against Pop, could relax into an idealistic aesthetic, and the "sophisticated" spectator (those consuming criticism) could be reassured that their comfortable dedication to Pop was worth respecting.

One of the great fears for critics was the erasure of lines distinguishing the fine arts and mass culture. The implication was always present that Pop equaled "kitsch." The attention lavished on the artists' "adjustments" of popular sources, the formalists' strategy, is very problematic. Indeed, the implications contained in this approach run directly counter to the intentions of Pop as they are defined by most of the artists.

Lawrence Alloway, in contrast, maintained that Pop could make use of the visual languages of both the majority and fine arts worlds.

> *The term was, in the first place, part of an expansionist aesthetics, a way of relating art to the environment. In place of an hierarchic aesthetics keyed to define greatness and to separate high from low art, a continuum was assumed which could accommodate all forms of art....*[23]

171

Although undoubtedly true in many important ways, it is also true that this dimension of Alloway's criticism smacked of a Utopianism that is more a reflection of British Pop than of the American experience, of which he rightly notes that, "From about 1961 to 1964, the term *Pop art* was narrowed to mean paintings that included a reference to a mass-medium source."[24] Art culture in England, including Pop, had sought a basis in theory, had willingly adopted the mantle of the avant-garde, and had approached modernism according to the rules of modernism. It coincided neatly with modernism's tradition of self-critique. Indeed, performing "critique from the inside" was one of the most powerful ways of validating one's self as modern. Thus, looked at in this way, Alloway's argument posed no threat to traditional critics. He and his theories of Pop could easily be granted a certain impunity, assigned a place as acceptable radicalism, respected and quoted. Alloway's discourse caused little disturbance among other discourses...his tolerance for art was reassuring.

> *What is characteristic and entirely American about Pop art is the high level of technical performance. Johns' mastery of paint handling, Rauschenberg's improvisatory skill, Lichtenstein's locked compositions, Warhol's impact as an image maker, reach the point that they do because of the high level of information about art in New York. In the background are the abstract expressionists, setting an aesthetic standard of forceful presence and impeccable unity.*[25]

Conservative critics, accustomed to tolerating liberal texts such as Alloway's, realized, however, that something more serious was at stake. The fact is, there was a criticism occurring outside the art world that had little to do with artistic radicalism, and that threatened to absorb art criticism into "its" criticism. Put crudely, what was most threatening about Pop was its disclosure of "real" culture and its embarrassment of "mythical" culture and its Platonic texts.

Convinced by the art world of the inferiority of his/her "real" culture — to the point of not recognizing it as culture — "everyman" was now being confronted by the reconstitution of that (their) culture by (as) art. American Pop raised to visibility existing cultures to which art criticism was unable to respond. The avant-garde's habit of preaching to the converted was suddenly echoed in Pop's preaching (or, at least, seeming to be) to its converted. In the latter case, however, the converted were comprised of an audience having little need of the art critic; indeed, the critic was functionally irrelevant.

Pop artists were, at least to a degree, perceived as spokespersons for the audience. Although prepared to speak of themselves as artists, and unembarrassed by the privileges this role historically carried with it, the relationship of the audience to the creator was dramatically changed; that is, there was less stress placed on "creator culture" and more on culture as created for audiences and "reception."

When asked by Gene Swenson, "Is pop art despicable?" Roy Lichtenstein answered in a way that seemed to validate the mass audience's acceptance of its environment. Imputing neither goodness nor badness to it, and declining to view that environment morally, the artist severely undercuts the agenda of idealistic art and criticism.

> That doesn't sound so good, does it? Well, it is an involvement with what I think to be the most brazen and threatening characteristics of our culture, things we hate, but which are also powerful in their impingement on us....Outside is the world; it's there. Pop art looks out into the world; it appears to accept its environment, which is not good or bad, but different — another state of mind.
> "How can you like exploitation? How can you like the complete mechanization of work? How can you like bad art?" I have to answer that I accept it as being there, in the world.

> Are you anti-experimental?

172

> I think so, and anti-contemplative, anti-nuance, anti-getting-away-from-the-tyranny-of-the-rectangle, anti-movement-and-light, anti-mystery, anti-paint-quality, anti-Zen, and anti all those brilliant ideas of preceding movements which everyone understands so thoroughly.[26]

A number of critics suspected that besides admitting the reality of the environment, the Pop artists shared in a "positive taste" for it. The crisis here was not whether their art suffered in the process so much as it was a question of whether it was admissable at all to like both high art and vernacular culture. Allan Kaprow, however, was ready to go even further.

> If pop art's use of popular imagery and methods contains a strong note of irony, the movement is too pervasive to hide, as well, a positive taste for such ingredients. These may be seemingly appreciated only as they exist in the ad, the TV commercial or theater marquee. That is, we may say that like so much other art, pop art is about art rather than the world. But commercial art, while also influenced by its own professionalism, does more vividly and robustly illuminate the real material world and our attitudes towards it, than any painting and sculpture during the last century. There is no doubt that fine artists must be very interested in this real stuff of life but can only approach it once removed, indirectly.[27]

Andy Warhol, the most unrelenting critic of "creator culture," comes close to parody in his account of creativity.

> It's hard to be creative and it's also hard not to think what you do is creative or hard not to be called creative because everybody is always talking about that and individuality. Everybody's always being creative. And it's so funny when you say things aren't....[28]

What Pop permitted was a concept of the spectator, including the artist, as critic. The Pop spectator, including the art critic, animates a process for which there is no right or wrong conclusion. With Pop, the audience was as fluent as the artist in many of its essential questions, and often a good deal more so than many of the critics.

One of the most disturbing aspects of Pop, then, involved a redrawn concept of ideologies. Ideologies were still present; they were more forcibly present than ever, but present as "givens" within which one transacted culture. Idealistic aesthetics had always required ideology, but as justification of its metaphysical agenda for which there were no secure, or even imaginable institutional bases. For example, Lichtenstein's painting threw into clear relief that formalism in art is a "tradition" and that one can consider "formalism as formalism," or "art as art," in a way that implicates it as part of popular culture. If high art is not mass culture, it is, in an important sense, mass culture's. For Lichtenstein, "composition" is stated through the content of formalism where the traditional roles of the two are surprisingly and wrenchingly reversed.

With formalism reduced to its conceits, the work was easily and effectively accessed by Pop's audiences. I do not mean to imply by this that the public understood formalism; it probably did not. But that does not really matter and has nothing to do with that public's "possession" of it. Artists willingly submitted their art to this situation since most of them were well aware that formalism no longer represented vital or even interesting artistic problems. To quote Lichtenstein again:

> There is no neat way of telling whether a work of art is composed or not; we're too comfortable with ideas that art is the battleground for interaction, that with more and more experience you become more able to compose. It's true, everybody accepts that; it's just that the idea no longer has any power.[29]

Contemporary criticism failed to note that it was precisely through comics, Americana, etc., that formalism was accessed or, at least, made more easily accessible. Taking away the comics would have created problems; but with accessing, not with formalism. For the audience (and for many of the artists) the question of right or wrong accessing (an odd idea if applied to almost other aspect of the majority culture that Pop constantly quoted) was treated with indifference because no one cared; not the audiences and not the artists...only the critics.

In spite of all this, the artists were artists and the public wanted art, and here is where the stress on traditional criticism became almost unbearable. The Pop audience was always confronted with a dilemma. It had to apply a discount to the very content giving them access to the work, in order to protect their notion of art. Art had to be available but not at the expense of reducing the spectator to banality. The balance, interestingly enough, was held by the artist and not by the critic. The artist wrote the contract and the public accepted or rejected it.

Lichtenstein (and Claes Oldenburg in a very different way) achieved a beautiful balance. Others, such as John Wesley and Mel Ramos, created veritable collisions. Wesley, for example, tested the audience by advancing the "decorative" (albeit historically derived "decoration") in the place where Lichtenstein advanced the "formal" (formalistic). Content was forced to the surface in a way that stretched credibility well beyond what Lichtenstein's work requires. Vulgar to the point of being objectionable, Wesley's work left the spectator and critic stranded between a form and a content equally incapable of saving the other and equally unwarrantable in their own rights. From our position in the 1990s, it is easy to appreciate Wesley's strategy. For formalist critics of the sixties, there was literally nothing to work with.

Ramos, although less so in the earlier painterly work represented in this exhibition, later began to validate negative and conservative criticism of Pop, but in ways that revealed the criticism to be more

173

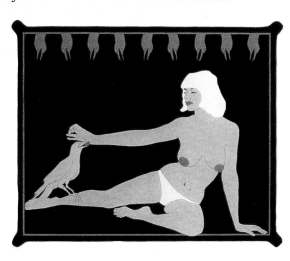

JOHN WESLEY
Bird Lady, 1965
Acrylic on canvas, 42 x 51 1/2 inches
Private collection

MEL RAMOS
Tourist, 1960
Oil on canvas, 50 x 44 inches
Collection of Joyce and Jay Cooper, Phoenix

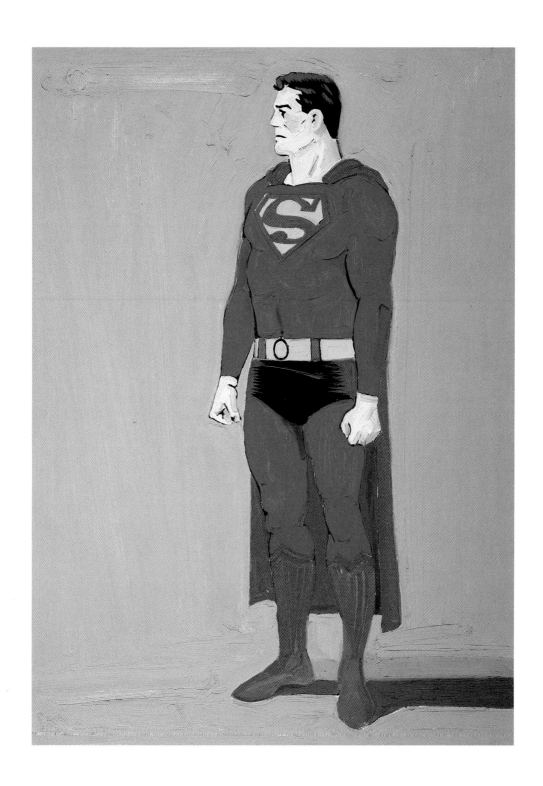

MEL RAMOS
Superman, 1961
Oil on canvas, 40 x 30 inches
Collection of Skot Ramos, Burbank, California

objectionable than the painting. The doubtful formal value in Ramos's painting is less interesting, and less to the point, than the fact that he makes it hard to be willing to approach it formally.

What the formal apparatus failed to accomplish, the content did. Unerringly sexist, crudely conceived in pictorial terms, and artistically depraved, Ramos's works were funny only for those who could afford to be amused; and those who could least afford to be amused were the critics. The problem was not the works' merits or demerits; the problem was that they could not be dismissed by conventional criticism any more than they could be embraced by it, and it is here that Pop's strategies intersect most with those of Duchamp. Here, art criticism is not only rendered irrelevant; it is rendered completely dumb. And it may be here, consequently, that the public felt most in need of criticism and that the critic felt most exonerated—a sorry situation for criticism to say the least.

The metamorphosis of critical roles has typically been understood by scholars, and by critics themselves, within boundaries self-imposed by the art world. That is, critical changes are conceived to occur "in reaction to" (distinct from "as a result of") social circumstances requiring critique or correction. Criticism, it is maintained, evolves in attempts to achieve its own stated, rather than culturally determined, purposes. As our understanding of the subject grows, it becomes clearer that what has been described as internally derived mandates for criticism may be nothing more than the outdated reflections of its actual source and location in larger culture; the culture responsible for its very existence; the culture that authored the critic's role. In place of a criticism that worked towards something, the late fifties and early sixties witnessed a criticism that worked; worked operationally (processually) rather than ideologically (prescriptively).

Pursuit of such a perspective suggests that any crisis of criticism has been an identity crisis. Increasingly deprived of its autonomy (ironically won with the loss of its "place" in culture), and devalued in terms of the stated objectives of its mission, criticism attempted to resecure itself through theories extrapolated from its own programs. The idealism of its history had been part of a story it did not author but could only recite; its "goodness" part of a cultural myth it more believed and participated in than produced or understood. Concern over criticism's possible complicity with culture (Greenberg et al.) was increasingly perceived, by more attentive minds, as the naive voice, thinly veiled in the language of betrayal, of those discovering that they had never possessed, and had failed to establish, a power base in their own agenda.

Only those "acting out" criticism (as opposed to using it) could have imagined that their thinking was in any way special.

> The artist [and critic], *trapped in the relativism inherent in modern societies, clings to an absolute definition of his role to compensate for the actual weakness of his position. In many cases he acts, often making himself look ridiculous, as a man "inspired," as though his creative themes were dictated to him by a religious power of which he is the representative on earth.*[30]

The crisis of twentieth-century criticism involved the increasing difficulty in sustaining that imaginative act in good faith.

Coupled with the sunset of modernism and its understanding of criticism, the culture boom of the fifties and sixties reconfigured the art world in irreversible ways. It was not a problem for the artist, who was finally acculturated, nor for the spectator, who was finally enfranchised. Only criticism lost its conventional platforms. Embarrassed beyond endurance, idealistic criticism became a partner in a new modernism through which its idealistic intentions were degraded, but at the same time, made purchasable, popular, and easy. Normal criticism witnessed a failure of "problems."

> *Bruce Glaser: How did you get involved with pop imagery, Andy?*
> *Andy Warhol: I'm too high right now. Ask somebody else something else.*[31]

Back row: Robert Rauschenberg (holding tree stump), Jasper Johns (head peeking out behind tree), Roland Pease. Middle row: Grace Hartigan (leaning against tree); Mary Abbott (sitting on tree); Stephen Rivers (son of Larry Rivers); Larry Rivers (in straw hat); Herbert Machiz (in sunglasses); Tibor de Nagy; John Myers; Sondra Lee (in front of Herbert Machiz). Front row: Maxine Groffsky (in sunglasses); Joe Hazan; Jane Freilicher. Water Mill, Long Island, 1959 *Photo: John Gruen*

1   For a discussion of this and related concepts, see Herbert Gans, *Popular Culture and High Culture* (New York: Basic Books, 1974), pp. 62-64. This is an American analysis of the mass culture critique, especially relevant because of its proximity in time to the work discussed here.

2   Christin J. Mamiya, *Pop Art and Consumer Culture: American Super Market* (Austin: University of Texas Press, 1992), pp. 169-71.

3   Clement Greenberg, "Avant-Garde and Kitsch" (1939), in *Art and Culture* (Boston: Beacon Press, 1961), p. 13. More sophisticated discussions from the same point of view can be found in Leo Lowenthal, "Historical Perspectives of Popular Culture" (1950) and Dwight MacDonald, "A Theory of Mass Culture" (1953), in Bernard Rosenberg and David Manning White, eds., *Mass Culture: The Popular Arts in America* (New York: The Free Press, 1964).

4   For a discussion of Greenberg's philosophy of history, see Stephen C. Foster, *The Critics of Abstract Expressionism* (Ann Arbor, Mich.: UMI Research Press, 1980).

5   Morse Peckham, "Art and Disorder" (1966), in Richard Kostelanetz, ed., *Esthetics Contemporary* (Buffalo: Prometheus Books, 1978), p. 95.

6   Gans, *Popular Culture and High Culture*, p. 62.

7   Jean Duvignaud, *The Sociology of Art*, trans. Timothy Wilson (New York: Harper and Row, 1972), p. 25.

8   Jacques Barzun, *Classic, Romantic, and Modern* (Garden City, N.J.: Doubleday, 1961), p. 154.

9   Ibid., p. 153.

10   Max Kozloff, "Pop Culture, Metaphysical Disgust and the New Vulgarians" (1962), in Carol Anne Mahsun, ed., *Pop Art: The Critical Dialogue* (Ann Arbor, Mich.: UMI Research Press, 1989), p. 21. Mahsun's anthology is an invaluable source for the criticism of this period.

11   Greenberg, "After Abstract Expressionism" (1962), in Mahsun, *Pop Art*, p. 36.

12   Peter Selz, "The Flaccid Art" (1963), in Mahsun, *Pop Art*, p. 78.

13   Herbert Read, "Disintegration of Form in Modern Art" (1965), in Mahsun, *Pop Art*, p. 104.

14   Edward Schils, "Panel Discussion" in Norman Jacobs, *Culture for the Millions*, quoted in Gans, *Popular Culture*, p. 61.

15   Erle Loran, "Cézanne and Lichtenstein: Problems of 'Transformation'" (1963), in Mahsun, *Pop Art*, p. 87.

16   Thomas Hess, "Mixed Media for a Soft Revolution" (1963), in Mahsun, *Pop Art*, p. 8.

17   Alan Solomon, "The New Art" (1963), in Mahsun, *Pop Art*, p. 52.

18   Allan Kaprow, "Pop Art: Past, Present and Future" (1967), in Mahsun, *Pop Art*, pp. 68-70.

19   Lawrence Alloway, "Anthropology and Art Criticism," *Arts Magazine* 45, no. 4 (February 1971): 23.

20   George Dickie, "The Artist and the Institution of Art" in Stephen C. Foster, Rainer Rumold, and Estera Milman, *The Metamorphoses of the Avant-Garde Artist and Author: 1908-1938* (forthcoming).

21   Gans, *Popular Culture*, pp. 3-4.

22   Read, "Disintegration of Form," p. 102.

23   Alloway, *American Pop Art* (New York: Macmillan, 1974), p. 18.

24   Ibid. For further discussion see Alloway, "Pop Art: The Words" (1962), in *Topics in American Art Since 1945* (New York: Norton, 1975), pp. 119-22.

25   Alloway, *American Pop Art*, pp. 18-19.

26   Gene Swenson, "What is Pop Art?" (1963-64), in Mahsun, *Pop Art*, pp. 111-12.

27   Kaprow, "Pop Art," p. 70.

28   Swenson, "What is Pop Art?," pp. 118-19.

29   Ibid., p. 113.

30   Duvignaud, *Sociology of Art*, p. 33.

31   Glaser, "Oldenburg, Lichtenstein, Warhol: A Discussion" (1966), in Mahsun, *Pop Art*, p. 141.

177

MEL RAMOS
Red Kangaroo, 1968
Oil on canvas, 40 x 30 inches
Private collection

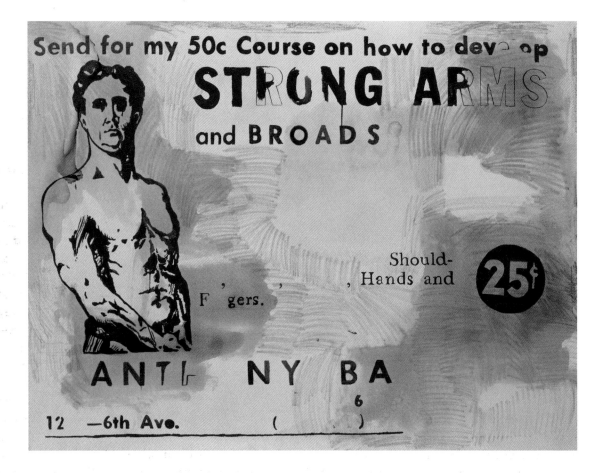

ANDY WARHOL
Strong Arms and Broads, 1960
Synthetic polymer paint, black Japan, and crayon on canvas,
45 x 61 inches
Private collection

Kenneth E. Silver

Modes of Disclosure:
The Construction of Gay Identity and the Rise of Pop Art

In memory of Zack

The epistemology of the closet is not a dated subject
or a superseded regime of knowing...there can be few gay people, however courageous and forthright by habit,
however fortunate in the support of their immediate communities, in whose lives
the closet is not still a shaping presence.

Eve Kosofsky Sedgwick, *The Epistemology of the Closet* (1990)

"The moment you label something, you take a step — I mean, you can never go back again to seeing it unlabeled."[1] These are Andy Warhol's words, which in their typically halting rhythm, anti-lapidary syntax, and use of commercial vernacular — note that he says "label" rather than name — express a simple truth: that the act of labeling is, like the U.S. Navy tattoo on the arm of the young man he drew in ca. 1957, indelible. Along with a number of other key figures in the art world of the late 1950s and early 1960s, Jasper Johns and Andy Warhol began to label something — male homosexuality — that had hitherto been considered too unworthy or too dangerous to name. As they were for the civil rights movement, the fifties and sixties were the key years of *naissant* gay political activism, when pre-Stonewall organizations like the Mattachine Society were founded.[2] Early Pop, or proto-Pop, is closely allied with burgeoning gay identity in the art worlds of New York and London.[3] In the waning years of the Abstract Expressionist hegemony homosexuality began to acquire a visual language, with the vocabulary provided by the gay artists themselves.

It is to state the obvious to say that Abstract Expressionist painting, like all non-representational art, does not label or name, but suggests: how could it be otherwise, as the content is meant to be ineffable? To be sure, we sometimes sense tragedy in an especially dark and monumental painting, or joy in another buoyant, brightly-colored composition. Of course the title of a picture, be it Willem de Kooning's *Excavation* or Jackson Pollock's *Sounds in the Grass*, sometimes points us in the direction of more specific evocations, but this is all guesswork, since we are provided with neither objects nor words in the images

179

ANDY WARHOL
Untitled (Boy with USN Tattoo), 1957
Ballpoint ink on sketchbook paper, 16 3/4 x 14 inches
The Andy Warhol Foundation for the Visual Arts, Inc., New York

themselves. In 1955 Leon Golub, in an article critical of what he considered to be Abstract Expressionism's vagueness, wrote "There are few common verbal equivalents of any such discursive motion and as observer recognition is not constant (except on rather illustrative levels in regard to the artist's undetermined intent), descriptive comment tends to be hyperbolic."[4] Not only does Abstract Expressionist art evoke rather than name, it also engenders a critical language of exaggerated claim equal in scale to the size of the works themselves.

Yet there are subjects so compelling, at least to certain artists at certain moments, that invocations of the ineffable and appeals to the non-specific will not satisfy the need for a clear, or clearer, summoning forth. In a provocative 1984 article on the art of Jasper Johns, Charles Harrison and Fred Orton make the important point that in the historical circumstance of the 1950s, this was easier said than done: "…we might say that the ambitious artist of Johns's generation (and since perhaps), who knows his or her Modernism and understands what 'American-Type' painting has to be in order to succeed as Modernism, has a real problem if he or she wants to express and to deal with subject-matter and to express feelings as subject matter."[5] Johns's *Painting with Two Balls* (1960), is at once a meditation on this dilemma of signification and a resolution of the generational problem. Here he calls into question the discursive system of high abstract art, a master narrative if there ever was one, by unpacking — and literally exposing — its gendered rhetoric. In this case, objects and labels are crucial to the enterprise.

Painting with Two Balls both embraces and betrays Abstract Expressionism: the hatched brushstroke, brilliant of hue, conveys the pleasure that Johns takes in the painterly abandon of Action Painters like Pollock, de Kooning, and Clyfford Still; the tripartite horizontal division recalls the rectilinearity that ordered the free play of paint in the work of artists like Mark Rothko and Barnett Newman. But of course in an early work by Johns even the seemingly most spontaneous handling is a feint; these are not traces of impetuosity, but its representation — the strokes are always smaller, shorter, and more controlled than those of his predecessors, and the various coloristic campaigns are more evenly distributed over the canvas. The use of encaustic here and in so many other works of this period serves to "mummify" what had been signs for vitality, so that we sense ourselves distanced from both the work as a record of activity and, one might add, from the artist whose activity is recorded.

180

JASPER JOHNS
Painting with Two Balls, 1960
Encaustic and collage on canvas with objects,
65 x 54 inches
Collection of the artist

We have entered into the realm of the simulacrum, a place of lost innocence with perhaps a residual nostalgia for the belief in originating acts and primal gestures. Needless to say, while Johns situates himself as the ironic "conservator" of Abstract Expressionism's "instinctual" gestures, he casts doubt on the very notion of instinctive gestures and unfettered aesthetic play. Not that he was alone in this strategy: Robert Rauschenberg's *Factum I* and *Factum II* (both 1957), which offer for all intents and purposes nearly identical renderings of post-Abstract Expressionist "authenticity," and Roy Lichtenstein's *Brush Stroke* (1965), with its cartoon rendering of monumental Action Painting brushstrokes, mark the terminus post and ante quem of this younger generation's parodic recasting of Abstract Expressionism's pictorial system. But Johns goes much further in his dis-illusioning of that painterly rhetoric by first wedging two small balls between the two top panels, and then inscribing the three-inch high words "PAINTING WITH TWO BALLS/1960/J JOHNS" along the bottom edge. This double transgression has the effect of turning the high seriousness of abstract New York painting into low comedy — the two "real," three-dimensional balls are experienced as an absurd, banal intrusion into the two-dimensional paradigm of non-specific and limitless aesthetic field, while the words below perform a related operation, labeling or naming not a psychic state or metaphysical event but that which is merely before us. Irony is the sign under which this work by Johns, and almost all his art, operates.

The irony of this deflationary procedure is that, by means of the insertion of the twin balls, Johns has performed a kind of counter-castration of the body of Abstract Expressionism (of its pictorial rhetoric and critical discourse). As Rosalind Krauss saw so clearly in 1965: "The objects undoubtedly refer to the myth of masculinity surrounding the central figures of Abstract Expressionism, the admiration for the violence with which they made their attack on the canvas, and the sexual potency read into their artistic acts."[6] Krauss is referring to readings like Harold Rosenberg's famous statement in "The American Action Painters," that "the painter no longer approached his easel with an image in his mind; he went up to it with material in his hand to do something to that other piece of material in front of him. The image would be the result of this encounter,"[7] or Elaine de Kooning's terse pronouncement: "Franz Kline's image found its virile originality in his response to non-art or life."[8]

By way of the addition of two silly balls, and the words naming them, Johns enunciates the unspoken term of Action Painting's puissance: he gives us the proverbial "painting with balls," the "ballsy" art that was New York painting's special purchase on modernist abstraction. Moreover, the frankly artificial nature of the entire enterprise of *Painting with Two Balls*, its myriad transgressions of the rhetoric of its predecessor, points to a specific moment in the master narrative, what we should perhaps call the "master equation" of Abstract Expressionism: artistic authenticity is the concomitant of identifiably masculine behavior, even an attribute of masculinity; tough, non-literary, serious art is made only by rough-hewn, spontaneous, male artists (sub-text: sissies can't make real art). In effect, Johns has torn asunder the rhetorical veil of Action Painting's look and commentary, revealing not a pair of Taurean globes of potency, but two little balls. Let there be no mistake: there is a great deal of rage contained in Jasper Johns's visual pleasantry.

But of course *Painting with Two Balls* tells us nothing of homosexuality per se; at issue is only the equation between stereotypical maleness and a certain kind of art. Yet the dismantling of Abstract Expressionism's rhetoric of the image was the precondition, or attendant strategy, for Johns's forging of a gay identity in his art, for his mapping of gay desire. On the other hand, so densely coded, so camouflaged, and so elusive are the homosexual thematics of Jasper Johns's work, that the myriad evasions which to a large extent determine both his form and content are inconceivable without the Abstract Expressionist code of non-specificity which he himself undertook to subvert. This is probably why we sense both pleasure and disdain in the meta-brushstrokes of his pseudo-gestural pastiches of de Kooning and Pollock. So implicated is Johns's art in the "abstracting" procedures of Abstract Expressionism that it would be to overstate and dehistoricize the case to think of Johns's homosexual references of the period as constituting "gay art." As Eve Sedgwick has termed it, we are dealing with the "epistemology of the closet." Still, there are closets and there are closets; if the

182

JASPER JOHNS
In Memory of My Feelings—Frank O'Hara, 1961
Oil on canvas with objects, 40 x 60 inches
Stefan T. Edlis Collection, Chicago

doors to Jasper Johns's aesthetic are not exactly flung open for all to examine, neither are they, nor were they intended to be, completely closed to us. As Marcel Duchamp, one of Johns's key influences, set out to demonstrate in his *11 rue Larrey* (1927-64), by hinging a door in the jamb between two openings, "a door need not be either opened or closed." It may be both.

In the manner that we have seen adumbrated in *Painting with Two Balls*, the gay component in Johns's art is constituted by means of objects (readymade objects) and words which are assemblaged into an Abstract Expressionist-like, painterly field, with its associations of deep, powerful "feelings." But the words — some contained within the pictorial fields and others serving only as titles in the traditional sense — are themselves ready-mades, inasmuch as they take the form of allusions to poets and their works, specifically to three gay American poets: Frank O'Hara, Hart Crane, and Walt Whitman. Johns also alludes in these works to the art of two gay American painters, Marsden Hartley and Charles Demuth. Needless to say, as is always the case with art which makes extensive use of allusion, Johns's work requires, insists upon, hermeneutical investigation; only an intense voyage *inward*, along a rather tortuous path, will reveal its meanings.[9]

In a sense, this movement inward rehearses the dynamics of "closeted" behavior, the result being that the traditional art historical exegesis — the investigator's journey into the work's meaning, the revealing of "hidden" or buried signification — bears an unfortunate but necessary relationship to "outing." But there is no choice really, to the extent to which Johns's allusions, his references both subtle and plain, may be said to constitute his authorial voice. Indeed, the artist has said that early on he had "worked in such a way that I could say that it's not me...not to confuse my feelings with what I produced. I didn't want my work to be an exposure of my feelings."[10] Yet, if we cannot offer airtight interpretation of his art — would we want to? — we may nonetheless point to a range of possibilities, and look in the direction of Johns's own glance. And we *can* say this: that in the name of vacating the place of his own feelings, Johns performs a kind of ventriloquism. The voices that speak through the vessel of his art are those of O'Hara, Crane, Demuth, Hartley, and Whitman.

Roberta Bernstein was the first to point out that Johns's two main literary interests, at least as evidenced by his paintings, were both gay poets, O'Hara and Crane.[11] Harrison and Orton have provided a useful and sensitive approach to Johns's 1961 painting *In Memory of My Feelings — Frank O'Hara*, where, as in *Painting with Two Balls*, the full title, signature, and date are stenciled along the bottom. In this case Johns puts to dramatic use the very pictorial rhetoric he had demythologized the year before: three-quarters of the canvas is covered in a dense matrix of hatched strokes *en grisaille*, intended in Abstract Expressionist fashion to suggest powerful feelings, presumably those recollected and/or mourned in the "title" (which of course is not a title in the usual sense, a verbal equivalent existing outside the work, but an element of the pictorial structure itself, smack up against the picture plane). The upper left quarter of the picture is covered only by a gray wash, against which a coupled fork and spoon hang attached by a wire. The painting is actually composed of two panels, hinged like a religious diptych, suggesting that sacred information is being conveyed. Also implied by the hinges, again in association with traditional religious imagery, is the potential for closing this work in upon itself, for concealment or protection of the contents.

Yet, for all that Johns freights his work with signs of concealment, *In Memory of My Feelings — Frank O'Hara* is notable for how much it reveals. First, of course, is what we can know from O'Hara's poem of the same title, written in 1956, a work about the attempt to distance oneself from the feelings of desolation caused by love lost. It begins, "My quietness has a man in it, he is transparent," and ends, some two hundred lines later, "and I have lost what is always and everywhere present, the scene of my selves, the occasion of these

JASPER JOHNS
Diver, 1962
Oil on canvas with objects, 90 x 170 inches
Collection of Irma and Norman Braman, Miami

ruses, which I myself and singly must now kill and save the serpent in their midst." Although difficult to see, Johns has stenciled the words "DEAD MAN" at the lower right corner of the painting.

Then there is the inclusion of Frank O'Hara's name, which insists that we attend not only to his art but to his person: even before his accidental death on Fire Island in 1966, O'Hara had achieved near-legendary underground status in the New York art world. An associate curator in the Department of Painting and Sculpture at the Museum of Modern Art, an editor at *Art News*, a prodigious writer of poetry and art criticism, O'Hara was renowned for his brilliance, personal charm, and intense loyalty to his friends. Moreover, from the point of view of a gay history, he was remarkable for the extent to which he was more or less openly gay, both in his work and his life, in the repressive and hyper-masculinist atmosphere of 1950s America. Finally, O'Hara was also crucial as a kind of linchpin between the older generation of the mostly heterosexual Abstract Expressionists and the younger group of artists and writers, among whom homosexuality and bisexuality were common. Johns's inclusion of both the title of an O'Hara poem about love and the poet's name—which is coupled on the right panel with the painter's own name and date—insures that only a willful ignorance can suppress the gay allusions. Whether this is a portrait of O'Hara's poem, or a portrait of O'Hara the man, Johns has asked us to meditate before this "altarpiece" of loss.

In fact, Harrison and Orton go further, relating *In Memory of My Feelings—Frank O'Hara* to Johns's own feelings of desolation during the turbulent final years of his love affair with Robert Rauschenberg, a relationship of more than six years duration (they would definitively break the following year). Considered in this light, then, the "hanged" knife and fork may convey a sense of the "death of the ordinary," the terrible dawning realization, at the end of a longstanding relationship, that one has lost not only love in its romantic form, but also in its daily, mundane aspect.

Even more crucial than O'Hara to Johns's art is Hart Crane—again, important to Johns both for his poetry and his life. Johns created a veritable gallery of images devoted to Crane, who committed suicide in April 1932 by jumping from the ship *Orizaba*, at sea three hundred miles north of Havana. Most direct is *Periscope (Hart Crane)* of 1963, which derives its title from one of the best-known images in Crane's great poem "Cape Hatteras": "time clears/Our lenses, lifts a focus, resurrects/A periscope to glimpse what joys or pain/Our eyes can share or answer—then deflects/Us, shunting to a labyrinth submersed/Where each sees only his dim past reversed...." Johns here makes reference, somewhat in the manner of *In Memory of My Feelings*, not only to the poem but to the poet as well: for this memorial to Crane the artist uses his own handprint as a surrogate for the drowning poet's, and draws in charcoal an arrow pointing downward, at the lower right, to the watery deep. Two works of the previous year are also homages to Crane: *Passage*, whose title comes from another Crane poem, and *Diver*, an obvious reference to the suicide itself, invoked by Johns's handprints at the center moving outward from the body like a swan dive. And there are other works, including the lithograph *Hatteras*, and the painting *Land's End*, made the same year as *Periscope*, which is, again, a coded portrait of the poet: now the hand reaches up from the deep at the lower left—again represented by Johns's own handprint—with an even more prominent downward pointing arrow at the lower right.

But there is more to Johns's interest in Hart Crane and "Cape Hatteras" than this—"Cape

JASPER JOHNS
Land's End, 1963
Oil on canvas, 67 x 48 inches
San Francisco Museum of Modern Art
Gift of Mr. and Mrs. Harry W. Anderson

184

Hatteras" is *already* a memorial, Hart Crane's memorial to his gay poetic ancestor, Walt Whitman. It begins with a citation from Whitman and ends with Crane's own words: "Yes, Walt, afoot again, and onward without halt, not soon nor suddenly—no, never/let go/ My hand/ in yours, Walt Whitman, so..." which, it is important to recognize, is Crane's specific response to Whitman's own opening lines of "Salut au Monde!" in which he calls to himself: "O take my hand Walt Whitman! Such gliding wonders, such sights and sounds! Such joined unended links, each hooked to the next, each answering all, each sharing the earth with all." By substituting his hand for Crane's in the paintings, Johns closes the circle, so that the hands of these three gay American artists are linked, "each hooked to the next," through their work.

Indeed, Johns appears to have appropriated elements of his "portrait" of Crane for his two self-portraits of 1964, *Souvenir 1* and *2*. Not only have the words "red, yellow, blue" been transferred from the Crane works to the souvenir plate on which we find the artist's photograph, but, more importantly, a flashlight and mirror (a car's sideview mirror?) have been affixed to the canvas so that they function as a periscope, where light bounces off a mirror angled at forty-five degrees, allowing the underwater viewer to see what is above water. Johns so places himself here that he is the "submersed" viewer.

There is a precedent for Johns's tribute to Crane in Marsden Hartley's painting *Eight Bells Folly: Memorial for Hart Crane*, painted the year after the poet's suicide. Here is Hartley's description of his Crane picture:

> It has a very mad look as I wish it to have—there is a ship foundering—a sun, a moon, two triangular clouds—a bell with an eight on it—symbolizing eight bells—or noon, when he jumped off—and around the bells are a lot of men's eyes—that look up from below to see who the new lodger is to be —on one cloud will be the number 33, Hart's age—and according to some occult beliefs a dangerous age for a man—for if he survives 33 he lives on—Christ was supposed to be 33....[12]

The painting is filled with occult references that seem to be Apocalyptic: the sun and the moon are present simultaneously.

It's possible that Johns knew Hartley's homage to Crane[13]; certainly his interest in his predecessor's art has long been noted.[14] *Land's End* has several things in common with Hartley's picture: the blue, black, and white palette punctuated with powerful touches of yellow-orange, and the raised arm and hand in *Land's End*, which parallels the upward-thrusting diagonal from lower left towards the center in *Eight Bells Folly*. But whether or not Johns knew Hartley's homage, the fact remains that both gay American artists have chosen to depict Crane's suicide. This seeming coincidence is not surprising, given that Hart Crane, his remarkable poetry and the fact of his suicide, have long been part of gay mythology: the great gay artist, tortured by social constraints and finally driven to take his own life, would be High Cornball, were it not for the reality it serves to remember. Gay remembrance—gay memorializing, even before the advent of AIDS —has throughout the modern period had the double sense not only of recollecting actual death, but of speaking for death-in-life: of the need to kill one's desire, of the sense of impending retribution from society, of the constant deadening of one's sensitivities in order to defend against what society considers an indefensible disposition. The death of the (gay) poet, be it Crane's or Oscar Wilde's, or even Frank O'Hara's accidental death on, of all places, Fire Island, is a trope for the persistent agon of homosexual experience.

Johns's early work is situated in a discourse, for those who could decipher it, of gay identity. Or

185

JASPER JOHNS
Souvenir 2, 1964
Oil and collage on canvas with objects, 28 3/4 x 21 inches
Collection of Mrs. Victor Ganz

perhaps I should say gay identification, so consistently does Johns speak through his gay antecedents, and they through him. But there is at least one more important figure in Johns's "family tree" of gay male artists, and that is Charles Demuth. Johns was surely struck, as so many gay American artists and critics have been ever since, by the fact that arguably the two most important modernist American painters of the years between the wars, Demuth and Hartley, were gay (even if this information was passed along *sub rosa*, until recently). As has been long recognized, Johns's *Figure 5* (1955), is an homage to Demuth's coded portrait of William Carlos Williams, *I Saw the Figure 5 in Gold* (1928); and this number 5, along with other numbers later, became a kind of talisman for Johns, appearing repeatedly over the years.[15]

Demuth's homosexuality was an important aspect of his art. He made both out-and-out raunchy pornographic watercolors, which he kept to himself, and more subtle, allusive images of sexuality between men, like the well-known *Acrobats* (1919), which he exhibited. But even more important for the art of Johns, I think, is that the need Demuth felt to keep his sexual interests hidden from public scrutiny also disposed him toward coded images and picture-puzzles. These include his well-known poster portraits of the late twenties, of both gay and straight friends, including *Love, Love, Love (Homage to Gertrude Stein)* and *I Saw the Figure 5 in Gold*. In these portraits, words, word fragments, letters, numbers, and imagery combine to both encode and reveal, to those who could decipher them, the identities of Demuth's sitters.

Johns's interest in Demuth was closely allied to his interest in Hartley: Demuth and Hartley were good enough friends for Demuth to have made a study for a poster portrait of Hartley, which seems never to have gone beyond the planning stage. In fact, Demuth really owed Hartley a portrait, inasmuch as he had got his idea for the coded, secret portraits from Hartley in the first place. I am referring to Hartley's well-known German military series of 1914-15, pictures that daringly combine Cubist elements and symbols —letters, numbers, flags, insignias, and war medals—for example, *Portrait of a German Officer* (1914). This and numerous others like it are all coded portraits of Lieutenant Karl von Freyburg, the young Prussian officer, killed in October 1914, who was Hartley's close friend and probably his lover.[16]

Max Kozloff long ago noted the striking similarity between Hartley's and Johns's surfaces,[17] which result from the wedding of two conflicting systems: the thickly built-up surface—a rich geography of paint in Hartley's case, and newsprint with encaustic in Johns's—covered by a thinly applied, colored layer on top. The two layers are so conjoined that we remain conscious of a lower stratum of indistinct activity and an upper level of delineation, strangely "out-of-sync" with what lies below. Given the "iconographic" impetus that Johns shared with Hartley, there is all the more reason for this commonality of surface, at once a private emotional geography beneath and a public emblem above. In Hartley's and Demuth's modernist, symbolic, emblematic, esoteric portraits, I think Johns found, or simply sensed, a way to give public form to his intensely private experience of being gay. In the work of his gay predecessors Johns found a language—shaped, as it

right:
MARSDEN HARTLEY
Portrait of a German Officer, 1914
Oil on canvas, 68 1/4 x 41 3/8 inches
The Metropolitan Museum of Art
The Alfred Stieglitz Collection, 1949

far right:
MARSDEN HARTLEY
**Eight Bells Folly: Memorial to
Hart Crane,** 1933
Oil on canvas, 30 5/8 x 39 3/8 inches
University Art Museum, University of Minnesota
Gift of Ione and Hudson Walker

JASPER JOHNS
Figure 8, 1959
Encaustic and collage on canvas, 9 x 6 inches
The Sonnabend Collection, New York

JASPER JOHNS
Numbers 0 Through 9, 1961
Oil and charcoal on canvas, 54 1/8 x 41 3/8 inches
Hirshhorn Museum and Sculpture Garden,
Smithsonian Institution, Washington, D.C.
Gift of Joseph H. Hirshhorn, 1966

were, by the closet — which could vouchsafe his passage as a modernist, American, gay painter.

It is, in fact, the very imagery of the closet which impresses itself upon us in that most famous early work of Johns's, *Target with Plaster Casts* (1955), an assemblage which he made the same year as his first neo-Demuth, *Figure 5*. Harrison and Orton, who had already noted that *In Memory of My Feelings* more or less coincides with the end of Johns's relationship with Rauschenberg, also made the significant point that the making of *Target with Plaster Casts* coincides in date with the beginning of that relationship. But they did not offer a reading of it. And again we are faced with a trap which Johns himself has set for us: to attempt to interpret the work is to violate the Surrealist-inspired ethos of free, imaginative play; yet to refuse to do so is an act of willful ignorance, which requires that one pretend that a target does *not* presuppose an archer, whose place is identical with the viewer's (whose gaze might be said to be the equivalent of arrows). Typically, Johns creates a work which is highly provocative, but which freezes the spectator in his or her attempt at response.

Nonetheless, if we accept the risk of reading, and of misreading, we can make the following observations: 1) the hinged doors, one for each compartment, may be either opened or closed, revealing or concealing a specific part of the anatomy; 2) the juxtaposition of target and fragmented body parts encourages us to attempt to make them cohere in signification; 3) any significance we can construct will involve both danger and sexuality.

These observations then allow us to go further. This kind of fetishistic dismemberment before our eyes or concealed from us (typical of Surrealist procedures) is usually reserved for women, whereas the only gender we can positively ascribe to any of the body parts is male: the penis and part of the testicles, in the third (green) compartment from the right. The nipple (in the pink compartment in the center) appears to be a male's and the foot at the far left (red) compartment looks male as well. Johns has told me in a letter that the casts were made from the bodies of both men and women[18]; nonetheless, the genitalia are male, and even if the ear, nose, and mouth are all female body parts, their presence has a relatively low psychic valence. The same cannot be said for the penis and nipple, the presence of which, especially in the art of a modern male artist, catches the spectator completely off-guard.

The simple enumeration of body parts might be called Whitmanesque. I am thinking of "I Sing the Body Electric," which after 130 lines, draws to a close with one of those plain-speaking, American catalogues of experience for which Whitman is so famous: the list.

> *Mouth, tongues, lips, teeth, roof of the mouth, jaws and the jaw-hinges,*
> *Nose, nostrils of the nose, and the partition,*
> *Cheeks, temples, forehead, chin, throat, back of the neck, neck-slue,*
> *Strong shoulders, manly beard, scapula, hind-shoulders, and the ample side-round of the chest,*
> *Upper arm, armpit, elbow-socket, lower-arm, arm-sinews, arm-bones,*
> *Wrist and wrist-joints, hand, palm, knuckles, thumb, forefinger, finger-joints, finger-nails,*
> *Broad breast-front, curling hair of the breast, breast-bone, breast-side,*
> *Ribs, belly, backbone, joints of the backbone,*
> *Hips, hip-sockets, hip-strength, inward and outward round, man-balls, man-root, ...*
> *O I say these are not the parts and poems of the body only, but of the soul,*
> *O I say now these are the soul!*

188

far left:
JASPER JOHNS
Figure 5, 1955
Encaustic and collage on canvas, 17 1/2 x 14 inches
Collection of the artist

left:
CHARLES DEMUTH
I Saw the Figure 5 in Gold, 1928
Oil on composition board, 36 x 29 3/4 inches
The Metropolitan Museum of Art
The Alfred Stieglitz Collection, 1949

JASPER JOHNS
Target with Plaster Casts, 1955
Encaustic and collage on canvas with objects, 51 x 44 x 3 1/2 inches
Collection of Leo Castelli, New York

This matter-of-fact list is strong stuff: it not only presupposes that the poet has fixed his gaze on the male body, but the poem itself is the trace of that gaze. Indeed, even if the observation is of himself in the mirror (which it is not in the fiction of the poem), this kind of narcissism is certainly not considered appropriate for men, indeed implies "femaleness," where narcissism is figured as a reasonable facsimile of the male objectification of women. At any rate, one can easily imagine Johns's interest in Whitman's non-inflected catalogue of the male body. Perhaps his numerous images of American flags and maps of the United States are more Whitmanesque than we have previously thought.[19]

But to return to the work in its entirety: the juxtaposition of salient male body fragments and target presents us with the highly unusual association, in modern art, of *danger* with the nude male body, and especially the male sexual organs. Again, one need only think of Surrealist imagery: the female body has often been represented by men as both dangerous (the "vagina dentata" immediately comes to mind) and endangered (how many breasts presented to male eyes and hands, how many bound or otherwise captive nude female figures?). So we must ask: under what circumstances is the male body endangered by the gaze? Under what regime of looking, or knowing, do men come under the same kind of scrutiny as women? What system of understanding will make sense of the target and the body, especially a target and body produced in the United States in 1955?

The answer, it must be obvious, is the male homosexual experience. For whatever else it may be, Johns's *Target with Plaster Casts* is first a portrait of the homosexual man of the postwar period, an era of extreme sexual repression; the besieged gay body—and gay psyche—is fragmented and sorted into compartments, each one capable of being alternately closeted or exposed. Moreover, the general realm of gay social and political repression alluded to here is simultaneously the site of personal, sexual, and romantic experience: in positive terms, the male body is offered as a target for Cupid's arrow, and in negative terms as a target for the ego fragmentation that can result from frustrated or thwarted desire. Moreover, in the context of the gay American subculture, the parceled-out body and secreted presences are redolent of the kind of anonymous and legally hazardous sexual practices—the use of so-called "glory holes" in public toilets—that are the concomitant of society's extreme limitations on homosexual contact.[20]

There is a precedent in more distant art history for this image of the nude male as target for the arrows of malevolent archers, one taken up often in gay subculture of the late nineteenth and early twentieth centuries: the martyrdom of Saint Sebastian[21]; we might say that in *Target with Plaster Casts* Johns has created an image of gay martyrdom in a demystified age. And there is a more immediate precedent for this kind of image; again we find the figure of Marsden Hartley. In 1939 Hartley painted *Sustained Comedy (Portrait of an Object)*. Hartley has portrayed his sitter—almost certainly a self-portrait—as a living target: his eyes are pierced with flaming arrows, and on his chest is a picture of the crucified Christ. Once again, whether or not Johns was consciously aware of Hartley's painting, the fact of their extraordinarily close manipulation of given imagery argues for a commonality of interest and intention. Finally, we might even ask, in the light of Harrison and Orton's observation that the work dates from the precise moment of the beginning of Johns's and Rauschenberg's relationship, whether *Target with Plaster Casts* ought not to be read in tandem with Robert Rauschenberg's *Bed*, made the same year (1955), under the same roof (the Pearl Street building where they both lived). The two works offer us some approximation—an inchoate and impulsive bodying forth, in the Abstract Expressionist sense—of the excitement, intensity, and danger of two men falling in love.

MARSDEN HARTLEY
Sustained Comedy (Portrait of an Object), 1939
Oil on board, 28 1/8 x 22 inches
The Carnegie Museum of Art, Pittsburgh
Gift of Mervin Jules in memory of Hudson Walker

190

JASPER JOHNS
4 the News, 1962
Encaustic and collage on canvas with objects, 65 x 50 1/4 inches
Kunstsammlung Nordrhein-Westfalen, Düsseldorf

ANDY WARHOL
Girl Sucking Forefinger, ca. 1956-58
Oil and graphite on primed linen, 48 x 41 inches
The Andy Warhol Foundation for the Visual Arts, Inc., New York

ANDY WARHOL
Flag, ca. 1956
Tempera on paper, 22 1/2 x 28 1/2 inches
The Andy Warhol Foundation for the Visual Arts, Inc., New York

Although Andy Warhol had been a working commercial artist in New York since 1949, and had even exhibited his "fine art" in galleries in New York during the 1950s, his desire to be a full-time (and big-time) artist did not come to realization until 1960. We should not be surprised then, given this chronology, that it was Jasper Johns and Robert Rauschenberg who were his idols, to use the terminology of Hollywood: not only were they the most important young artists in New York, they were gay, and they were lovers. As Rauschenberg said recently to the critic Paul Taylor about his relationship with Johns: "It was sort of new to the art world that the two most well-known, up-and-coming studs were affectionately involved."[22] What more appropriate role models for Warhol than these two mavericks? Warhol even made several silkscreen homages to Rauschenberg, *Let Us Now Praise Famous Men*, unabashedly proclaiming his devotion and admiration for the strikingly handsome Texan. But all did not go as Warhol had hoped—he felt slighted by the storybook couple, ignored despite his entreaties. Here is the passage from *POPism: The Warhol '60s* in which Warhol recounts the luncheon at which he finally summoned up the courage to ask his good friend, the filmmaker Emile De Antonio, what the problem was:

> As we sat at "21"...we talked about the art around town.... De was such good friends with both Jasper and Bob that I figured he could probably tell me something I'd been wanting to know for a long time: why didn't they like me? Every time I saw them, they cut me dead. So when the waiter brought the brandy, I finally popped the question, and De said, "Okay, Andy, if you really want to hear it straight, I'll lay it out for you. You're too swish, and that upsets them."
>
> I was embarrassed, but De didn't stop. I'm sure he saw that my feelings were hurt, but I'd asked him a question and he was going to let me have the whole answer. "First, the post-Abstract Expressionist sensibility is, of course, a homosexual one, but these two guys wear three-button suits —they were in the army or navy or something! Second, you make them nervous because you collect paintings, and traditionally artists don't buy the work of other artists, it just isn't done. And third," De concluded, "you're a commercial artist, which really bugs them because when they do commercial art—windows and other jobs I find them—they do it just 'to survive.' They won't even use their real names. Whereas you've won prizes! You're famous for it!"...
>
> What De had just told me hurt a lot.... Finally I just said something stupid: "I know plenty of painters who are more swish than me." And De said, "Yes, Andy, there are others who are more swish—and less talented—and still others who are less swish and just as talented, but the major painters try to look straight; you play up the swish—it's like an armor with you."
>
> There was nothing I could say to that. It was all too true. So I decided I just wasn't going to care, because those were all things that I didn't want to change anyway, that I didn't think I should want to change. There was nothing wrong with being a commercial artist and there was nothing wrong with collecting art that you admired. Other people could change their attitudes, but not me—I knew I was right. And as for the "swish" thing, I'd always had a lot of fun with that—just watching the expressions on people's faces. You'd have to have seen the way all the Abstract Expressionist painters carried themselves and the kinds of images they cultivated, to understand how shocked people were to see a painter coming on swish. I certainly wasn't a butch kind of guy by nature, but I must admit, I went out of my way to play up the other extreme.[23]

It must be said, before I proceed to analyze this rich account, that we are dealing with Warhol's recollections of his feelings about an afternoon nearly twenty years previous. We will never know just what De Antonio said to him, nor whether Johns and Rauschenberg ever told De Antonio what he claims they communicated. But this is of little importance; what concerns me is what Warhol believed he heard (and for all we know, he may have heard and recounted things precisely as they happened) and how he felt about it. In order to indicate that

193

Robert Rauschenberg and Jasper Johns at Tibor de Nagy Gallery, New York, 1959
Photo: Fred W. McDarrah

ultimately this is Warhol's narrative, and no one else's (except perhaps Pat Hackett's, his co-author on *POPism*), I will refer to Johns, Rauschenberg, and De Antonio as they are invoked by Warhol: as "Jasper and Bob" and as "De," in quotation marks.

As Warhol tells it, according to "De" it is precisely what Andy shares with "Jasper and Bob" —homosexuality—that creates an unbridgable distance between them: Andy's effeminacy, as it used to be called—his "swishiness" in gay parlance—is an embarrassment. For "Jasper and Bob" the private and the public are two distinct and essentially separate realms; the self which inhabits one is not necessarily co-extensive with the other. For Warhol, on the other hand, the private and the public, if hardly identical, were a pair of interconnecting chambers: swishiness is the public sign he wears for his private desires, and which he, as he has just told us, clings to fiercely.

Moreover, Warhol's queerness—which seems the appropriate term for a system of sexual signification which parades its "inappropriateness,"—"I must admit I went out of my way to play up the other extreme"—was manifested not only in his comportment; "Jasper and Bob" may also have been offended by the homosexuality manifested in Warhol's pre-Pop art, which was quite well known in New York at the time.[24] Not that we are dealing with an artist whose (homo)sexuality was "out" in the sense that that of a young artist in 1992 might be: Warhol was enough a man of his times that his sexual "identity"—even his purported asexuality—was accentuated or de-emphasized depending on moment, medium, and context. For instance, during the early Pop art years, 1960-65, as distinct from the periods both before and after, representations of frank sexuality are almost completely displaced from the realm of the pictorial to the filmic, as in *Blow Job* (1963), which Stephen Koch has referred to as the "apotheosis of the reaction shot, never to be surpassed."[25] The entire film is made up of the facial reactions of its fortunate, fellated star; except for a very brief glimpse of a leather-jacketed shoulder, the other participant and the act itself are withheld from the spectator. Furthermore, in contrast to the relatively direct "boy drawings" of the 1950s, full appreciation of Warhol's early Pop paintings and silkscreens required at least a certain gay-attuned sensibility and a sense of humor. A case in point is the *Thirteen Most Wanted Men* mural which Warhol created for Philip Johnson's New York State Pavilion at the 1964 World's Fair, which was—for those who could decipher it—a punning reference not only to the FBI's desire, but to Warhol's own. That "wanting men" was here synonymous with criminal activity must have made the joke all the better to Warhol. As local post offices across America offered, if unintentionally, male pinups to the American public, Warhol can be said to have collaborated with the U.S. government in cultivating gay sensibility. Inasmuch as Warhol was asked to hide his mural from public view before the Fair opened (which he did by painting over his "most wanted men" with silver paint), it may be that some of his "inside" jokes were, at least subliminally, too close to the surface.

But let us return to "De's" statement to Warhol that the first reason that "Jasper and Bob" don't like him is that he is too swish. If this were only a question of the personal reaction of two particular gay artists to the behavior of another gay artist, it would not, it seems to me, merit a great deal of attention. But the 21 Club anecdote is not idiosyncratic, it's exemplary; it provides us with another glimpse into the gendered nature of the discourse of postwar American art. We know what Warhol is talking about when he says, "You'd have to have seen the way all the Abstract Expressionist painters carried themselves and the kinds of images they cultivated to understand how shocked people were to see a painter coming on swish." But "De" continues: "Second, you make [Jasper and Bob] nervous because you *collect* paintings, and traditionally artists don't buy the work of other artists, it just isn't done. And third, you're a commercial artist, which really bugs them, because when they do commercial art—windows and other jobs I find them—they do it just 'to survive.' They won't even use their real names. Whereas *you've* won prizes! You're *famous* for it!"

Andy Warhol *was* proud of his commercial work, and with good reason: he was one of New York's

194

best-known and highest paid commercial artists of the fifties. But there is special pleading in "Jasper and Bob's" objections to Warhol's willingness to "own" his commercial reputation: as "De" recounts, they also did commercial assignments. Specifically, they designed windows for Gene Moore at Tiffany and Bonwit Teller, both working under the same pseudonym: Matson Jones. There is a parallelism, then, between Warhol's willingness to wear his "swishiness" as a sign and to wear his "commercialism" as a sign, just as there is a symmetry in "Jasper and Bob's" twin refusals to do either. Moreover, these two buttoned-down guys were surely aware that moonlighting as a window dresser was not quite the same thing as moonlighting as a security guard: to dress Tiffany's windows was, and often still is, a typically gay pursuit; it is highly lucrative; and it is perilous because it is morphologically close to the making of paintings. Warhol's insistence on being both a commercial and a fine artist wreaked havoc on the kinds of binarisms — social, economic, sexual, aesthetic, and political — that structured, and still do to a large extent, the discourse of art.

      I will return to the issue of commercialism, but we must first attend to "Jasper and Bob's" third objection, that Warhol has committed trespass in being an art collector. To say that Andy Warhol was a collector is to risk understatement — Warhol was King of the Collectors. In his later years he was a fixture on

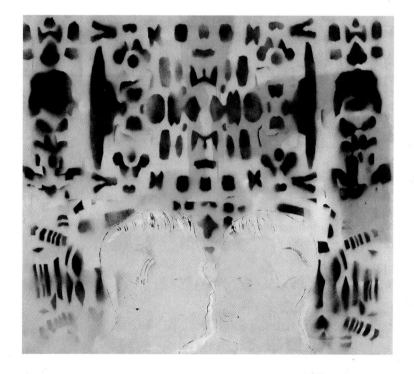

Madison Avenue and at the Sixth Avenue Flea Market, where he collected the good, the bad, and the ugly. He not only collected the work of his contemporaries, he also accumulated cookie jars, jewelry, furniture, illustrated books, gay pornography, Native American art, eighteenth-century silver, you name it.

      But we still don't know precisely what it is that is so objectionable about Andy's collecting; "De" himself isn't certain either — he concludes with the phrase: "it just isn't done." The trick here, I think, is to change our terminology: collector is another word for shopper, a *fancy* word for shopper, one who shops for high-class goods. Both shoppers and collectors are consumers, and this leads us again to the threshold of gender. Warhol is disliked by his gay predecessors because he acts like a *consumer*, when he is supposed to act like

195

ANDY WARHOL
Two Heads, ca. 1952-57
Oil, ink, and commercial spray paint on primed linen, 42 x 47 3/4 inches
The Andy Warhol Foundation for the Visual Arts, Inc., New York

ANDY WARHOL
Where is Your Rupture?, 1960
Synthetic polymer paint on canvas, 70 x 54 inches
Private collection, courtesy of Gallery Bruno Bischofberger, Zurich

a *producer*. This is another way of saying that Warhol acts like a *woman*, not like a *man*. In the postwar world that provides the context for Pop art, consumerism — especially consumerism of the supermarket — was associated with women. The supermarket was the domain of women shoppers, the place where mothers and wives went to seek sustenance for their families. Only an unmanly man ventured forth to the market, according to the stereotype. So, in a very real sense, to say that Warhol is too "swishy" and to say that he is a collector is to say more or less the same thing — that he has transgressed his proper gender identification, that he has taken on the attributes of a woman.

Furthermore, Andy Warhol was not only a "sissy," he was a "momma's boy," and seemingly as proud of *that* as he was of being a commercial artist. Again Warhol displays as part of his identity the very things he is supposed to keep hidden by the codes of adult maleness. But these two identities — mother-identified man and commercial artist — are inextricably bound together: Warhol had made his reputation, above all else, as an illustrator for the women's "carriage trade." As is well known, mother and son at times collaborated on various projects, commercial and otherwise. In 1958 the Art Director's Club actually bestowed an award on Julia Warhola, which referred to her in mock hand-drawn calligraphy, as if it were her name, as "Andy Warhol's Mother."

Yet something remarkable happened when Warhol left commercial art for his own art

— although he still thought about commerce, he now thought about commercialism and consumerism not through the eyes of a *Vogue* reader or Bonwit shopper, but through his mother's eyes. In terms of his iconography, Andy's grown-up world in New York was relinquished for a return to the world of Pittsburgh and his childhood. Cross and Blackwell was traded in for Campbell's. It was a "blue-collar" woman's world that Warhol offered New York's sophisticated art consumers. In a Duchampian transference, women *and* men who never did their own shopping or cleaning were sent to the Stable Gallery and Leo Castelli's to buy Campbell's and Brillo, just like Mrs. Warhola and the vast majority of American women. And it was of course his same working-class woman's world that Warhol held up to us in his portraits of movie stars. In the repetition of images, the off-register printing, and the general lack of nuance, Warhol's portraits of stars reveal their source in the daily newspaper and the fan magazines, those halfway houses between fact and fiction.[26]

ANDY WARHOL
Dr. Scholl, 1960
Synthetic polymer paint on canvas, 48 x 40 inches
The Metropolitan Museum of Art, New York
Gift of Halston

197

For Warhol, his past and his present could now be made to cohere. His class origins and his sexual preferences could be expressed in one utterance, for on the common ground of "camp," that is to say in popular culture, the working class and the homosexual meet. The year that Warhol made his first Troys and Marilyns, 1962, is the same year that Susan Sontag published her "Notes on Camp," in which she made available to the general population the gay, cult sensibility which embraces all that good taste abhors: the popular, the outré, and the forgotten. How felicitous that mother and son could share a taste for Troy Donahue and for an Art Deco club chair (which in the case of Andy's mother and her friends survived in the living room because they could not afford to replace it with a more up-to-date specimen).

Indeed, Warhol's *Campbell's Soup Can* of 1962 now begins to look like a "feminine" response to Johns's "masculine" *Painted Bronze* of two years earlier: supermarket vs. saloon, shopping vs. drinking, nourishment vs. escape. But the comparison, I think, is instructive in other ways as well. Both, obviously, are "portraits" of objects drawn from popular culture, and both are intended as Duchampian demonstrations of the power of the art context to determine value (Johns's work apparently originated as a dare, when someone commented that Leo Castelli was such a superb salesman that he could even sell a couple of beer cans to a collector, if he had to). More specifically, both works are representations of vessels that can be found in any supermarket or grocery store. In both cases the labels, the "text" that would have been so anathema to Abstract Expressionist artists, make up a good part of the image.

But at that point the similarities end. Obviously in the case of the Johns we are dealing with sculpture, a work in three dimensions, and Warhol's work is a two-dimensional representation; but the example could have been reversed, with a Warhol Campbell's Soup crate and the Johns print of his subject. This distinction does not seem important. What is important, though, is the means of manufacture: Johns has made a bronze cast which he subsequently hand paints, Warhol a photographic silkscreen. Although both are in effect derived from a template which, in theory, can be used to reproduce itself, the Johns work, after all the trouble he has gone to, ends up as a handmade object, which of course is the point. The hand of the artist turns ale cans into "art," whereas Warhol's silkscreen simply reiterates — on canvas instead of paper — the original mode of the referent's manufacture. It may now be art, but that simply means that art's definition has been pulled "down" to include supermarket items; Johns's hand-painted Pop objects have, on the contrary, had their originals brought "up" to the museum.

But this leads us to the spectator and the way in which each work is to be apprehended. We must still perform the hermeneutical pursuit of meaning to read Johns's *Painted Bronze*; we must get beneath its "skin," we must know of its multiple moments of realization, and we must sense and savor the contrariness of object and appearance. In Warhol's *Campbell's Soup Can* we remain where Warhol always insisted we remain: on the surface. There is no place to go "into" the work, no depths to plumb, no mysteries to unravel. Indeed, if we are to go anywhere it is outward, back into our own space and the cultural codes which determine how we evaluate the relative worth of things in the world. We might say that if with Johns we are required to move at a ninety-degree angle into the work, perpendicular to the picture plane, or into the body of the objects, like one of the arrows that would pierce his *Target with Plaster Casts*, with Warhol we can only move laterally, or find ourselves bounced back to where we stand, reflected. That is to say, if with Johns the irony which structures

far left:
JASPER JOHNS
Painted Bronze, 1960
Painted bronze, 5 1/2 x 8 x 4 3/4 inches
Museum Ludwig, Cologne

left:
ANDY WARHOL
Big Campbell's Soup Can 19¢, 1962
Acrylic on canvas, 72 x 54 1/2 inches
The Menil Collection, Houston

ANDY WARHOL
Peach Halves, 1960
Synthetic polymer paint on canvas, 70 x 54 inches
Staatsgalerie Stuttgart

the work pulls us ineluctably further in, with Warhol's "camp" facsimile — camp being the poor relation of irony — we remain outside, laughing perhaps, and maybe recognizing how artificial, how arbitrary, are our systems of representation. Indeed, I have come to think that Warhol's insistence on our taking his art at face value, his insistence that we remain on the surface of things, derived from acute awareness that "depth," intellectual or pictorial, could all too easily begin to assume the shape of "the closet," from the depths of which one might never reemerge. One could hide in deep, dark places, be those the spaces of high Abstract Expressionism, or the spaces we construct for ourselves by means of less-than-forthright behavior. "So I decided I just wasn't going to care," Warhol comments on "Jasper and Bob's" censure, "because those were all things that I didn't want to change anyway, that I didn't think I *should* want to change.... Other people could change their attitudes, but not me — I knew I was right."

Now, lest I give the impression that Warhol took all his cues from mass culture, and was somehow oblivous to high art discourse (as distinct from Johns's more rarified system of reference and understanding), I should point out that the battle lines were clear even at the highest levels: an inviolable distinction between the popular and the elite had long been inscribed in American art discourse. It was in 1939, after all, that Clement Greenberg — the most powerful, serious American critic of Warhol's era — published "Avant-Garde and Kitsch," an essay written against the terrifying background of European fascism on the eve of World War II.[27] The essay is well known in part because it is here that the young Greenberg exhibited his supposed left-wing sympathies. The essay ends with a paraphrase of Marx: "Today we no longer look toward socialism for a new culture — as inevitably as one will appear, once we have socialism. Today we look to socialism *simply* for the preservation of whatever living culture we have right now." Yet, as has been discussed by Robert Storr, this encomium of socialism occurs at the end of an extended indictment of popular culture, which Greenberg saw as essentially fascist.[28] In order to do this, of course, he had to construct a proletariat which was both powerless and benighted: "There has always been," Greenberg writes," on one side the minority of the powerful — and therefore the cultivated — and on the other the great mass of the exploited and poor — and therefore the ignorant. Formal culture has always belonged to the first, while the last have had to content themselves with folk or rudimentary culture, or kitsch." And Greenberg continues:

> Where there is an avant-garde, generally we also find a rear-guard. True enough — simultaneously with the entrance of the avant-garde, a second new cultural phenomenon appeared in the industrial West: that thing to which the Germans give the wonderful name of kitsch: popular, commercial art and literature with their chromeotypes, magazine covers, illustrations, ads, slick and pulp fiction, comics, Tin Pan Alley music, tap dancing, Hollywood movies, etc. etc....to fill the demand of the new market, a new commodity was devised: ersatz culture, kitsch, destined for those insensible to the values of genuine culture, but who are hungry nevertheless for the diversion that only culture of some sort can provide.

Without debating the validity of these attitudes, I want nonetheless to point to one final passage in Greenberg's essay, which brings us yet again to the threshold of gender. Greenberg says that "If the avant-garde imitates the processes of art, kitsch, we now see, imitates its effects." This is Greenberg's shorthand way of saying, as he explains a bit more clearly elsewhere in the essay, that avant-garde art requires the spectator to sympathetically involve him or herself with the making of art — the processes — whereas kitsch makes no demand on the spectator — he or she has simply to consume the end result: the effects. But we may usefully understand this distinction as the same one we have already encountered, the very same one that "Jasper and Bob" found so odious in the Warhol scenario: if the avant-garde is allied with processes, according to Greenberg, it is an expression of production, of the world of men; if kitsch is allied with effects, again according to Greenberg, it is an expression of consumption, of the world of women.

Andy Warhol at Eleanor Ward Gallery, New York, 1964
Photo: Fred W. McDarrah

Once launched in the New York art world, this gendered distinction between avant-garde and kitsch had a particular tenacity, although never with the slightest self-consciousness (as in all ideological constructs, an auto-critique would have vitiated the power of the mythicizing assumptions).[29] In 1962, the year of Warhol's first Campbell's Soup cans, his paint-by-number pictures, and his Green Stamps, Greenberg in his essay "After Abstract Expressionism," coined the term "homeless representation." He wrote:

> This manner, as returned to abstract art by de Kooning himself and the countless artists he influenced, I call "homeless representation." I mean by this a plastic and descriptive painterliness that is applied to abstract ends, but which continues to suggest representational ones. In itself "homeless representation" is neither good nor bad, and maybe some of the best results of Abstract Expressionism in the past were got by flirting with representation.[30]

It is interesting to note, by the way, that after discussing the art of Jasper Johns, Greenberg concludes that the artist is, in effect, the last Abstract Expressionist: "Johns sings the swan-song of 'homeless representation,'" he writes, "and like most swan-songs, it carries only a limited distance."[31]

Of course, Greenberg's use of the term "homeless representation" is intended to point us *away* from the "home," away from figuration (even in its orphaned, late-abstract, or Johnsian incarnation), towards the color-field painters he was championing. But his choice of terminology is significant, and must have been especially resonant at the very moment that not only Warhol, but also Jim Dine, Roy Lichtenstein, Claes Oldenburg, and numerous other Pop artists were creating such a sensation with their images of consumer culture in general and of the home in particular. Indeed, the trope of the "anti-domestic" was inscribed in the discourse of Abstract Expressionism by at least the early 1950s, if not sooner.

A case in point is the article published in 1951 in *Art News*, "Pollock Paints a Picture," by Robert Goodnough, which accompanied the well-known photographs by Hans Namuth of Jackson Pollock at work in his studio in East Hampton. Here is the gospel of Pollock according to Goodnough:

> Before settling on the Island, Pollock worked for ten years in a Greenwich Village studio. Intermittently he made trips across the country, riding freight trains or driving a Model A Ford, developing a keen awareness of vast landscape and open sky. "You get a wonderful view of the country from the top of a freight car," he explains. Pollock loves the outdoors and has carried with him and into his painting a sense of the freedom experienced before endless mountains and plains, and perhaps this is not surprising in an artist born in Cody, Wyoming, and raised in Arizona and Northern California.[32]

At the very moment of the successful domestication of the American artist within American culture, of the "Triumph of American Painting," we are asked to recall, as we gaze at Pollock working in the barn alongside his Long Island house, the "natural habitat" of the species. In fact, just months before Namuth took his photographs, Pollock showed himself to be not only domesticated, but a paradigmatic 1950s consumer: he traded in his Model A Ford for a Cadillac.[33] The moral of Goodnough's postwar tale is a variation on the one which Johns will send up in *Painting with Two Balls*, i.e., that only authentic American males can make authentic art. Now the critic says: *in spite of appearances*, with all evidence to the contrary, the American male painter is still not a part of the domestic world of women. The excessive need to insist upon the wide-open expanses of the virilizing American landscape, the need to affirm what is neither domestic or commercial, is precisely the same need which so many Pop artists — and by no means only the gay ones — took such pleasure in

ANDY WARHOL
Marilyn, 1962
Acrylic and silkscreen on canvas, 20 x 16 inches
Collection of Douglas S. Cramer, Los Angeles

201

parodying. So essential to postwar art criticism was the anticonsumerist, antidomestic, masculinizing construction, that in 1952, in "The American Action Painters," we find Harold Rosenberg not only decrying the arrival in America of mass good taste — "Modern furniture and crockery in mail-order catalogues; Modern vacuum cleaner, can openers," but also describing the abstract painting he considered empty as "apocalyptic wallpaper" which he further says we may recognize by "a few expanses of tone or the juxtaposition of colors and shapes purposely brought to the verge of bad taste in the manner of Park Avenue shop windows...."[34]

We perhaps should not be surprised that Warhol, in his typically matter-of-fact reification of the disdained terms of art and behaviorial rhetoric, went right to the heart of this Abstract Expressionist no-man's-land in 1966: he produced wallpaper, with which he papered Ileana Sonnabend's gallery in Paris and Leo Castelli's gallery in New York.[35] Wallpaper: housewives, consumers; Park Avenue shop windows, fairy decorators; cows. Not only did the cow remind Americans of that era of Elsie, the Borden Dairy company logo, but in Warhol's paper the female of the species' benign gaze is a campy deflation of the imperious bull's glare, that look of masterful control that had become more or less synonymous with a certain kind of male, avant-gardist authority.

So, when it came time five years later for Andy Warhol's retrospective at the Whitney Museum, in 1971, what more economical gesture, what more succinct way of expressing his allegiances — in terms of gender identification, sexual orientation, and class origins — than his decision, before hanging his paintings, to paper the immense fourth floor of Marcel Breuer's brutalizing, modernist building. With the pananche of a big-time decorator or a strong-willed housewife, Warhol transformed the public space he was given into a jumbo-sized simulacrum of the domestic interior. By way of making the Whitney's vast rooms look cozy, he dressed up the galleries designed for the display of avant-garde "production" in the trappings of kitsch "consumption." Obviously, this is a kind of transvestism. Warhol was willing to have a decade of his painting and sculpture look like so many gaudy accessories on a cheap dress in order to unleash, yet once more, the free play of gender, sexuality, and class signification that was his special field of knowledge.

202

PABLO PICASSO
Still Life with Red Bull's Head, 1938
Oil and enamel on canvas, 38 1/4 x 51 1/4 inches
The Museum of Modern Art, New York
Gift of Mr. and Mrs. William A. M. Burden

1 Andy Warhol and Pat Hackett, *POPism: The Warhol '60s* (New York: Harcourt Brace Jovanovich, 1980), p. 40.

2 The Mattachine Society was founded in Los Angeles in 1950 and the Daughters of Bilitis in San Francisco in 1955. The Stonewall Riots took place in New York in June 1969. For a moving oral history of the early gay liberation movement, see Eric Marcus, *Making History: The Struggle for Gay and Lesbian Equal Rights 1955-1990* (New York: HarperCollins, 1992).

3 This article is based on a series of lectures that I delivered between 1986 and 1991: "Belated Notes on Camp: Homosexuality, Representation, and the Decline of Abstract Expressionism" (College Art Association Annual Meeting, New York, 1986, and the University of Pennsylvania, 1986); "The Body Electric: Jasper Johns' Song of Himself" (Lesbian and Gay Studies Conference, Yale, 1988; Simon Watson Gallery, New York, 1989); and "Andy Warhol, Soup to Nuts" (The Museum of Modern Art, 1989; the Getty Center for Art History and the Humanities, 1989; UCLA, 1989; Harvard, 1990; Stanford, 1990). I am especially grateful to Jim Salsow, John Goodman, Jim Herbert, Annette Michelson, and Romy Golan for their help and suggestions at various stages. I also want to thank Kurt Forster and the Getty Center for Art History and the Humanities for inviting me, as a Visiting Scholar, to refine my ideas on Warhol.

4 Leon Golub, "A Critique of Abstract Expressionism," *College Art Journal* 14, no. 2 (Winter 1955): 143.

5 Charles Harrison and Fred Orton, "Jasper Johns: 'Meaning What you See'," *Art History* 7, no. 1 (March 1984): 97.

6 Rosalind Krauss, "Jasper Johns," *Lugano Review* 1, no. 2 (1965): 97.

7 Harold Rosenberg, "The American Action Painters," *Art News* 51, no. 8 (December 1952): 22.

8 Elaine de Kooning, "Franz Kline: Painter of His Own Life," *Art News* 61, no. 7 (November 1962): 31.

9 On the issue of Johns's "evasions," see Jill Johnston, "Trafficking with X," *Art in America* 79, no. 3 (March 1991): 102-111, 164-65.

10 Vivien Raynor, "Jasper Johns: 'I Have Attempted to Develop my Thinking in Such a Way That the Work I'm Doing is Not Me'," *Art News* 72, no. 3 (March 1973): 22.

11 Roberta Bernstein, *Jasper Johns' Paintings and Sculptures 1954-1974: "The Changing Focus of the Eye"* (Ann Arbor, Mich.: UMI Research Press, 1985). This is a revision of her Ph.D. dissertation for Columbia University, New York, 1975.

12 Marsden Hartley to Adelaide Kuntz, December 5, 1932, quoted in Barbara Haskell, *Marsden Hartley* (New York: Whitney Museum of American Art, 1980), p. 94.

13 I asked Johns in a letter of October 8, 1988, if he knew either Hartley's homage to Crane or *Sustained Comedy (Portrait of an Object)* (1939); in a letter of October 17, 1988, Johns wrote to me: "The two Hartley titles mean nothing to me. I might recognize the paintings if I saw them, but I have no way of looking them up at the moment."

14 See, for instance, Max Kozloff, *Jasper Johns* (New York: Abrams, 1967), pp. 11-12.

15 Ibid.

16 For a discussion of the German military portraits in the light of Hartley's homosexuality, see Haskell, *Marsden Hartley*, pp. 31-32, 43-45.

17 See Kozloff, *Jasper Johns*, p. 12.

18 "The casts in my *Target with Plaster Casts* were taken from several (4, I think, or perhaps, 3) models, male and female." Letter from Jasper Johns to the author, October 17, 1988.

19 Philip Fisher alludes to Jasper Johns's maps of the United States in "Democratic Social Space: Whitman, Melville, and the Promise of American Transparency," *Representations* 24 (Fall 1988): 99-100.

20 Moira Roth discusses Johns's work in terms of McCarthy-era investigations and codes in "The Aesthetic of Indifference," *Artforum* 16, no. 3 (November 1977): 46-53. Jonathan Katz is currently at work on a Ph.D. dissertation for Northwestern University, the subject of which is the art of Johns and Rauschenberg in the context of Cold War politics.

21 Dr. Annemarie Springer delivered a paper at the College Art Association annual meeting in New York in 1986, on this subject: "Saint Sebastian from the 15th to the 20th Centuries: A Study in Homoerotic Imagery."

22 Robert Rauschenberg interviewed by Paul Taylor, *Interview* 20, no. 12 (December 1990): 147.

23 Warhol and Hackett, *POPism*, pp.11-13.

24 For an excellent study of gay imagery in Warhol's pre-Pop art, see Trevor Fairbrother, "Tomorrow's Man," in *"Success is a Job in New York...": The Early Art and Business of Andy Warhol* (New York: Grey Art Gallery, New York University, in association with the Carnegie Museum of Art, 1989).

25 Stephen Koch, *Stargazer: Andy Warhol's World and His Films* (New York and London: Marion Boyars, 1985), p. 48.

26 For an insightful study of Warhol's movie-star portraits, see Cecile Whiting, "Andy Warhol, the Public Star and the Private Self," *Oxford Art Journal* 10, no. 2 (1987): 58-75.

27 Clement Greenberg, "Avant-Garde and Kitsch," *Partisan Review* (Fall 1939); all citations here are from the essay as published in *Clement Greenberg: Collected Essays and Criticism*, vol. 1, ed. John O'Brian (Chicago: University of Chicago Press, 1988), pp. 5-22.

28 Robert Storr, "No Joy in Mudville: Greenberg's Modernism Then and Now," in *Modern Art and Popular Culture: Readings in High and Low* (New York: Abrams, 1990).

29 The seminal essay on the subect of the gendered nature of modernism and mass culture, and particularly of Greenberg's place in the discourse is Andreas Huyssens, "Mass Culture as Woman: Modernism's Other," which originally appeared in *Studies in Entertainment: Critical Approaches to Mass Culture*, ed. Tania Modleski (Bloomington, Ind.: University of Indiana Press, 1986).

30 Clement Greenberg, "After Abstract Expressionism," *Art International* 6, no. 8 (October 25, 1962): 25.

31 Ibid., p. 27.

32 Robert Goodnough, "Pollock Paints a Picture," *Art News* 50, no. (May 1951): 38-41, 60-61.

33 Steven Naifeh and Gregory White Smith, *Jackson Pollock: An American Saga* (New York: Harper Perennial, 1989), p. 627.

34 Rosenberg, "The American Action Painters," p. 49.

35 Thomas B. Hess first suggested that Warhol's cow wallpaper might be read as a response to attitudes about modern art: "It is as if Warhol got hung up on the cliche that attacks 'modern art' for being like 'wallpaper,' and decided that wallpaper is a pretty good idea, too." Hess, review of Andy Warhol at Castelli, *Art News* 63, no. 9 (January 1965): 11. I am grateful to my student Joelle LaFerrara for this reference. Benjamin Buchloh relates the cow wallpaper to Rosenberg's proscription in "Andy Warhol's One-Dimensional Art: 1955-1966," in *Andy Warhol: A Retrospective* (New York: The Museum of Modern Art, 1989), p. 56.

203

Installation view of the exhibition "Andy Warhol" (1971)
at the Whitney Museum of American Art, New York

Ex.1 - Laying a Standard.

JESS
Laying a Standard (Translation #1), 1959
Oil on canvas, 23 1/2 x 15 inches
Courtesy of Odyssia Gallery, New York

Dick Hebdige

Fabulous C o n f u s i o n! Pop Before Pop?

[Pop] is basically a U-turn back to a representational visual communication, moving at a break-away speed in several sharp late models...some young painters turn back to some less exalted things like Coca-Cola, ice-cream sodas, big hamburgers, super-markets and "EAT" signs. They are eye-hungry; they pop...[They are] not intellectual, social and artistic malcontents with furrowed brows and fur-lined skulls.... Robert Indiana[1]

To be confused by culture is to know culture. To study culture is not to understand it, but to maintain that confusion. The cultural object is not only the object (thing) under analysis but also the object (aim) of analysis: it is both the reason for enquiry and the reason for not concluding the enquiry. To conclude the enquiry is then to present the findings, to close the text and shut the case. When this is done, all simultaneity and immediacy evaporate in a discourse that presents evidence to state that there were things not evident in the "original" object; that there was little to be discovered in the immediate and simultaneous experience of the object's material effects. The evidence is intended to prove a point of view — when it should be proving the object. Philip Brophy[2]

I.

Philip Brophy's call for the maintenance of a principled and rigorous confusion on the part of cultural critics is likely to appeal to anyone who wants to write on Pop but doesn't want to be identified with Indiana's dog-eared malcontents. After all, who among the fortysomethings — among those, at least, for whom "square" and "straight" are more than merely geometric figures — would *volunteer* for exile to the Land of the Uncool?! But in the case of hand-painted Pop, a certain amount of confusion is not only desirable but necessary. It can scarcely be avoided when the object of study is itself as confused, as imperspicuous, transitional, and jumbled as the "moment" just before Pop proper emerged from the mud of abstraction and assemblage, brushed itself down, jumped into its shiny, sharp-edged vehicles and took off at breakneck speed for the art history books and international auction houses. How do we go about "proving" the object when the object is itself a question? Pop before Pop!?!

After a decade of postmodernism, Neo-Geo, Neo-Pop, after Peter Halley, Richard Prince, Cindy Sherman, Barbara Kruger, and Jeff Koons, the adjectival linkage of "Hand-Painted" to "Pop" may seem willfully perverse. "Pop" has been wedded for decades to a brazenly Mechanical Bride. The word "Pop" is indissolubly associated with *industrial* technologies of reproduction—with epidiascopes, xerox machines, polaroid cameras, silkscreen printing. In the standard invocations of Pop art's primal scene, the paintbrush figures, if at all, as a tool of last resort. ("One work began as an assemblage assisted with paint," wrote Richard Hamilton, the British Pop "painter" in 1962, "was then photographed, the photography modified and a final print made which was itself added to paint and collage.")[3]

And no resume of Pop, however brief, would be complete without a mention of Roy Lichtenstein's *Brushstrokes (Little Big Painting)* (1965), when the grandiose truth claims of the expressive oily trace which had supported the epic tradition of postwar U.S. painting were reduced in one fell swoop to a huge, flat, florid joke.

> *What is needed, first, is more attention to form in art. If excessive stress on* content *provokes the arrogance of interpretation, more extended and more thorough descriptions of* form *would silence. What is needed is a vocabulary—a descriptive, rather than prescriptive, vocabulary—for forms.*   Susan Sontag[4]

According to the Orthodox Version of twentieth-century art history, Pop stripped the overlarded canvas of Abstract Expressionism bare for clean-lined figuration with the chemical efficiency of a specialist cleansing agent applied to a graffiti-covered subway train. The story of Pop's clean break has now become so securely enmeshed in the order of things that an advertising agency in Britain recently judged it to be familiar enough to the relevant market segment to hinge a campaign promoting the services of a major business consultancy firm entirely around it. In May of this year, readers of *The London Independent* newspaper were confronted with a centerfold, which consisted of a color photograph, with accompanying text, of a vast, horizontally elongated "painting" hanging on a gallery wall. A fire extinguisher positioned in the bottom left-hand corner

206

Advertisement for Andersen Consulting in *The London Independent*,
May 31, 1992

served to establish both scale and location (the latter confirmed by the wooden floor, white wall and an identification plaque placed next to the "painting" identifying it as METAMORPHOSIS by ANDERSEN CONSULTING).

Scanning from left to right of the depicted artwork, a parody of "spill and spatter" Pollock gradually resolves into pastiche Lichtenstein. In the right-hand corner sits a 1960s stereotyped office beauty, her skin composed of Ben-Day dots, her lemon hair and scarlet blouse exactly matching the red and yellow blobs and squiggles in the "Jackson Pollock" section. Her face, framed between the cartoon computer blinking on the desk and a filing cabinet that picks up the green of "Pollock's" wobbly stripes, wears a startled expression, turned toward the viewer. The blue eyes are wide behind the spectacles. The lips are parted. One varnished fingernail rests on a prominent cheekbone. Light streams in through the window (this is the moment of illumination): a trail of bubbles leads from the secretary's head past the angle-poise lamp to a thought balloon enclosing the words: WOW! WHAT A DIFFERENCE! The clinching slogan in bold type runs across the top of both pages: *We've got turning confusion into order down to a fine art.*

Here a moment from art history is frozen, turned into a moral fable. This is history painting for the nineties: Pop's "capitalist realism" caught in the heroic act of saving fine art, the business community, the female service role, good office practice, instrumental rationality, and the public from the toils of the depth model. The copy underneath reads:

> *Moving a business forward to keep your competitive edge can sometimes seem confusing....We work with you to create a seamless link between strategy, technology, business processes and people. In this way, a metamorphosis can be achieved across your whole company. This will give you better results, not to mention a clear picture of the future.*

Finally, in italics, the clinching one-liner: *"Metamorphosis in a world of change."*

The message of this ad is as cloudless as the future it predicts for all its client's clients. It is conjugated in a transformational grammar familiar to anyone capable of distinguishing a de Kooning from a Rosenquist: Pop out of Ab-Ex = Objective Realism out of Subjective Mess = cybernetics out of romanticism = U.S. corporate values *über Alles* = Us out of Them = Use Value ("purposelessness for purposes") out of Uselessness ("purposefulness without purposes") = Order from Confusion.

...We remain suspended with the works assembled for this exhibition in the interval between these transformations, in the murky middle section of Andersen's colossal *Metamorphosis*. At the central point of the "canvas" where the grid of the graph on the computer screen bleeds off into a series of horizontal white lines that blur into abstraction...at the central point just before the squiggly red and yellow stripes acquire graphic definition, turn into cables and get plugged into the computer's power inputs...there is a hiatus that is motionless, where the direction of the flows, the nature of their dynamism, their origins and destinations remain forever undecidable. And we...(GASP!)...we're still stuck there...

207

ROY LICHTENSTEIN
Little Big Painting, 1965
Oil and synthetic polymer on canvas, 68 x 80 inches
Whitney Museum of American Art
Purchase, with funds from the Friends of the Whitney Museum of American Art

JESS
If All the World Were Paper and All the Waters Ink, 1962
Oil on canvas, 40 x 50 inches
Courtesy of Odyssia Gallery, New York

II.

The contemplation of things as they are, without error or confusion, without substitution or imposture, is in itself a nobler thing than a whole harvest of invention. Francis Bacon[5]

Transparence *is the highest, most liberating value in art — and in criticism — today. Transparence means experiencing the luminousness of the thing in itself, of things being what they are.... What we decidedly do not need now is further to assimilate Art into Thought, or (worse yet) Art into Culture.*

Susan Sontag[6]

So what and where exactly *is* hand-painted Pop? To confer a single identity on the heterogeneous work produced from the mid-1950s to early 1960s by a diverse group of young and youngish painters dispersed along both continental seaboards is a bit like naming Jacques Lacan's "*hommelette*": the egoless bundle of uncoordinated drives that constitutes the infant prior to the Mirror Phase. The act of naming may be a gratifying ritual for the parents and the name itself should, under normal circumstances, function in the future as a socializing agent operating retrospectively to nail the little rascal into the appropriately gendered position reserved for it in the Symbolic Order. But we can't disguise the fact that there's no "one" there (yet) to answer to the name. What, after all, could possibly bind together the diversity of styles and projects embedded in the work in this exhibition? If, to quote Richard Hamilton's famous list from 1956, the relevant desiderata for Pop at that time were: "Popular (designed for mass audience), Transient (short-term solution), Expendable (easily forgotten), Low-cost, Mass-produced, Young (aimed at youth), Witty, Sexy, Gimmicky, Glamorous, Big Business"[7] then what, for instance, are Cy Twombly's delicate, Classically inspired scribblings doing here? To take another case only slightly less incongruous, Grace Hartigan's immersion in storefront displays, in billboards and the visual cacophony accompanying what Lawrence Alloway called in 1959 "the drama of possessions"[8] might indicate a proto-Pop concern with consumption and the street. ("I am assaulted, as we all are, by images," she wrote, "The images I choose have come to me through the mail, through windows, through various chance encounters.")[9] However, the way she *translated* found imagery into paint on canvas from 1955 to 1957 is something else again. A "free lyrical variant of de Kooning..."[10] is how one critic has described a style which borders, at times, in its generous and luminous intensity, on a spiritual exstasis which seems to emanate from sources bearing little ostensible relation to those directing the detached, laconic gaze of Edward Ruscha, say, or Andy Warhol. Similarly, while Jess's densely worked paste-ups of the fifties and sixties sometimes took off from comic book motifs, nonetheless, as Michael Auping has observed, they "present an introverted and fantasized character that seems distant from the sardonic...cool message of Pop."[11] The arcane nature of the narrative allusions in a Jess collage, the mysterious "Egyptian" image strands, the painstaking process of assemblage (what the artist called the "chain of action" which sometimes leads him to hang on to an image for years before it "finds its place" in a work) — all owe more to Magick and the Tarot than to Madison Avenue or the idea of planned obsolescence.

What binds this work together and links it to the more instantly identifiable early Pop of Oldenburg or Lichtenstein is, of course, the move away from pure abstraction, though the shift occurs unevenly. The departures rarely reach "breakaway speed" and they lead off in a number of quite different directions. The routes and rates of acceleration are determined by contingent factors: individual biographies, conscious and unconscious influences, preferences, desires, aversions, commitments. The route may be circuitous — a looping back and forth through border country rather than a straight line from A(bstract Expressionism) to B(anal Figuration). Thus Twombly might scale down Action Painting's epic strokes to a web of pencil-slim inscriptions. He might replace the flat-bed canvas with an overwritten surface that ends up looking like a fragment of a wall found in some dilapidated ancient city. But his project still involves a stretching out beyond or

209

BILLY AL BENGSTON
Untitled, 1957
Oil on canvas, 13 x 17 inches
Collection of the artist

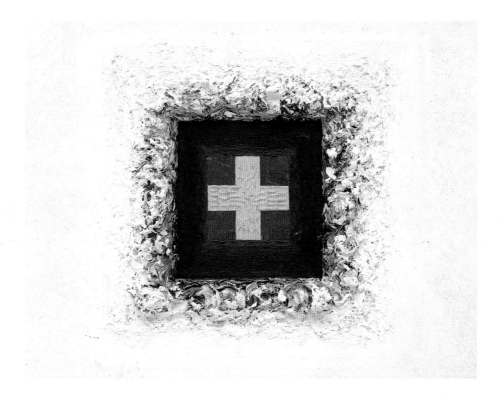

through the phenomenal world towards more hesitantly cohering forms than those named in experience, and that stretching is accomplished in a spirit of open-ended inquiry that brings him closer to de Kooning or Paul Klee than to any of the other artists represented in this exhibition.

210

Nor is (relative) physical proximity any guarantee of common ground here. To take the regionally pertinent examples, Jess, Mel Ramos, Billy Al Bengston, Joe Goode, and Ed Ruscha all lived and worked in California in the late fifties and their paintings were shaped, in part, by recognizably local cultural and environmental features. However, there is a world of difference between San Francisco and L.A. There is little shared space (or sense of space) uniting the inward-looking beatnik scene, concentrated in the fifties in the Bay Area, to which Jess was for a time affiliated, and the decentered car and motorcycle culture of Southern California's lunar strips and ribbon highways that spat out Kenneth Anger in the 1950s with one breath and drew in Bengston, Goode, and Ruscha from the midwest in the next. Bengston's BSA motorcycle emblems, isolated at the center of the frame, are bathed in the radiance of an altogether harsher (though no less loving) light than the glow produced by the cleansing fires that flicker at the edges of Jess's strange, nocturnal compositions. ("My earlier work took off from things I saw in the street: cars, signs, etc. — man-made things that we see in harsh California light." [Bengston][12]).

> To reject that part of the Buddha that attends to the analysis of motorcycles is to miss
> the Buddha entirely.   Robert M. Pirsig[13]

And while Ruscha and Jess (or Oldenburg for that matter) are driven by an allergy to the obvious that "shows" itself in a will to allegory that obviates definitive interpretation, Ruscha's tactic of laid-back verbal play is quite distinctive — quintessential West Coast cool:

Billy Al Bengston, Ascot short track, 1963
Photo courtesy of the artist

BILLY AL BENGSTON
Untitled, 1957
Oil on canvas, 13 x 17 inches
Collection of the artist

Hebdige

[Ruscha] slid a painting from the rack.
"I haven't finished this one," he said, "I don't know why."
"What is it?"
"Norms," he said.
"Norms?" I said.
"Norms Restaurant, you know, on fire."
"Like the Standard station?"
"Yeah, and the Los Angeles County Museum."
"Didn't one Standard station have a torn-up penny Western?"
"Yeah, that's why I set it on fire."[14]

In his exchanges with Dave Hickey on the subject of his burning restaurant, gas station, and museum series, Ed Ruscha complies with Susan Sontag's injunction in "Against Interpretation" "to show *how it is what it is,* even *that it is what it is,* rather than to show *what it means.*"[15] The conversation is as oblique,

lateral, tightly organized (and as elliptically competitive) as "The Route," one of the tracks laid down by Art Pepper and Chet Baker in Hollywood for Pacific Records in 1956. The phrases are spaced out evenly like telegraph poles on a smoother, emptier road than any highway Jack Kerouac and the Beats ever blustered down. "I had probably been wrong about the Standard station," Hickey concedes in the wake of that dialogue, (re)covering his tracks with a subtle *post-hoc* exegesis.

It wasn't a standardized *station but a* station which dispensed standards, *like a* restaurant which served norms, *or a* museum which did both.... *It seemed to me that you could say that Ruscha's work was generally negative toward what was "normal" or "standard," while being generally positive toward what was "typical" or "ordinary." (A recent "grand horizontal" painting goes so far as to present the* Mean *as* Hell.*)*[16]

Billy Al Bengston at Ferus Gallery, Los Angeles, 1962
Photo: Marvin Silver, courtesy of the artist

211

212

BILLY AL BENGSTON
Grace, 1959
Oil on canvas, 49 3/4 x 42 1/2 inches
Collection of Betty Asher, Beverly Hills

This "generally positive" attitude toward the ordinary, itself a typically West Coast understatement, constitutes probably the single most important common strand in Pop. Once the verbal constraints of cool were lifted, as, for instance, in Oldenburg's *Street* and *Store Days* publications, the voicing of that preference could approach the garrulous intensity of Walt Whitman in full flow:

I am for art that flaps like a flag, or helps blow noses, like a handkerchief....

I am for the art of neck-hair and caked tea-cups, for the art between the tines of restaurant forks, for the odor of boiling dishwater....

I am for the art of slightly rotten funeral flowers, hung bloody rabbits and wrinkly yellow chickens, bass drums and tambourines, and plastic phonographs.[17]

To recapture the power of what some readers may be tempted to dismiss as the deluded juxtaposition of awe and ordinariness requires us to question much of the "wisdom" accumulated in hindsight round Pop (and, incidentally, round that other much abused critical category, the banal). One way to recover the sense of emergency (*emergency*, a coming to light, an arising) surrounding those transitional forms and projects that bridged the gap between one "decisive" moment in American art (Abstract Expressionism) and the next (Pop) is to go back to beginnings. For insofar as hand-painted Pop appears, at first glance, to be a contradiction in terms, it issues a challenge to the sequential and thematic orders of recent art history and its preferred developmental narratives. Where better to begin (again) than by tracing the derivation of the word itself with the aid of a dictionary? (Unfortunately there's no guarantee that we've got the right entry):

BILLY AL BENGSTON
Count Dracula II, 1960
Oil on canvas, 48 x 48 inches
Newport Harbor Art Museum
Purchased by the Acquisition Council with a matching grant from
the National Endowment for the Arts, a federal agency

populace *mass of people; Italian popolo, PEOPLE with pejorative suffix (: — Latin -ACEOUS).*
So popular pertinent to the people C15th; finding favour with the people C17th…populous full of people
— late Latin populosus Classical Latin populari = ravage, pillage   Oxford Dictionary of English Etymology

One of the most persistent myths about Pop art today concerns the imagined intimacy of its relationship to popular taste and the notional mass audience drawn together in the fifties by advertising, film, and TV. Despite the transparency of the representational codes borrowed from commercial forms by artists like Ramos and Warhol, the affinity between Pop and the *popular* which now appears so natural proves to be, on closer inspection, a convenient but unconvincing fiction. It is, in the long run, about as historically and sociologically accurate as those TV retrospectives on the sixties that insist on putting every woman in a miniskirt and every man in an Afro wig and flares.

Pop's notoriety was founded on its ambivalence both to its sources in mass-mediated imagery and to the connotative baggage attached to painterly technique (e.g., the paradox of Lichtenstein's "hand-made readymades"). That ambivalence was guaranteed to antagonize as well as to seduce some, at least, of Pop's potential audiences (critics, dealers, established artists committed to "pure" painting, other larger, less directly "interested," publics). There is plenty of anecdotal evidence indicating the hostility directed at early Pop by the threatened coterie of Abstract Expressionists. Warhol describes the welcome he and Robert Indiana received when they arrived with Marisol at a party given by the Ab-Ex painter, Yvonne Thomas, to which Marisol alone had been invited:

ROBERT INDIANA
Terre Haute, 1960
Oil on canvas, 59 7/8 x 35 7/8 inches
Collection of the artist
Courtesy of Salama-Caro Gallery, London

When we walked into that room, I looked around and saw that it was chock full of anguished, heavy intellects. Suddenly the noise level dropped and everyone turned to look at us. (It was like the moment when the little girl in The Exorcist *walks into her mother's party and pees on the rug.) I saw Mark Rothko take the hostess aside and I heard him accuse her of treachery: "How could you let* them *in?"*[18]

The *reductio ad absurdum* of expressionist histrionics in Jasper Johns's dead-eyed targets and frozen canvas flags threatened the whole foundation of Abstract Expressionist theory, and, as Leo Steinberg pointed out later, "it was the painters who resented it most."[19] But it is also probable that Pop art's oxymorons produced confusion and offense beyond the narrow confines of an avant-garde elite pledged to defend authentic Art from kitsch. If the scandal of Johns's "hand-painted Pop" punctured the Ab-Ex balloon by indicating that the strokes and drips of the de Kooning school were "after all only a subject-matter of a different kind"[20]

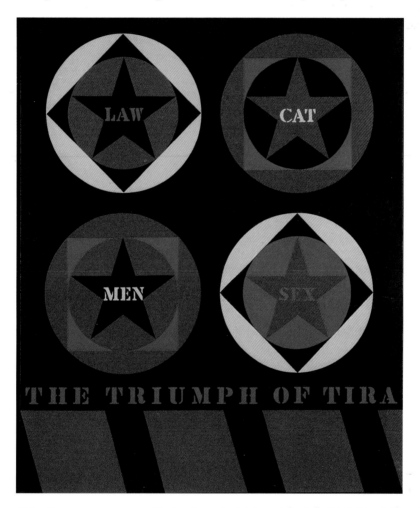

then a thirsty John Doe was no more likely than the ghost of Jackson Pollock to find satisfaction in a hand-painted beer can cast in bronze.

Pop never spirited away the hierarchical distinctions between "high" and "low," "minority" and "mass." It simply blurred the line by the postmodern strategy of double coding that made it possible, in David Deitcher's words "for privileged spectators to enjoy their cultural aloofness from the 'mob' while standing in its midst before the very same object."[21]

ROBERT INDIANA
Triumph of Tira, 1961
Oil on canvas, 72 x 60 inches
University of Nebraska-Lincoln, Sheldon Memorial Art Gallery, Nebraska Art
Association, Nelle Cochrane Woods Memorial Collection, 1964

EDWARD RUSCHA
Schwitters, 1962
Oil and collage on paper, 11 3/4 x 11 inches
Collection of the artist

216

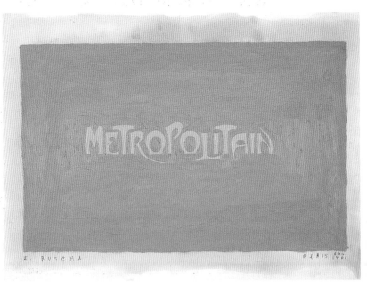

EDWARD RUSCHA
Metro, 1961
Photo-collage and oil on paper, 14 3/8 x 11 15/16 inches
Collection of the artist

EDWARD RUSCHA
Metropolitain, 1961
Oil on paper, 19 3/4 x 26 5/8 inches
Collection of the artist

The popular currency of Pop art's dominant image-repertoire is no more in dispute here than its success in attracting a more socially diverse audience for contemporary art than any other twentieth-century movement. Nonetheless, nobody using conventional sociological and market research criteria could claim that Pop art was any more "the people's choice" in 1962 than Cubism had been in its day or Jeff Koons is in ours. The conflation of analytically distinct problematics, objects, and practices (e.g. "admass" iconography/fine art transpositions and annexations of that iconography; consumer culture/the art of consumption/consumption of art, etc.) recurs as an asserted objective or a *fait accompli* in many of Pop's corporate mission statements. But Rauschenberg's imperative, issued at the outset to himself and circulated ever since amongst his followers, to "act in the gap between art and life" has probably done much to muddle important distinctions between Pop's rhetorical strategies, its "dumb" and ironic modes of address, the responses of actual audiences, and the postmodern "structures of feeling" ("camp" or "cool") which Pop helped to articulate, circulate, legitimize. It also obscures the specificity of Pop art's conditions of emergence, including the emergence of the name itself.

As Daniel Wheeler has remarked:

> *One of the many ironies to be savored in Pop is that as both a term and a concept it was first defined in England...where distance made it possible for a group of artists and intellectuals to regard imported American movies, rock recordings, science fiction, and glossy, ad-filled magazines with something other than the horror and disdain felt by their kitsch-hating counterparts across the Atlantic.*[22]

British Pop's hybrid parentage in, on the one hand, the paintings and collage work of Eduardo Paolozzi and Richard Hamilton and, on the other, the analysis of 1950s popular culture undertaken at the London Institute of Contemporary Arts by members of the Independent Group should not obscure the fact that the artists got there first. The terms "Pop Culture" and "Pop Art" had been current in Britain some years before "Pop" became the preferred designation for the new figurative painting in New York around 1960-61. Both terms had been coined originally by the critic and curator Lawrence Alloway to refer, more or less interchangeably, to "mass-produced" imagery and the exploration/exploitation of that imagery within contemporary painting. However it should not be forgotten that Alloway had taken his cue from the artists, not vice versa.

The word POP first appeared in Britain in a fine art context with an exclamation mark in a cartoon cloud of smoke fired from a cutout image of a gun adjacent to a girly pinup on a dimestore book cover, above a postcard of a wartime bomber and sliced-up cherry pie and Coca-Cola ads in a 1947 collage by Paolozzi called *I Was a Rich Man's Plaything*. It began to stick as a label after its second appearance nine years later on the wrapper of a giant POPsicle held by a generic piece of beefcake in Richard Hamilton's collage *Just what is it that makes today's homes so different, so appealing?* — the image which, transferred to the cover of the 1956 *This is Tomorrow* catalogue at London's Whitechapel Gallery, effectively launched Pop as a movement in Europe.

217

> *People talk about the subject entirely too much. The subject is chosen because it enables me to demonstrate something about the physical condition of nature.* Claes Oldenburg[23]

John Coplans's caveats about distinguishing Pop's provenance as a "regional movement" in Britain, primarily focussed on an anthropological interest in broad patterns of cultural change, from the specificity of Pop *art's* project (which he defines as "altering the perception of art itself") have to be taken seriously.[24] They are especially pertinent in this case given that the latter project was largely realized independently of British influence in the States. Some of the currently favored stories about Pop need revising in the light of that distinction, particularly those which lay inordinate stress on the ostensible "content" of the work. Pop's links to pop(ular) culture were always prominently there even in the hand-painted proto-Pop discussed in this catalogue.

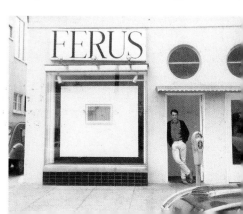

Edward Ruscha at Ferus Gallery, Los Angeles, 1963
Photo courtesy of the artist

EDWARD RUSCHA
Ace Radio Honk Boss, 1961
Tempera on paper, 15 5/8 x 20 inches
Collection of the artist

They are visibly there on canvas in the deadpan quotations from comics, commercial packaging, the rapturous language of pop and film star fandom. But these links were in the long run often incidental, sometimes tenuous, in large part instrumental.

This particular confusion between Pop and Pop art has, in the past, proved attractive to cultural critics, the present author included. It provides an easy alibi for anyone who sets out to stress the social contexts of artistic production over detailed consideration of the artworks in themselves, the manner of their execution, or the quality of their reception. Despite the revival of critical interest in Pop in the eighties, sparked by publications and major retrospectives in New York, Sydney, and London, and by the rearticulation of the Pop aesthetic in Neo-Geo and post-Pop art, that confusion has persisted. If anything, it has intensified so that it threatens today to inhibit fresh thinking on precisely what it was that made Pop "pop." Ten years ago, I concluded an essay on the subject with the following reflections:

> *The final destination of pop art, pop imagery and pop representational techniques lies not inside the gallery but rather in that return to the original material, that turning back towards the source which characterised so much of pop art's output in its "classic" phases. Its final destination lies...in the generation, regeneration not of Art with a capital "A" but of popular culture with a small "p.c."...*[25]

Such assertions can be accepted or rejected...(though I would add, in passing, that the only destination that looks final now is death [and even that finality remains, I hope, in doubt]). Either way, they should not prevent us from acknowledging that Pop's *origin* lies somewhere else again in a dimension that can't be mapped by polarized abstractions like Gallery versus Street; Art versus the People (a dimension, moreover, untroubled by the inadvertently anticipated specter of "political correctness" [p.c.] which endows the second term in each of those pairs with a spurious materiality and moral force). Turning back from England towards the sources of U.S. Pop requires, as a preliminary move, an exact inversion of the original terms of that argument. For we would surely be on firmer ground, etymologically speaking, if we were to assert instead that the authentic derivation for American Pop lies not in the heroic and abused body of the "populus" as imagined by generations of European intellectuals, nor in the "popular culture" constructed round that figure and now installed in the academy as *the* lost object of critical inquiry, but in the short, sharp shock administered to the senses, to logic, syntax, grammar by the sound the word makes in the mouth:

POP.....
 like DADA, infantile, nonsensical, onomatopoeic.

EDWARD RUSCHA
Annie, 1961
Tempera on paper, 6 7/8 x 8 5/8 inches
Collection of the artist

218

IV.

Pop *substantive; verb; interjection; and adverb; of imitative origin. The earliest uses (C14th) have reference to rapping or knocking; not recorded for abrupt explosive sound before C16th; vb put, pass, move suddenly…pop the question C18th; effervescing beverage C19th, compounds; pop CORN for popped corn C19th (U.S.); pop-eyed-eyes (having) prominent eyes C19th; pop GUN C17th (Hobbes).*

Oxford Dictionary of English Etymology

Pop — even in, especially in, its hand-painted infancy — was always first and foremost suddenly put. It was always a rapping or knocking from somewhere outside ("Outside is the world; it's there. Pop art looks out into the world" [Roy Lichtenstein][26]) even if it worked (when it worked best) to turn the inside/outside opposition inside-out ("Pop art took the inside and put it outside, took the outside and put it inside." [Andy Warhol][27]). If, as the neo-Kantians insisted, modern art really was about levelling the depicted field to the plane of its material support, if modern painting since Manet really did involve, to hijack Clement Greenberg's analogy, the "progressive flattening of the pictorial stage…'until its backdrop has become the same as its curtain,'"[28] even if, to hitch a ride on Harold Rosenberg's alternative theatrical analogy, the canvas had become "an arena in which

219

to act — rather than…a space in which to reproduce, re-design, analyze or 'express' an object"[29] then Pop was a loud report from somewhere off: an abrupt explosion in the wings. To the front-row metropolitan cognoscenti it looked like an invasion by outsiders acting in another medium:

> *It was like a science fiction movie. You Pop artists in different parts of the city, unknown to each other, rising up out of the muck and staggering forwards with your paintings in front of you.* Henry Geldzahler[30]

For all Pop's vaunted fascination with the pixillated visual detritus of what pundits in the fifties were already calling "an image-saturated society," for all its fixation on used-up mythologies (the comic book superhero/the painter-priest) and secondhand sources, Pop's visceral impact and didactic effects (the two were related) could be surprisingly immediate and direct. For those Americans intent in 1960 on approaching the canvas with the question "What Is Art?" Pop was a slap in the face as sharp, timely, and unexpected as any blow administered by a Zen master to an overintellectualizing novice dawdling on the road to enlightenment. Contrary to appearances, Pop was not "about" appearances. It was not "about" consumer culture, painting, serial

EDWARD RUSCHA
Ace Radio Honk Boss, 1961
Tempera on paper, 15 5/8 x 20 inches
Collection of the artist

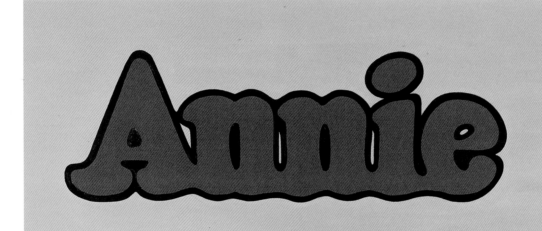

EDWARD RUSCHA
Annie, 1962
Oil on canvas, 72 x 67 inches
Private collection

EDWARD RUSCHA
Ace, 1962
Oil on canvas, 71 3/8 x 66 3/4 inches
San Diego Museum of Contemporary Art
Museum purchase in memory of Lois Person Osborn

WAYNE THIEBAUD
Cigar Counter, 1955
Oil on panel, 25 7/8 x 43 7/8 inches
Private collection

222

WAYNE THIEBAUD
Store Window, 1957
Oil on board, 11 x 12 inches
Private collection
Courtesy of Allan Stone Gallery, New York

WAYNE THIEBAUD
Ribbon Store, 1954-57
Oil on canvas, 28 3/4 x 34 7/8 inches
Private collection

WAYNE THIEBAUD
Bakery Counter, 1961-62
Oil on canvas, 54 3/4 x 71 3/4 inches
Collection of Foster and Monique Goldstrom, Oakland, Calif., and New York

224

WAYNE THIEBAUD
Desserts, 1961
Oil on canvas, 24 1/8 x 30 1/8 inches
Collection of PaineWebber Group Inc., New York

production, repetition, TV, flatness, advertising, art's commodity status, the implosion of object-subject distinctions, the "disappearance of the depth model," the "banality" of everyday life, the futility of "radical" gestures, the prevalence and power of the code of the cliche or the manufactured stereotype or the systematic logic of commodity-signs. In fact it wasn't "about" anything at all. Pop presented, and what it presented it presented in the face and on the face of what it represented. (Or as Marshall McLuhan put it rather more succinctly: the Medium is the Message).

It did without "about." It was exactly what the dictionary told us it should be: an effervescent beverage (Coca-Cola), Pop corn, Pop eye, Pop gun: a moving line of image-objects rolling through canvas after canvas and on towards the viewer like the prizes wheeled out for the camera and the overwhelmed contestants in the memory test finale of a 1950s TV game show. Pop was visual onomatopoeia — the revenge of the clunky referent on modernism's aspiration to transcend the mere materiality of things, to purge away the lust for more with less and less and less. Pop was a sharpening of the wits asserted against the ascetic urge of the avant-garde to exchange the noisy tyranny of the visible for the clean air of abstraction.

I think a picture is more like the real world when it is made out of the real world.   Robert Rauschenberg[31]

[Lichtenstein] has made a sow's ear out of a sow's ear.   Brian O'Doherty[32]

Hand-painted Pop approached the condition of a different kind of silence — an absolute merger of paint and depicted subject matter. (If you listen to that silence, O'Doherty's insult is turned into a compliment.) It strove towards a more morally responsible and spiritually enabling sense of arbitrariness than that enclosed in the superannuated rationalism of the always-empty sign. The silence grows deafening in the case of Wayne Thiebaud:

I like to see what happens when the relationship between paint and subject-matter comes as close as I can get it — white, gooey, shiny, sticky oil paint [spread] out on top of a painted cake to "become" frosting. It is playing with reality — making an illusion which grows out of an exploration of the properties of materials.[33]

The drive to merge sign and referent accelerates at "break-away speed" with Rauschenberg's all-inclusive combines, *Rebus* paintings, and ghostly blueprint paper silhouettes which bear the imprint of actual absent bodies. Here, and in the work of Jasper Johns, the "as if" which haunts European modernism's disenchanted body is replaced by the "as is" which comes equipped with its own material and concrete magic. As Leo Steinberg demonstrates in his analysis of Johns's fanatically literalist oeuvre, the neo-Dada label just will not do.

Johns's images do not seek [Magritte's] immunity of the unreal. You can't smoke Magritte's painted pipe but you could throw a dart at Johns's target, or use his painted alphabets for testing myopia.[34]

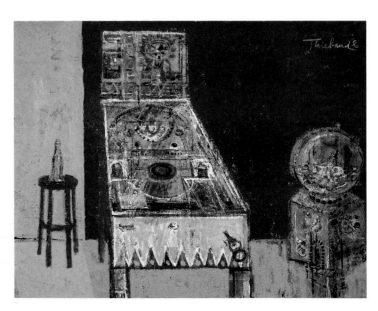

WAYNE THIEBAUD
Pinball Machine, 1956
Mixed media on presswood, 37 x 49 1/2 inches
Private collection

225

JOE GOODE
Milk Bottle Painting (Green), 1961-62
Oil on canvas with oil on glass milk bottle, 67 1/2 x 66 inches
Collection of James Corcoran, Malibu, Calif.

JOE GOODE
Milk Bottle Painting (Two-Part Blue), 1961-62
Oil on canvas with oil on glass milk bottle, 68 1/2 x 66 inches
Collection of the artist

V.

Perception, then, is neither a matter of aesthetic education nor a god-given talent. It is developed — through exercise and practice. If the brain is "the seat of sensation" (as in the Oxford Shorter Dictionary*) I furthermore regard it as a muscle.... When was the last time a critic, teacher or theoretician submitted to either a hearing or seeing test?*   Philip Brophy[35]

What is important now is to recover our senses. We must learn to see *more, to* hear *more, to* feel *more.*

Susan Sontag[36]

Brophy's kill-or-cure prescription for the geriatric ailments of critique — perceptual calisthenics and early retirement for those who can't keep up — may sound needlessly harsh. But it is absolutely of a piece with Pop. His recipe for the recovery of the object (and the dignity of writing *on* the object) is "to write without claiming meanings, staking values...declaring notions...constituting a writing that describes the *experience* that created the writing."[37] He thus restates, albeit more aggressively, the argument set out in 1964 in "Against Interpretation," Susan Sontag's prescient assault on the "hermeneutics of suspicion" — the self-validating urge of the critic to dig beneath the surface of the artwork for the subtext that explains it all (away). In that essay, Sontag argued that interpretation betrays "a contempt for appearances," and creates a "shadow world of meanings" that threatens to engulf the original forms in order to replace them. For Sontag interpretation thus represents "the revenge of the intellect upon art." Art responds by seeking to escape:

> *The flight from interpretation seems particularly a feature of modern painting. Abstract painting is the attempt to have, in the ordinary sense, no content; since there is no content, there can be no interpretation. Pop Art works by the opposite means to the same result; using a content so blatant, so "what it is," it, too ends by being uninterpretable.*[38]

Since the publication of that essay, cultural criticism has changed as much as art itself, along with the institutions that support them both. After thirty years of expansion in arts education, after structuralism, poststructuralism, deconstructionism, Minimalism, Conceptualism, "Art and Language," postmodernism...the boundary between art and its "shadow" has imploded like the Berlin Wall, precipitating similar confusions: elation, migration, disappointment, despair: strange and unpredictable effects.

Post-Pop Neo-Geo "illustrates" Jean Baudrillard: the tail now wags the dog. And Baudrillard has a specific "take" on Pop. While he approves of Pop's collusion with the system of commodity-signs ("Pop...is the first movement to explore the very status of art as a 'signed' and 'consumed' object."[39]) he is flummoxed by "the ideology of Nature, Revelation ('Wake Up!') and authenticity which evokes the better moments of bourgeois spontaneity." Here Pop's "logical enterprise" ("the secularization of the object") is contradicted by

> *...a bewildering sort of behaviourism produced by the juxtaposition of things as they appear (something resembling an impressionism of consumer society) coupled with a vaguely Zen or Buddhist mysticism stripping the Ego and Superego down to the "Id" of the surrounding world, with a dash of Americanism thrown in for good measure!*[40]

Bewildered here not fabulously confused...the object (Pop) is admonished for failing to fulfill its destiny, i.e. to manifest the critic's point of view.

Baudrillard's dismissal of *satori* ("a vaguely Zen or Buddhist mysticism") and "Americanism" as irrational aberrations is symptomatic of that more general reluctance on the part of European intellectuals to leave Europe (and the European Enlightenment) far enough behind to "prove" the object, as Brophy, the Australian critic, puts it — to see the object clearly in all its crystalline confusion. The dream of the "pure" object is fatally flawed (this, perhaps is the true "revenge of the crystal"): the object looks at us but when we turn to

Joe Goode, 1962
Photo: Patrick Blackwell, courtesy of Edward Ruscha

227

meet its gaze we find ourselves projecting: "It is naive to imagine that you avoid the risk of projecting merely by not interpreting. In desisting from interpretation, you do not cease to project. You merely project more unwittingly...."[41] The two-way passage of projections back and forth across both the Atlantic and the "United" States itself delineates another set of questions around Pop's emergence, to do with identity and difference, national, regional, and local networks of affiliation and belonging. Those projections helped to bind Pop together as an (inter)national "movement," an art historical "moment," and as a common sensibility or set of dispositions. At the same time, the turbulence generated in the wake of their hectic circulation threatened to split asunder each of those precarious forms of imaginary coherence.

> *The farther west we drove, the more Pop everything looked on the highways. Suddenly we all felt like insiders because even though Pop was everywhere—that was the thing about it, most people still took it for granted, whereas we were dazzled by it—to us, it was the new Art. Once you "got" Pop, you could never see a sign the same way again. And once you thought Pop, you could never see America the same way again.* Andy Warhol[42]

228

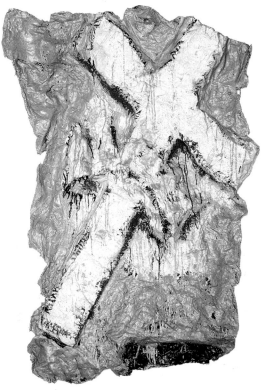

It would be reasonable to assume that the sheer unadulterated weirdness of American vernacular forms in 1955 or 1962 had been less immediately apparent to American than European artists. After all, the Americans had grown up with them. Warhol's recollections of this trip from New York to L.A. in 1962, to attend the opening of his second solo show there, disabuses us of this reasonable assumption. Part of the astonishment and awe registered by North American Pop artists when confronted by what the Canadian broadcaster Sidney Newman once called "the marvellous world of the ordinary"[43] stemmed from the fact that they, no less than Kerouac and the Beats, were discovering their own country for the first time. Federal investment in highway construction made migration and internal travel easier than it had ever been before.

CLAES OLDENBURG
Store Cross, 1961
Muslin soaked in plaster over wire frame, painted with enamel
52 3/4 x 40 1/2 x 6 inches
The Museum of Contemporary Art, Los Angeles
The Panza Collection

I didn't ever want to live any place where you couldn't drive down the road and see drive-ins and giant ice cream cones and walk-in hot dogs and motel signs flashing! Andy Warhol[44]

I drove around the city one day with Jimmy Dine. By chance we drove along Orchard Street....It seemed to me that I had discovered a new world....I began wandering through the different stores as if they were museums. I saw the objects displayed in windows as precious works of art. Claes Oldenburg[45]

The sense of exhilaration that runs through Oldenburg's lists of mundane discoveries made in the early sixties in the streets and garbage cans of New York's Lower East Side reverberates throughout much of the writing produced on U.S. pop culture in the period. A similar sense of astonishment comes through, for instance, in Tom Wolfe's breathless forays into the West Coast tangerine-flake streamlined-surfboard-teen-and-custom-car culture and in Robert Venturi's open-mouthed reactions to Las Vegas—that sense we get of being led by a Parisian flaneur on a walk around the moon (Mon Dieu! Wow! this place *does* exist![46]) Most of the artists clustered in Los Angeles, San Francisco, and New York had come from somewhere else. (David Hickey refers to the "pop-culture nullity of [Ruscha's home state] Oklahoma"[47]).

The situation was further complicated by traditional East-West rivalries, mutual distrust, and incomprehension. If Irving Blum could describe living in L.A. in the fifties as "like slowly sinking into a bowl of warm farina,"[48] if, as far as the (L.A.!) art dealer James Corcoran was concerned, Los Angeles was "Omaha with a beach,"[49] then there were also plenty of sophisticated Californians willing to dismiss Manhattan as a "jungle," a "nightmare" or a "headache."

The differences in response to U.S. ephemera and commercial signage on the part of Pop artists based in Europe and the States can be overestimated. It is certainly true that distance and austerity served to enhance both the curiosity *and* the irritation value of imported Americana for Europeans in the early postwar period. (Anti-Americanism was the one thing European intellectuals of both Left and Right agreed on in the

CLAES OLDENBURG
Pepsi-Cola Sign, 1961
Muslin soaked in plaster over wire frame, painted with enamel
58 1/4 x 46 1/2 x 7 1/2 inches
The Museum of Contemporary Art, Los Angeles
The Panza Collection

Claes Oldenburg
in his studio, 1961
Photo courtesy of the artist

CLAES OLDENBURG
Stockinged Thighs Framed by Skirt, 1961
Muslin soaked in plaster over wire frame, painted with enamel
34 3/8 x 41 3/8 x 6 inches
Collection of Holly Solomon, New York

CLAES OLDENBURG
Mu Mu, 1961
Muslin soaked in plaster over wire frame, painted with enamel
63 1/3 x 41 1/3 x 4 inches
The Museum of Contemporary Art, Los Angeles
The Panza Collection

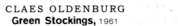

CLAES OLDENBURG
Blue and Pink Panties, 1961
Muslin soaked in plaster over wire frame, painted with enamel
62 1/4 x 34 3/4 x 6 inches
The Museum of Contemporary Art, Los Angeles
The Panza Collection

CLAES OLDENBURG
Green Stockings, 1961
Muslin soaked in plaster over wire frame, painted with enamel
43 1/4 x 18 inches
The Museum of Contemporary Art, Los Angeles
The Panza Collection

CLAES OLDENBURG
Green Legs with Shoes, 1961
Muslin soaked in plaster over wire frame, painted with enamel
46 x 42 x 8 inches
Museum Ludwig, Cologne

CLAES OLDENBURG
Chocolates in Box (Fragment), 1961
Muslin soaked in plaster over wire frame, painted with enamel
44 x 32 x 6 inches
The Museum of Contemporary Art, Los Angeles
The Panza Collection

231

CLAES OLDENBURG
Cigarettes in Pack Fragment, 1961
Muslin soaked in plaster over wire frame, painted with enamel
32 3/4 x 30 3/4 x 6 3/4 inches
The Museum of Contemporary Art, Los Angeles
The Panza Collection

CLAES OLDENBURG
Red Tights with Fragment 9, 1961
Muslin soaked in plaster over wire frame, painted with enamel
69 5/8 x 34 1/4 x 8 3/4 inches
The Museum of Modern Art, New York
Gift of G. David Thompson, 1961

CLAES OLDENBURG
Man's Shoe, 1961
Muslin soaked in plaster over wire frame, painted with enamel
23 1/2 x 43 1/4 inches
The Museum of Contemporary Art, Los Angeles
The Panza Collection

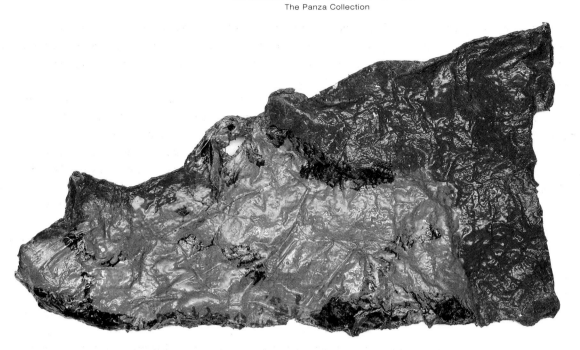

232

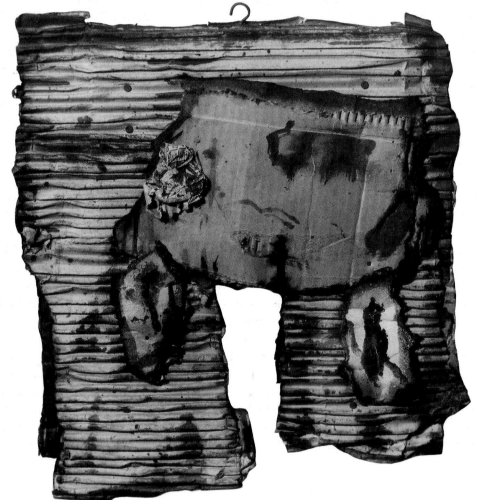

CLAES OLDENBURG
Truck-Pants, 1960
Painted cardboard with charcoal, 22 1/2 x 20 1/2 inches
The Sonnabend Collection, New York

fifties). In fact, it was precisely the discrepancy between those two responses — curiosity/irritation, attraction/repulsion — and the opportunity it afforded for playing up and playing out the class-based antagonisms that underwrote opposing taste formations in Britain at the time that gave British Pop its early dynamism and guaranteed the power of its schlocky shock effects.[50]

However, the Greenbergian hegemony on kitsch had produced a repression of the "popular-ordinary" in the New York art world no less systematic (or desperate) than that implemented by the BBC when it set about rationing the amount of jazz or Elvis heard by British listeners on the airwaves (a move that succeeded only in provoking a mass defection of the younger audience to Radio Luxembourg).[51] The significant lines of antagonism accompanying Pop's emergence in the States were less easily confused with the old hierarchies of social class than in Europe, but they served to articulate conflicts of interest and affiliation which were as contradictory and finely nuanced as anything produced by the elaborate machinations of the British class system.

The divisions around which the States-side taste war fought round Pop were organized would, however, hardly have occurred to Karl Marx. After all, the articulation of those divisions only began in earnest some time after Marx had left the scene — to be precise, *the day after* the Axis Powers had surrendered to the Allies when, as if at a prearranged signal, a series of unofficial fronts were opened up on North American soil. U.S. Pop was just the latest battle in the bloody, ongoing civil war waged inside America in the post-1945 period.

The relevant forces ranged against each other in 1960 cut across traditional social and territorial boundaries and, then as now, they were largely nonaligned. They included "East Coast" vs. "West Coast," "hipster" vs. "beat," "hip" vs. "straight," "camp" vs. "straight," "swish" vs. "straight," "queer" vs. "straight." The list of combatants is by no means exhaustive and it is important to note that the four "straights" mentioned above are not necessarily the same "straight," that the same lines cut into the social and individual body at different points from different angles, that the war, in other words, was more like the current conflict in what was once called Yugoslavia than either the revolt of the Confederacy or a colonial war of national liberation.

However, unlike those other wars, back in 1960 at least (before Vietnam, the riots and assassinations and the backlash of the Nixon years, before recession and the new conservatism, before the decline of the American city had reached crisis point, most importantly, before AIDS) the American taste and lifestyle "war" could still feel like a game. It was still being played out on the surface, on the tensile skin that lay across the seriously social, in the lag between the "normal" and the "ordinary" (i.e., before the system got too nervous, before the "norm" bit back): "As for the swish thing, I'd always had a lot of fun with that — just watching the expressions on people's faces," Warhol said later.[52] Warhol's rejection of the "hard-driving, two-fisted" machismo of the Cedar crowd went hand in hand with his celebration of the artificial and man-made ("I was glad those slug-it-out routines had been retired — they weren't my style, let alone my capability"[53]). Like the movies Jack Smith produced with the "flaming creatures" of Manhattan's lower East Side — the transvestites and transsexuals of the emergent "out" gay scene — Warhol's project involved a committed, surgical examination of masculinity and femininity as masquerade.

As Andrew Ross has noted in a fine analysis of Frank O'Hara's poem, "The Day Lady Died," late fifties and early sixties camp was "proto-political" insofar as it was structured round the possibility of "imagining a different relation to the existing world of too strictly authorized and legitimized sexual positions."[54] Its investment in surface and disguise entailed a rejection not only of the imaginary transparency of "real men" (and women) but of the patriarchal order which kept women in parenthesis and "politics" firmly up there in the ether — in Washington and voting booths and Great Affairs of State — rather than at home or work or on the street in the places where we live. It recognized, in Ross's words, "that history, for the most part, is...made

233

out of particulars, by people whose everyday acts do not always add up to the grand aggregates of canonical martyrdom which make for real *politics*."[55]

Despite the presence of Grace Hartigan and Jean Follett in the current exhibition, hand-painted Pop in both its "cool" and "campy," hetero- and proto-gay modes was dominated, like every other moment in the history of modern painting from Braque to Basquiat, by men and it articulated masculine concerns. Yet the styles of masculinity it inhabited could hardly be confused with the sincere-but-agonized, tough-and-heavy "manly" types promoted in Ab-Ex. Larry Rivers, a transitional figure, who Warhol classified as "very Pop" (because "he rode...a motorcycle...had a sense of humor about himself" and had once won $49,000 on a TV quiz show), conveys the flavor of the expository (or "flashing") style of self-disclosure that sometimes passed for social interaction on the Ab-Ex scene: "There were always great discussions going on, and there was always some guy pulling out his poem and reading it to you. It was a very heavy scene...."[56] The recycling of that stereotype (the second time as farce) in Pop's deconstruction of the comic book superhero is so familiar that its subversive impact on the gender front is sometimes overlooked. The rendering via "heroic" brushwork of equally heroic juvenile role models established an equivalence between the two which enhanced the status of the latter at the expense of the former. It exposed the infantile pretensions surrounding the mythology of painting as a battlefield. The sense of cool deliberation implied in such analogues and visual puns seems totally alien to

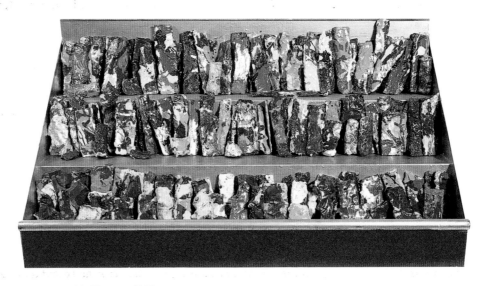

234

the "engaged," intensely *situated* Ab-Ex sensibility.

Pop unravelled the threads out of which the strongly gender-marked identities of the fifties were woven in ways that anticipated the postmodern strategy of ironic simulation. Some of Jess's paste-ups from the 1950s look like pages torn straight from a comic book. It is only when the viewer steps forward to inspect them that the transformations become apparent: the speech balloons are stuffed with word salad, the letters in the name "Dick Tracy" have been turned into an anagram...our Hero stands unmasked as one "Tricky Cad." Coming somewhat later, Lichtenstein's clean-jawed pilots, "blond hunks," and "dark and handsome" bohemian types imply acts of identification on the part of both the artist and the male viewer that takes the work close in spirit (and possibly intention) to Cindy Sherman's *Untitled Film Stills* from the late 1970s and early 1980s. These are self-portraits of Lichtenstein as mediated Everyman.

Hand-painted Pop's subversions of the "straight" are, on the whole, less blatant and direct. Consider, for instance, the delicacy with which Joe Goode leaves a real, hand-painted milk bottle by the

CLAES OLDENBURG
Candy Counter with Candy, 1961
Plaster, enamel paint, painted steel and wood case
11 1/2 x 34 3/4 x 21 3/4 inches
Anne and William J. Hokin Collection, Chicago

metaphorical stoop at the bottom of each section of the soft, evenly colored canvas of his *Milk Bottle* paintings. In one economical gesture, Color-Field Abstraction is quietly domesticated. Listen to the way Jess Collins discreetly drops his surname, shuts the door, and slips into the twilight zone between the genders. Rauschenberg's renunciation of ego and the will to mastery becomes at time so perfect that he sounds like a "New Man" before his time addressing some p.c. Artists' Collective:

I really didn't trust my own taste. .. I didn't want color to serve me, in other words—didn't want to use green to intensify red, because that would have meant subordinating green.[57]

The relations between gendered identity, sexual orientation, and taste dispositions (camp/cool/ straight) in early Pop form one productive focus of inquiry. The networks of galleries, studios, bars, and clubs in the various cities where Pop artists lived and worked functioned as the closet (this, after all, was Pop: emotions were generally kept on a tight leash) in which the psychodrama of mutual fear and admiration, suspicion and desire could be acted out. But the positions available within those "scenes" for identification were multiple and mobile and any links between a particular "type," an individual artist, and an individual work can only be tentatively posited and hypothetical.

The moratorium imposed by Pop on the "hard" and "serious" masculine stereotypes inherited from Fordism and reinforced by compulsory military service during World War II and the Korean War nonetheless remains one of Pop's enduring legacies. Daniel Wheeler describes how, in 1961, in the simulated

235

magical environment of Oldenburg's *Store* on East Second Street, the artist acted out a fantasy of passing, as "not only the capitalist entrepreneur, but also the…baker, plasterer, house painter, tailor, window dresser, shop clerk, and lighting expert."[58] Oldenburg's approach to the production of both (extra)ordinary goods (plaster pastries, soft sinks) and "ordinary" masculine identities is neither "camp" nor "cool." It allegorizes Pop's overall performance on material forms by shaking lazy notions of what constitutes real art, real life, real people —by demonstrating (WAKE UP!) that the "common man" (as both Universal Subject and as the one essential masculinity common to all men) and the "common object" (as both empiricism's raw material and as universal end and aim of History) are insubstantial figments of modernity's imagination which are melting into air.

Nonetheless, one common "place" (or more accurately, "horizon") towards which all the work on show here, including even Twombly's, might be said to be heading is the horizon of the commonplace itself. (Alternative names considered for American Pop before its official christening included *Commonism* and *Common-Image Popular Culture*.) The relation of hand-painted Pop to the "ordinary-banal" is, however, no more straightforward than its relation to the "ordinary-popular."

CLAES OLDENBURG
Money (Used in "Ray Gun Spex" Performances), 1960
Mimeograph on paper, printed on both sides (ten denominations,
each on blue, pink, and white paper), 2 x 4 1/2 inches each
Collection of Claes Oldenburg and Coosje van Bruggen, New York

VI.

banal *pertinent to all the tenants of a feudal jurisdiction C18th; open to all, (hence) commonplace
C19th; Old and modern French banal, f. ban BAN In the earliest uses "proclamation, summons to arms,"
"body of vassals summoned" C13th*   Oxford Dictionary of English Etymology

There was nothing intrinsically new about Pop's lowering of the threshold of attention to encompass the mundane details of daily life in art. The meticulous transcription onto canvas of humble objects and domestic scenes can be found as far back as the seventeenth century in Dutch genre painting. Modernists had been incorporating found imagery and urban detritus into pictorial space since the invention of collage. Pop's lineage has been traced back in this respect directly to Dada, Duchamp, Art Brut, Junk Art, Assemblage, and the Ashcan School. In addition, there are literary precedents not just for Pop's disciplined attention to surface (the "realist" novel from Fielding and Defoe onwards) but for the later experiments with accentuated focus and inverted scale (Oldenburg and Rosenquist are visual art's reply to Lawrence Sterne and Alain Robbe-Grillet). Even the efforts made by Oldenburg and Rauschenberg to integrate chance and coincidence into their daily work routines have their literary equivalents—Baudelaire's "botanizing on the asphalt"; Joyce's epiphanies; Dos Passos's "newsreel" novels; Burroughs's cut-ups.

But the roots of Pop's investment in "ordinary" surface are more profound and widely spread than such purely formal comparisons and linear chronologies will allow. There are other standards by which the quality of Pop's attachment to the structured contingencies of everyday life can be assessed. After all, Sigmund Freud had developed the conjectural "science" of psychoanalytic method by re-viewing the underrated "ordinary," learning, in the process, (to use his own words), "to divine secret and concealed things from despised or unnoticed features, from the rubbish-heap, as it were of our observations."[59]

236

We are unable to seize the human facts. We fail to see them where they are, namely in humble, familiar, everyday objects.... Our search for the human takes us too far, too "deep." We seek it in the clouds or in mysteries, whereas it is waiting for us, besieging us on all sides.... "The familiar is not necessarily

CLAES OLDENBURG
Untitled (detail), 1960
Newspaper collage with watercolor on Rheingold Beer promotional pamphlet
13 x 10 1/2 inches
Collection of Claes Oldenburg and Coosje van Bruggen, New York

the known" said Hegel. Let us go farther and say that it is in the most familiar things that the unknown — not the mysterious — is at its richest.   Henri Lefebvre[60]

In the light of these remarks, Pop's "clean break" with abstraction is once more placed in doubt. One of the many legacies inherited from Abstract Expressionism (e.g., large-scale single-image structures) was the skepticism, manifest throughout Pop art and the Pop sensibility, toward all meta-narratives, Hegelian or otherwise. According to Daniel Wheeler, the mid-century collapse of "every solution — Marxist, nationalist, Utopian...along with all the art, whether representational or non-objective, that had accompanied it" had produced a "crisis of subject matter" which the Abstract Expressionists would resolve through the exposition of intensely private gestures embodying deeply felt social, psychological, and moral concerns.[61] Though Pop is often interpreted as a wholesale repudiation of both this crisis *and* solution, I believe it is more usefully regarded as a further exploration of the same predicament *by other means.*

I think the objects are more or less chosen as excuses or tangible things that I can hang my expression of what it feels like to be alive on.... And I think it's a more abstract concern than appears.   Claes Oldenburg[62]

One of Pop's most distinctive strategies involves moving in microscopically on the familiar to de-familiarize it. The eye is forced to make rapid adjustments of focus as the contours of some object that we feel we should recognize dissolve into patterns of fractal complexity. We are thrown *through* the object into Chaos. The world that William Blake held in a grain of sand is revealed to be a "Ball of Confusion." Here the seductive power of the object explored in Pop meets Abstract Expressionism's tortured expiation of the subject moving out onto the picture plane from the opposite direction. At the point of merger the artist, on either side, is rigorously decentered from the work. Thus, Pollock's manic immersion in the process of production ("When I am in my painting I'm not aware of what I'm doing"[63]) is matched in a cooler, more ironic mode by the Incredible Shrinking Man routines performed by Rosenquist in his billboard painting days, when, swinging in a cradle high above the street or studio floor, he reduced himself to the diminutive proportions of a human speck lost in outered space.[64]

As so often when we consider the relationship of Pop to Ab-Ex, the metaphor that most adequately "explains" the relations of misrecognition and mutual disavowal that simultaneously lock the two movements together and keep them perpetually apart is the mirror.

The inversions and reversals Pop performed on the flat-bed body of Ab-Ex (and vice-versa) were psychotically symmetrical. Oldenburg's stated ambitions to "spiritualize American experience" and "to look for beauty where it is not to be found"[65] bear facetious comparison with Barnett Newman's project, but the tactics he chose in projects like *The Street* and *The Store* for "othering" the industrial processes and retail rituals that make America tick were diametrically opposed to Newman's austere bracketing of the world beyond the frame. Oldenburg's baggy household appliances and "inedible edibles" turn Kant upside down to produce a new paradoxical order of confusion: the ridiculous sublime. If the Abstract Expressionists, in Newman's famous phrase, set about "making it out of ourselves," Oldenburg showed how it was possible to make ourselves out of it, how to make a subject out of an object. His objective, he once wrote: "to make hostile objects human."[66]

There is no poor subject. A pair of socks is no less suitable to make a painting than wood, nails, turpentine, oil and fabric.   Robert Rauschenberg[67]

237

VII.

Do not get yourselves entangled with any object, but stand above, pass on and be free. Master Rinzai[68]

Jesus said: Become passers by. The Gospel of St. Thomas[69]

Oldenburg's hyperrealizations of the "ordinary" and the "typical" in the sculptures and happenings of the early 1960s were motivated by the same will to transcendence through worldly imbrication that dictated early Pop's return to figurative painting. Both practices display that passionate and vigilant attachment to what Allan Kaprow called the "nameless sludge and whirl of urban events"[70] that marks the I-did-this-then-I-did-that style of Frank O'Hara's *Lunch-Time Poems*, the "uncontrolled shooting" and "open editing" of Direct Cinema, John Cage's aleatory music and philosophy, the meandering-inclusive style of a *spritz* by Lenny Bruce. Far from being a capitulation to the existing social order as critics more at home with Leftist theology or the tragic variety of existentialism are prone to suggest, early Pop and proto-Pop (*as well as* Jackson Pollock) formed part of that reaction to the social, cultural, and conceptual hierarchies associated with European influence which made a mature, independent critical culture in North America for the first time fully possible. That culture would be deliberately eclectic — as tuned into Buddhism and to *jijimuge*, "the unimpeded interdiffusion of all particulars,"[71] as to Parisian Surrealism, "automatic writing," Levi-Strauss, and *bricolage*. It would permit itself to let things happen ("A happening is…something that just happens to happen" [Kaprow][72]) as well as to act and to agonize on the edges of the action,

> *…to hold the mind in enormous concentration of purpose, yet utterly relaxed; to seek intensely, knowing that the effort itself bars us from success; to see that the littlest act is of vital importance yet what we do is of no importance at all.*[73]

It would respond to the

> *…art of the jolt…more subversive than violence [which]* does not grasp at anything…*is situated…floats and drifts between the desire which, in subtle fashion, guides the hand, and politeness, which is the discreet refusal of any captivating ambition.*[74]

And it would find that art not only in the place where Roland Barthes had found it, in the wisdom of Cy Twombly's painting, but wherever it occurs — in the break across the bars when it erupts in a John Coltrane or Charlie Parker solo, in the sudden mid-phrase stop that freezes, one beat back, then drags the note right down and off the scale in a Billie Holliday performance. It would find it in the moment when the man we had been watching on our television screens, writhing in silence beneath the blows administered by four other men, night after night, for more than a year, finally stood up again one day in April, 1992, stumbled painfully, blinking, out into the light, visibly distressed, supported by his lawyer and a circle of friends, to hold a press conference he clearly never wanted to give but felt he had to give. It would find it in the moment when, battling with shot nerves and emotions, this man looked into the cameras and said:

> *We're just here for a while. Can we all get along? Can't we stop making it horrible for the older people and the kids? It's just not right. It's not going to change anything. We'll get our justice. We'll have our day in court.*[75]

The equation of Pop with surface, of surface with "banality" in the pejorative sense originally attaching to that term in pre-revolutionary France, is to fail to acknowledge how a sustained and disciplined attention to the material circumstances of our lives is the only basis on which a humane, that is a genuinely other-centered ethic, might be built in a world where nothing, no outcomes and no values — including even the value of our witness — is ever guaranteed.

1   Quoted in G. R. Swenson, "What is Pop Art? Answers from Eight Painters, Part 1," *Art News* 62, no. 7 (November 1963): 27, 63.

2   Philip Brophy, "As Deaf as a Bat" in P. Brophy, S. Dermody, D. Hebdige, S. Muecke, *Streetwide Flash Art: Is There a Future for Cultural Studies?* Power Institute of Fine Arts Occasional Papers, no. 6. (Sydney: University of Sydney, 1987), p. 19.

3   Richard Hamilton, "An Exposition of $he," *Architectural Design* 32, no. 10 (October 1962): 73.

4   Susan Sontag, "Against Interpretation" in *Against Interpretation* (New York: Farrar, Straus & Giroux, 1961), p. 12.

5   Taken from Louis Marcorelles, *Living Cinema: New Directions in Contemporary Film-Making* (London: Allen & Unwin Ltd., 1973), p. 63.

"Albert Maysles (the Direct Cinema film-maker) and his brother once studied psychology and they quote with conviction his credo" (i.e. the Bacon quote). The context indicates that this is Francis Bacon (1561-1626), the British empirical philosopher, not Francis Bacon (1909-1992), the British painter.

6   Sontag, "Against Interpretation," p. 13.

7   Richard Hamilton, quoted in *Modern Dreams: The Rise and Fall and Rise of Pop* (Cambridge, Mass.: MIT Press, 1988), p. 42.

8   Lawrence Alloway, "The Long Front of Culture" (1959), ibid., p. 31.

9   Grace Hartigan, statement in a catalogue for a 1983 exhibition at the Avery Center for the Arts at Bard College entitled *Distinct Visions: Expressionist Sensibilities* (Annandale-on-Hudson, New York: Avery Center for the Arts, Bard College, 1983), unpag.

10   Daniel Wheeler, *Art Since Mid-Century* (London: Thames & Hudson, 1991), p. 187. The present essay is indebted to this excellent survey which is particularly impressive in its comprehensive and knowledgeable treatment of North American art in the designated period.

11   Michael Auping, *Jess: Paste-Ups (and Assemblies) 1951-1983* (Sarasota, Fla.: The John and Mable Ringling Museum of Art, 1983), p. 13.

12   Quoted in Leo Rubinfien, "Through Western Eyes," *Art in America* 66, no. 5 (Sept.-Oct. 1978), p. 78.

10   Robert M. Pirsig, *Zen and the Art of Motorcycle Maintenance* rev. ed. (Toronto and New York: Bantam, 1984), p. 76.

CLAES OLDENBURG
U.S.A. Flag, 1960
Muslin soaked in plaster over wire frame, painted with tempera
24 x 30 x 3 1/2 inches
Collection of Claes Oldenburg and Coosje van Bruggen, New York

14 David Hickey, "Available Light," in *The Works of Edward Ruscha* (San Francisco: San Francisco Museum of Modern Art, 1982), p. 24.

15 Sontag, "Against Interpretation," p. 14.

16 Hickey, "Available Light," p. 24.

17 From a statement written by Claes Oldenburg for the catalogue of a 1961 exhibition entitled "Environments, Situations, Spaces" at the Martha Jackson Gallery, New York. Reprinted in Barbara Rose, *Claes Oldenburg* (New York: Museum of Modern Art, 1970), p. 190.

18 Andy Warhol and Pat Hackett, *POPism: The Warhol '60s* (New York and London: Harcourt Brace Jovanovich, 1980), pp. 34-35.

19 Leo Steinberg, "Jasper Johns: The First Seven Years of His Art" in *Other Criteria: Confrontations with Twentieth-Century Art* (New York: Oxford University Press, 1972), p. 22.

20 Ibid.

21 David Deitcher, "Wild History," in *Comic Iconoclasm* (London: Institute of Contemporary Arts, 1987), p. 86.

22 Wheeler, *Art Since Mid-Century*, p. 122.

23 Quoted in Jeanne Siegel, *Artwords: Discourse on the 60s and 70s* rev. ed. (New York: da Capo Press, 1992), p. 184.

24 John Coplans, "An Observed Conversation" (with Leo Castelli, Alanna Heiss, Betsey Johnson, Roy Lichtenstein and Claes Oldenburg) in *Modern Dreams*, p. 87.

25 Dick Hebdige, "In Poor Taste: Notes on Pop," in ibid., p. 85.

26 Lichtenstein quoted in Simon Wilson, *Pop* (London: Thames & Hudson, 1974), p. 4.

27 Warhol and Hackett, *POPism*, p. 1.

28 Greenberg in "Abstract, Representational, and So Forth," quoted in Steinberg, "Other Criteria," in *Other Criteria*, p. 67.

29 Harold Rosenberg, "The American Action Painters," *Art News* (December 1952): 22-23.

30 Henry Geldzahler quoted in *POPism*, p. 3.

31 Quoted in Wheeler, *Art Since Mid-Century*, p. 131.

32 Brian O'Doherty, "Lichtenstein: Doubtful but Definite Triumph of the Banal," *New York Times*, 27 October 1963, quoted in Deitcher, "Wild History," p. 84. "Brian O'Doherty" is the pseudonym used by Patrick Ireland.

33 Quoted in Lucy R. Lippard, *Pop Art* (New York: Praeger, 1966.), pp. 153-54.

34 Steinberg, "Jasper Johns: The First Seven Years of His Art," p. 42.

35 Brophy, "As Deaf as a Bat," p. 19. The next few sentences develop the argument and "explain" the essay title:

"...Beethoven may have still composed when deaf, but how much analysing of other works did he do? If material effects are the primary means of facilitating our perceptual encoding, our focus should be scrutinized as much as our discourse. This possibility of inaccurate focus is the most pervasive and haunting fear of cultural studies. Like a nightmare effect erupting into the following day's domain, it exists in the morning papers, the weekly reviews, the term lectures, the quarterly journals, the yearly forums — as deaf as a bat."

36 Sontag, "Against Interpretation," p. 14.

37 Brophy, "As Deaf as a Bat," p. 20.

38 Sontag, p. 10.

39 Jean Baudrillard, *Revenge of the Crystal: Selected Writings on the Modern Object and Its Destiny, 1968–1983*, ed. and trans. Paul Foss and Julian Pefanis. (London and Concord, Mass.: Pluto Press, in association with the Power Institute of Fine Arts, University of Sydney, 1990), p. 82.

40 Ibid., p. 83.

41 Steinberg, "Objectivity and the Shrinking Self," in *Other Criteria*, p. 321.

42 Warhol and Hackett, *POPism*, p. 39.

43 Quoted in George Brundt, ed., *British Television Drama* (New York: MacMillan, 1976).

44 Warhol and Hackett, *POPism*, p. 40.

45 Claes Oldenburg quoted in Baudrillard, *Revenge of the Crystal*, pp. 82–83.

46 See, for example, Tom Wolfe, *The Kandy-Kolored Tangerine-Flake Streamline Baby* (1965), and *The Pump House Gang* (1968), and Robert Venturi, *Learning from Las Vegas*.

47 Quoted in Anne Livet, "Introduction: Collage and Beyond," in *The Works of Edward Ruscha*, p. 14.

48 Quoted in Henry T. Hopkins, "A Remembrance of the Emerging Los Angeles Art Scene," in *Billy Al Bengston: Paintings of Three Decades* (Houston: Contemporary Arts Museum; Oakland: The Oakland Museum; and San Francisco: Chronicle Books, 1988), p. 41.

49 Ibid.

50 Hebdige, "In Poor Taste: Notes on Pop," and "Towards a Cartography of Taste 1935-1962," in *Hiding in the Light: On Images and Things* (New York: Routledge, 1988), pp. 45-76, 116-143.

51 See Andrew Ross, *No Respect: Intellectuals and Popular Culture* (New York: Routledge, 1989).

52 Warhol and Hackett, *POPism*, p. 12.

53 Ibid., p. 15.

54 Ross, "The Death of Lady Day," in Lyn Hejinian and Barrett Watten, eds., *Poetics Journal*, no. 8 (June 1989): 74.

55 Ibid., p. 70. Ross's remarks on O'Hara's personal code are highly pertinent to the arguments put forward in the present essay:

"O'Hara's poetry rejects the big, global questions of politics and economics, even the big "artistic" questions of aesthetics. His is certainly not a heroic poetics of self-reliance or self-making in the transcendent, Emersonian tradition, nor does it make a pragmatic religion out of individualism, in the American grain. Instead it subscribes to the micropolitics of personal detail, faithfully noting down dates, times, events, feelings, moods, fears, and so on, and devoting a bricoleur's disciplined attention to details in the world and in the people around him. O'Hara's is a code of personal politics, which says that at some level you have to take responsibility for your own conduct in the everyday world and towards others; you can't rely on organized politics or unorganized religions to change that. It is a code which starts from what we find lying, unplanned, around us, rather than from achieved utopias of the body and mind. In 1959, well before the coming riots of self-liberation, this was a mannered way of saying: take things into your own hands."

56 Larry Rivers quoted in Warhol and Hackett, *POPism*, p. 14.

57 Quoted in Wheeler, *Art Since Mid-Century*, p. 129.

58 Ibid., p. 143.

59 Sigmund Freud, "The Moses of Michelangelo," in James Strachey, ed., *The Standard Edition of the Complete Psychological Works of Sigmund Freud* vol. 13 (London: Hogarth Press, 1966-73), p. 222.

60 Henri Lefebvre, *Critique of Everyday Life* vol. 1 (Paris, 1947). John Moore, trans. (London: Verso, 1991), pp. 132-33.

61 Wheeler, p. 25.

62 Quoted in Siegel, *Artwords*, p. 183.

63 Jackson Pollock quoted in Wheeler, p. 43. "When I am painting I have a general notion as to what I am about; I can control the flow of paint; there is no accident."

240

64 Rosenquist's interest in perceptual oddities led him in the 1960s to explore the mechanics of peripheral vision and "...a phenomenon called 'circles of confusion,' which are little balls of color that start moving around...there's a reflection in your eye that causes strange things to happen...[I]t was trying to see something while a person was looking into a vacant area like straight up into the sky, at a plain white wall, meditating. What happens if you look and look and look—you see spots in front of your eyes." Rosenquist quoted in Siegel, *Artwords*, p. 201.

65 Quoted in Wheeler, p. 142.

66 Ibid.

67 Ibid., p. 127.

68 From Irmgard Schloegl, trans., *The Zen Teachings of Rinzai* (Berkeley, Calif.: Shambhala Publications, 1976).

Lin-Chi (in Japanese, Rinzai) carried on the line of "sudden" Zen teaching introduced by Ma-tsu (709-788) and continued by Huai-hai, Huang-Po, and Hui-neng. Lin-Chi (814-866) founded the Rinzai sect which was taken by Master Ensai to Japan in the late twelfth century, where its rough, spontaneous and illogical style (enlightenment "provoked" by slaps, kicks, shouts, and violent paradox) found immediate favor with the Samurai class. The "sudden" school of zen enlightenment is contrasted with the gentler, more gradualist approach of the Soto school.

Humphreys elaborates:

"For Hui-neng nothing is, nor dust nor Mind and and there is nothing to be 'done' by anyone. (Cf. the Taoist Wu-wei, or 'action in inaction'). For him there is no How in life, nor What nor When nor Why. There IS—the rest is silence, and a finger pointing to the Way. That is what Dr. Suzuki calls 'dynamic demonstration,' and it ranges from utter silence, to anything, a gesture, or cough, or a blow, which will fully arouse the waking awareness of the agonized disciple."

Quoted in Christmas Humphreys, *Zen: A Way of Life* (London: English Universities Press, 1962), p. 89.

69 C. M. Tuckett, ed., *Nag Hammadi and the Gospel Tradition: Synoptic Tradition in the Nag Hammadi Library* (Edinburgh: T. & T. Clark, 1986).

70 Allan Kaprow quoted in Wheeler, p. 167.

71 *Jijimuge* is a key term in the Japanese Kegon School of Zen. Outlining the changes wrought on the Theravada ("Teaching of the Elders") body of Buddhist teaching by the emergence of the Mahayana School (with which Zen shares the Bodhisattva doctrine), Christmas Humphreys writes:

"The general effect of the change...of the Mahayana School was to raise a moral philosophy of right action to a mystical idealism of spiritual becoming which engaged the total man. Emphasis shifted from the Arhat ideal of the "worthy" one to that of the Bodhisattva, the master of compassion....In the field of philosophy and psychology there was a lift from a somewhat materialistic view of cause-effect and the cycles of becoming to the supernal doctrines of Sunyata, the Voidness of Emptiness of all things, and of *Jijimuge*, the Japanese term for the "unimpeded interdiffusion of all particulars," as Dr. Suzuki translates the term....If these concepts are still in the realm of duality, and in the field of Samsara, everyday life, they are surely near to the breakthrough to Non-duality, an awareness of the Absolute. The intellect...can never grasp directly, and can only know *about* the subject of inquiry. When *Jijimuge* is grasped even at the conceptual level the reach of concept is all but attained, and thought can go no further."

Humphreys, *Zen: A Way of Life* p. 58.

Elsewhere, Humphreys elaborates: "...the *Jijimuge* doctrine...destroys all false antitheses. The world of distinction is seen to be falsely imagined; discrimination falls away. In application, "there is nothing infinite apart from finite things," naught holy nor profane. There is neither here nor there, for all is always Here; there is neither now nor then, for all is Now; there is neither this nor that, still less a fusion of this and THAT, for there is only This, in a here and now."

Christmas Humphreys, *Buddhism* (London: Penguin, 1951), p. 17. See also pp. 151-52.

English-language translations of Zen teachings and accessible exegeses like those provided by Humphreys had an enormous impact (together with the constant pulse of trans-Pacific immigration/emigration to and from the West Coast) on the formation of a distinctive counter cultural ethos and aesthetic in the U.S.A. in the post-World War II period. Zen has "shaken" successive generations of (mainly white) American "dharma bums" from the Beats to the yippies and beyond. It shaped Merce Cunningham's theory of dance and John Cage's affirmative philosophy of contingency, happenstance and happy chance. To my knowledge there is little work as yet on the impact of Zen on African-American intellectual culture during this period, though the influence of Eastern traditions of art and thought on the sonic philosophy of, for instance, Pharoah Saunders, Alice Coltrane, Archie Shepp, Albert Ayler, and Sun Ra in the 1960s would be difficult to miss.

72 Allan Kaprow quoted in Wheeler, p. 179. Kaprow further defines a Happening as:

"an assemblage of events performed or perceived in more than one time and place. Its material environments may be constructed, taken over directly from what is available, or altered slightly; just as its activities may be invented or commonplace. A Happening, unlike a stage play, may occur at a supermarket, driving along a highway, under a pile of rags, and in a friend's kitchen, either at once or sequentially. If sequentially, time may extend to more than a year. The Happening is performed according to plan but without rehearsal, audience, or repetition. It is art but seems closer to life."

See Wheeler, p. 178.

73 Humphreys, *Zen: A Way of Life*, pp. 96-97.

74 Roland Barthes, "The Wisdom of Cy Twombly's Painting," from the catalogue of a 1979 one-man show held at the Whitney Museum of American Art, New York, quoted in Harold Szeemann, ed., *Cy Twombly: Paintings, Works on Paper, Sculpture* (Munich: Prestel-Verlag, 1987), p. 32.

75 Rodney King, quoted in the *Los Angeles Times*, 1 May 1992. A footnote to an article on early Pop would seem, on the face of it, hardly the place for a discussion of the events immediately following the public announcement on April 29, 1992 of the acquittal of LAPD officers Wind, Briseno, Powell, and Koon on a range of charges stemming from the "forceful apprehension" of Rodney King more than a year earlier. However, the proactive (rather than reactive) role of televised images in the chain of events leading from the chance video recording, taken by amateur cameraman George Holliday, of the beating administered to King in the early hours of March 3, 1991 to the "fly on the wall" shots taken by professional broadcasters (often hanging six hundred feet above the "action") of looted shops, burning buildings, and revenge attacks on white motorists raises questions about the equivocal value of "banal" or "mundane" witness which are germane to the present argument.

If an "ordinary" (white) bystander with no ostensible stake in the fate of a (black) stranger inadvertently succeeded in exposing the "standard" procedure adopted in the relevant circumstances by arresting officers, then the "normal" practices of "neutral" reportage undertaken by professional broadcasters certainly succeeded in provoking an "extra-ordinary" reaction (i.e., the notorious "heating up" effect of live, on-the-spot news coverage). It would not be stretching a point to say that hand-painted Pop, in its fascination with the power of mediated imagery, in its recognition of the subversive potential of the "typical" and the neglected "ordinary," falls between both these possibilities. Perhaps what is truly extraordinary about Mr. King's statement, given, unrehearsed, at the height of the L.A. riots, is that it went so directly against the grain of normal expectations. The affects and effects triggered by that statement and the events that preceded and provoked it will resonate for years to come. However, the sudden jolt to standard expectations will reverberate, too, in that moment when the "object" of public media and judicial attention transformed at last before our eyes and ears into a subject. What is perhaps extraordinary about that moment is that when the subaltern (finally) got to speak, he cut through all the (fabulous) confusion.

JIM DINE
Black Tools in a Landscape, 1962
Collage and oil with objects, 36 x 48 inches
Moderna Museet, Stockholm

Checklist of the Exhibition

BILLY AL BENGSTON

Untitled, 1957
Oil on canvas, 13 x 17 inches
Collection of the artist
Page 210

Untitled, 1957
Oil on canvas, 13 x 17 inches
Collection of the artist
Page 211

Grace, 1959
Oil on canvas, 49 3/4 x 42 1/2 inches
Collection of Betty Asher, Beverly Hills
Page 212

Count Dracula II, 1960
Oil on canvas, 48 x 48 inches
Newport Harbor Art Museum
Purchased by the Acquisition Council with a
matching grant from the National Endowment for
the Arts, a federal agency
Page 213

JIM DINE

The Checkerboard, 1959
Oil and collage on checkerboard
18 1/4 x 18 1/4 inches
Private collection, New York
Page 75

Crash Drawing with White Cross #1,
1959
Ink and gouache on paper
25 1/2 x 19 1/2 inches
Private collection, New York
Page 79

Crash Drawing with White Cross #2,
1959
Ink and gouache on paper
25 1/2 x 19 1/2 inches
Private collection, New York
Page 79

Green Suit, 1959
Oil and cloth, 62 x 24 inches
Private collection, New York
Page 75

The Blonde Girls, 1960
Oil, charcoal, and rope
2 panels: 78 x 50 inches each
Collection of Sarah Goodwin Austin, New York
Page 76

The Valiant Red Car, 1960
Oil on canvas, 53 x 132 inches
National Museum of American Art,
Smithsonian Institution, Washington, D.C.
Gift of Mr. and Mrs. David K. Anderson, Martha
Jackson Memorial Collection
Page 78

Flesh Tie, 1961
Oil on canvas
16 x 22 inches
Collection of Jasper Johns, New York
Page 75

The Red Bandana, 1961
Oil on canvas, 62 x 54 inches
Private collection, New York
Page 74

Black Tools in a Landscape, 1962
Collage and oil with objects, 36 x 48 inches
Moderna Museet, Stockholm
Page 242

Black Zipper, 1962
Oil and mixed media on canvas, 96 x 72 inches
The Sonnabend Collection, New York
Page 77

JEAN FOLLETT

Lady with the Open Door Stomach, 1956
Painted wood, gravel, and metal
46 3/4 x 48 x 3 inches
Whitney Museum of American Art, New York
Purchase, with funds from an anonymous donor
63.60
Page 71

Many-Headed Creature, 1958
Assemblage: light switch, cooling coils, window
screen, nails, faucet knob, mirror, twine, cinders,
etc., on wood panel, 24 x 24 x 4 3/4 inches
The Museum of Modern Art, New York
Larry Aldrich Foundation Fund, 1961
Page 72

JOE GOODE

Milk Bottle Painting (Green), 1961-62
Oil on canvas with oil on glass milk bottle
67 1/2 x 66 inches
Collection of James Corcoran, Malibu, California
Page 226

Milk Bottle Painting (Two-Part Blue),
1961-62
Oil on canvas with oil on glass milk bottle
68 1/2 x 66 inches
Collection of the artist
Page 226

244

Popeye, 1961
Oil on canvas, 42 x 56 inches
Collection of David Lichtenstein, New York
Page 48

Ring-Ring, 1961
Oil on canvas, 24 x 16 inches
Courtesy of James Goodman Gallery, New York
Page 84

Roller Skates, 1961
Oil on canvas, 42 x 40 inches
Collection of Pontus Bonnier, Stockholm
Page 106

Turkey, 1961
Oil on canvas, 26 x 30 inches
Collection of Mitchell Lichtenstein, New York
Page 107

Calendar, 1962
Oil on canvas, 48 1/2 x 70 inches
The Museum of Contemporary Art, Los Angeles
The Panza Collection
Page 8

Cherry Pie, 1962
Oil on canvas, 20 x 24 inches
The Sydney and Frances Lewis Collection,
Richmond, Virginia
Page 115

Cigarette, 1962
Oil on canvas, 12 x 34 inches
Private collection
Page 109

Curtains, 1962
Oil and magna on canvas, 68 3/4 x 58 1/2 inches
The Saint Louis Art Museum
Gift of Mr. and Mrs. Joseph Pulitzer, Jr.
Page 85

The Grip, 1962
Oil on canvas, 30 x 30 1/4 inches
The Museum of Contemporary Art, Los Angeles
The Panza Collection
Page 111

Like New, 1962
Oil on canvas, Diptych: 36 x 28 inches each
Collection of Robert and Jane Rosenblum,
New York
(Los Angeles only)
Page 47

Man with Folded Arms, 1962
Oil on canvas, 70 x 48 1/2 inches
The Museum of Contemporary Art, Los Angeles
The Panza Collection
Page 108

Sponge II, 1962
Oil on canvas, 36 x 36 inches
Collection of Peder Bonnier, New York
Page 119

Swiss Cheese, 1962
Oil on canvas
40 x 40 inches
Collection of David Lichtenstein, New York
Page 114

Large Jewels, 1963
Magna on canvas, 68 x 36 inches
Museum Ludwig, Cologne
Page 113

CLAES OLDENBURG

Untitled (Illustration for *Chicago* magazine),
1955
Charcoal on paper, mounted on cardboard with
masking tape, 6 3/8 x 7 inches
Collection of Claes Oldenburg and Coosje van
Bruggen, New York
Page 81

Skid Row Figure, 1957
Ink on paper, mounted on cardboard
10 3/4 x 5 1/2 inches
Collection of Claes Oldenburg and Coosje van
Bruggen, New York
Page 81

**Study for an Homage to Céline and
Dubuffet,** 1959
Pencil on paper, 11 x 8 1/2 inches
Collection of Claes Oldenburg and Coosje van
Bruggen, New York
Page 81

Self-Portrait, 1959
Oil on canvas, 68 x 47 1/2 inches
Collection of Claes Oldenburg and Coosje van
Bruggen, New York
Page 66

Money (Used in "Ray Gun Spex" Performances),
1960
Mimeograph on paper, printed on both sides (ten
denominations, each on blue, pink, and white
paper), 2 x 4 1/2 inches each
Collection of Claes Oldenburg and Coosje van
Bruggen, New York
Page 235

"Ray Gun Poster"—U.S. Death Heart #2,
1960
Monoprint, 17 3/4 x 11 7/8 inches
Collection of Claes Oldenburg and Coosje van
Bruggen, New York
Page 80

Truck-Pants, 1960
Painted cardboard with charcoal
22 1/2 x 20 1/2 inches
The Sonnabend Collection, New York
Page 232

Untitled, 1960
Newspaper collage with watercolor on Rheingold
Beer promotional pamphlet, 13 x 10 1/2 inches
Collection of Claes Oldenburg and Coosje van
Bruggen, New York
Page 236

U.S.A. Flag, 1960
Muslin soaked in plaster over wire frame, painted
with tempera, 24 x 30 x 3 1/2 inches
Collection of Claes Oldenburg and Coosje van
Bruggen, New York
Page 239

Blue and Pink Panties, 1961
Muslin soaked in plaster over wire frame, painted
with enamel, 62 1/4 x 34 3/4 x 6 inches
The Museum of Contemporary Art, Los Angeles
The Panza Collection
Page 230

Candy Counter with Candy, 1961
Plaster, enamel paint, painted steel and wood
case, 11 1/2 x 34 3/4 x 21 3/4 inches
Anne and William J. Hokin Collection, Chicago
Page 234

Chocolates in Box (Fragment), 1961
Muslin soaked in plaster over wire frame, painted
with enamel, 44 x 32 x 6 inches
The Museum of Contemporary Art, Los Angeles
The Panza Collection
Page 231

Cigarettes in Pack Fragment, 1961
Muslin soaked in plaster over wire frame, painted
with enamel, 32 3/4 x 30 3/4 x 6 3/4 inches
The Museum of Contemporary Art; Los Angeles
The Panza Collection
Page 231

Green Legs with Shoes, 1961
Muslin soaked in plaster over wire frame, painted
with enamel, 46 x 42 x 8 inches
Museum Ludwig, Cologne
Page 231

Green Stockings, 1961
Muslin soaked in plaster over wire frame, painted
with enamel, 43 1/4 x 18 inches
The Museum of Contemporary Art, Los Angeles
The Panza Collection
Page 230

INJUN Poster, 1961
Monoprint, 13 15/16 x 17 inches
Collection of Claes Oldenburg and Coosje van
Bruggen, New York
Page 80

Man's Shoe, 1961
Muslin soaked in plaster over wire frame, painted
with enamel, 23 1/2 x 43 1/4 inches
The Museum of Contemporary Art, Los Angeles
The Panza Collection
Page 232

245

246

ANDY WARHOL
Superman, 1960
Synthetic polymer paint and crayon on canvas
67 x 52 inches
Gunter Sachs Collection, Paris

Mu Mu, 1961
Muslin soaked in plaster over wire frame, painted
with enamel, 63 1/3 x 41 1/3 x 4 inches
The Museum of Contemporary Art, Los Angeles
The Panza Collection
Page 230

Pepsi-Cola Sign, 1961
Muslin soaked in plaster over wire frame, painted
with enamel, 58 1/4 x 46 1/2 x 7 1/2 inches
The Museum of Contemporary Art, Los Angeles
The Panza Collection
Page 229

Red Tights with Fragment 9, 1961
Muslin soaked in plaster over wire frame, painted
with enamel, 69 5/8 x 34 1/4 x 8 3/4 inches
The Museum of Modern Art, New York
Gift of G. David Thompson, 1961
Page 231

Stockinged Thighs Framed by Skirt, 1961
Muslin soaked in plaster over wire frame, painted
with enamel, 34 3/8 x 41 3/8 x 6 inches
Collection of Holly Solomon, New York
Page 230

Store Cross, 1961
Muslin soaked in plaster over wire frame, painted
with enamel, 52 3/4 x 40 1/2 x 6 inches
The Museum of Contemporary Art, Los Angeles
The Panza Collection
Page 228

MEL RAMOS

Tourist, 1960
Oil on canvas, 50 x 44 inches
Collection of Joyce and Jay Cooper, Phoenix
Page 174

Superman, 1961
Oil on canvas, 40 x 30 inches
Collection of Skot Ramos, Burbank, California
Page 175

The Joker, 1962
Oil on canvas, 50 x 44 inches
Guess, Inc., Marciano Collection, Los Angeles
Page 162

ROBERT RAUSCHENBERG

Hymnal, 1955
Combine painting, 64 x 49 1/4 x 7 1/4 inches
The Sonnabend Collection, New York
Page 35

Interview, 1955
Combine painting, 72 3/4 x 49 1/4 inches
The Museum of Contemporary Art, Los Angeles
The Panza Collection
Page 33

Untitled, 1955
Combine painting, 15 1/2 x 20 3/4 inches
Collection of Jasper Johns, New York
Page 31

**Untitled Combine (Man with White
Shoes),** 1955
Combine painting, 86 1/2 x 37 x 26 1/3 inches
The Museum of Contemporary Art, Los Angeles
The Panza Collection
(Los Angeles only)
Page 32

Interior, 1956
Combine painting, 45 1/4 x 46 1/2 x 7 1/2 inches
The Sonnabend Collection, New York
Page 35

Small Rebus, 1956
Combine painting, 35 x 46 inches
The Museum of Contemporary Art, Los Angeles
The Panza Collection
Page 34

Factum I, 1957
Combine painting, 61 1/2 x 35 3/4 inches
The Museum of Contemporary Art, Los Angeles
The Panza Collection
Page 28

Coca Cola Plan, 1958
Combine painting, 26 3/4 x 25 1/4 x 4 3/4 inches
The Museum of Contemporary Art, Los Angeles
The Panza Collection
Page 256

Broadcast, 1959
Combine painting, 61 x 75 x 5 inches
Collection of Kimiko and John Powers,
Carbondale, Colorado
Page 36

Inlet, 1959
Combine painting, 84 1/2 x 48 inches
The Museum of Contemporary Art, Los Angeles
The Panza Collection
Page 10

Kickback, 1959
Combine painting, 76 1/2 x 33 1/4 x 2 3/4 inches
The Museum of Contemporary Art, Los Angeles
The Panza Collection
Page 37

Photograph, 1959
Combine painting, 46 3/8 x 54 5/8 x 2 3/4 inches
Collection of Marcia and Irving Stenn, Chicago
Page 38

Octave, 1960
Combine painting, 78 x 43 inches
Collection of Mr. and Mrs. Bagley Wright, Seattle
Page 39

Reservoir, 1961
Combine painting
85 1/2 x 62 1/2 x 14 3/4 inches
National Museum of American Art,
Smithsonian Institution, Washington, D.C.
Gift of S. C. Johnson & Son, Inc.
Page 37

LARRY RIVERS

Washington Crossing the Delaware, 1953
Oil, graphite, and charcoal on linen
83 5/8 x 111 5/8 inches
The Museum of Modern Art, New York
Given anonymously
(Los Angeles only)
Page 18

Europe I, 1956
Oil on canvas, 72 x 48 inches
The Minneapolis Institute of Arts
Anonymous gift
Page 24

The Studio, 1956
Oil on canvas, 82 1/2 x 193 1/2 inches
The Minneapolis Institute of Arts
John R. Van Derlip Fund
Page 22

Buick Painting with P, 1960
Oil on canvas, 48 x 61 inches
Collection of Mr. and Mrs. Richard Titelman,
Atlanta
Page 25

The Final Veteran, 1960
Oil on canvas, 81 3/8 x 51 inches
Albright-Knox Art Gallery, Buffalo, New York
Gift of The Seymour H. Knox Foundation,
Inc., 1961
Page 25

JAMES ROSENQUIST

Astor Victoria, 1959
Billboard enamel on canvas
67 5/16 x 82 3/4 inches
Collection of the artist
Page 49

President Elect, 1960
Poster illustration and magazine advertisements
with pencil, paint, masking tape, and paper,
mounted on paper, 17 1/2 x 32 inches
Collection of the artist
Page 52

President Elect, 1960-61
Oil on masonite, 84 x 144 inches
Musée National d'Art Moderne, Centre Georges
Pompidou, Paris
Page 53

247

Pushbutton, 1960
Magazine advertisement with tape, pencil, paper,
and colored paper, mounted on paper
11 1/2 x 13 1/2 inches
Collection of the artist
Page 51

Zone, ca. 1960
Magazine advertisement on paper
13 1/2 x 14 inches
Collection of the artist
Page 50

I Love You with My Ford, 1961
Oil on canvas, 84 1/2 x 95 inches
Moderna Museet, Stockholm
Page 55

Pushbutton, 1961
Oil on canvas, Diptych: 82 3/4 x 105 1/2 inches
The Museum of Contemporary Art, Los Angeles
The Panza Collection
Page 51

Zone, 1961
Oil on canvas, 96 x 96 inches
Philadelphia Museum of Art
Purchase: Edith H. Bell Fund
Page 50

A Lot to Like, 1962
Oil on canvas, Triptych: 93 x 204 inches
The Museum of Contemporary Art, Los Angeles
The Panza Collection
Page 54

248

EDWARD RUSCHA

School Assignment, 1957
Tempera on board, 7 1/2 x 9 1/2 inches
Collection of the artist
Page 14

Dublin, 1959
Wood, newspaper, and ink on paper
13 1/2 x 13 inches
Collection of the artist
Page 56

E. Ruscha, 1959
Oil on canvas, 43 1/2 x 43 1/2 inches
Collection of the artist
Page 59

Dublin, 1960
Oil on canvas, 72 x 67 inches
Collection of the artist
Page 56

U.S. 66, 1960
Oil on paper, 13 1/16 x 13 inches
Collection of the artist
Page 58

Ace Radio Honk Boss, 1961
Tempera on paper, 15 5/8 x 20 inches
Collection of the artist
Page 219

Ace Radio Honk Boss, 1961
Tempera on paper, 15 5/8 x 20 1/8 inches
Collection of the artist
Page 218

Annie, 1961
Tempera on paper, 6 7/8 x 8 5/8 inches
Collection of the artist
Page 218

Ice, 1961
Oil on paper, 10 3/4 x 12 inches
Collection of the artist
Page 57

Metro, 1961
Photo-collage and oil on paper
14 3/8 x 11 15/16 inches
Collection of the artist
Page 216

Metropolitain, 1961
Oil on paper, 19 3/4 x 26 5/8 inches
Collection of the artist
Page 216

Para Pic, 1961
Oil on paper, 10 3/4 x 14 3/8 inches
Collection of the artist
Page 250

Ace, 1962
Oil on canvas, 71 3/8 x 66 3/4 inches
San Diego Museum of Contemporary Art
Museum purchase in memory of Lois Person
Osborn
Page 221

Actual Size, 1962
Oil on canvas, 72 x 67 inches
Los Angeles County Museum of Art
Anonymous gift through the Contemporary
Art Council
(Los Angeles only)
Page 63

Annie, 1962
Oil on canvas, 72 x 67 inches
Private collection
Page 220

Falling but Frozen, 1962
Oil on canvas, 72 x 67 inches
Collection of Tony Shafrazi, New York
Page 62

Heavy Industry, 1962
Oil on canvas, 67 x 71 5/8 inches
Collection of the artist
Page 60

Hotel, 1962
Oil on paper, 11 1/2 x 14 1/8 inches
Collection of the artist
Page 62

Schwitters, 1962
Oil and collage on paper, 11 3/4 x 11 inches
Collection of the artist
Page 216

War Surplus, 1962
Oil on canvas, 71 x 66 3/8 inches
Collection of the artist
Page 61

PETER SAUL

Icebox, 1960
Oil on canvas, 69 x 58 1/2 inches
Courtesy of Frumkin/Adams Gallery, New York
Page 64

Bathroom Sex Murder, 1961
Oil on canvas, 69 x 59 1/2 inches
Courtesy of Frumkin/Adams Gallery, New York
Page 166

Valda Sherman, 1961
Oil on canvas, 51 x 59 inches
Courtesy of Frumkin/Adams Gallery, New York
Page 167

WAYNE THIEBAUD

Ribbon Store, 1954-57
Oil on canvas, 28 3/4 x 34 7/8 inches
Private collection
Page 223

Pinball Machine, 1956
Mixed media on presswood, 37 x 49 1/2 inches
Private collection
Page 225

Store Window, 1957
Oil on board, 11 x 12 inches
Private collection
Courtesy of Allan Stone Gallery, New York
Page 222

Bakery Counter, 1961-62
Oil on canvas, 54 3/4 x 71 3/4 inches
Collection of Foster and Monique Goldstrom,
Oakland, Calif., and New York
Page 224

Desserts, 1961
Oil on canvas, 24 1/8 x 30 1/8 inches
Collection of PaineWebber Group Inc., New York
Page 224

CY TWOMBLY

The Geeks, 1955
Oil, crayon, and pencil on canvas
42 1/2 x 50 inches
Courtesy of Thomas Ammann, Zurich
Page 149

The Blue Room, 1957
Oil and crayon on canvas, 56 1/4 x 71 5/8 inches
The Sonnabend Collection, New York
Page 151

Untitled (Panorama), 1959
Oil, crayon, and pencil on paper
58 1/8 x 95 1/4 inches
Courtesy of Galerie Karsten Greve, Cologne
Page 146

(Study for) School of Athens, 1960
Oil and crayon on canvas, 49 1/4 x 65 inches
Courtesy of Galerie Karsten Greve, Cologne
Page 159

(Study for) Sunset, 1960
Oil and crayon on canvas, 49 1/4 x 65 inches
Courtesy of Galerie Karsten Greve, Cologne
Page 154

Untitled, 1960
Oil, crayon, and pencil on canvas
38 1/4 x 55 1/8 inches
Collection of Ralph and Helyn Goldenberg,
Chicago
Page 152

ANDY WARHOL

Two Heads, ca. 1952-57
Oil, ink, and commercial spray paint on printed
linen, 42 x 47 3/4 inches
The Andy Warhol Foundation for the Visual Arts,
Inc., New York
Page 195

Flag, ca. 1956
Tempera on paper, 22 1/2 x 28 1/2 inches
The Andy Warhol Foundation for the Visual Arts,
Inc., New York
Page 192

Girl Sucking Forefinger, ca. 1956-58
Oil and graphite on printed linen, 48 x 41 inches
The Andy Warhol Foundation for the Visual Arts,
Inc., New York
Page 192

Coca-Cola, 1960
Oil and wax crayon on canvas
69 5/8 x 52 1/4 inches
Dia Center for the Arts, New York
Page 92

Dick Tracy, 1960
Casein and crayon on canvas, 48 x 33 7/8 inches
Private collection
Page 87

Dr. Scholl, 1960
Synthetic polymer paint on canvas
48 x 40 inches
The Metropolitan Museum of Art, New York
Gift of Halston
Page 197

Icebox, 1960
Oil, ink, and pencil on canvas, 67 x 53 1/8 inches
The Menil Collection, Houston
Page 6

Peach Halves, 1960
Synthetic polymer paint on canvas
70 x 54 inches
Staatsgalerie Stuttgart
Page 199

Storm Door, 1960
Synthetic polymer paint on canvas
46 x 42 1/8 inches
Courtesy of Thomas Ammann, Zurich
Page 90

Strong Arms and Broads, 1960
Synthetic polymer paint, black Japan, and crayon
on canvas, 45 x 61 inches
Private collection
Page 178

Where is Your Rupture?, 1960
Synthetic polymer paint on canvas
70 x 54 inches
Private collection, courtesy of Gallery Bruno
Bischofberger, Zurich
Page 196

Telephone, 1961
Acrylic and pencil on canvas, 72 x 54 inches
The Museum of Contemporary Art, Los Angeles
Purchased with funds provided by an
anonymous donor
Page 94

Before and After II, 1962
Oil on canvas, 54 x 70 inches
Collection of Kimiko and John Powers,
Carbondale, Colorado
Page 89

JOHN WESLEY

Stamp, 1961
Oil on canvas, 24 x 24 inches
Collection of the artist
Page 169

American Eagle Badge, 1962
Oil on canvas, 24 x 24 inches
Collection of the artist
Page 170

Coat of Arms, 1962
Oil on canvas, 48 x 48 inches
Collection of the artist
Page 170

249

EDWARD RUSCHA
Para Pic, 1961
Oil on paper, 10 3/4 x 14 3/8 inches
Collection of the artist

Selected Bibliography

Monographs and Articles on the Artists

Billy Al Bengston

Billy Al Bengston: Paintings of Three Decades. Houston: Contemporary Arts Museum; Oakland: The Oakland Museum; and San Francisco: Chronicle Books, 1988.

Monte, James. *Billy Al Bengston*. Los Angeles: Los Angeles County Museum of Art, 1968.

Jim Dine

Gordon, John. *Jim Dine*. New York: Praeger, in association with the Whitney Museum of American Art, 1970.

Jim Dine: Exhibition, New Paintings. New York: Sidney Janis Gallery, 1963.

Shapiro, David. *Jim Dine: Painting What One Is*. New York: Abrams, 1981.

Joe Goode

Joe Goode: Work Until Now. Fort Worth: The Art Center Museum, 1972.

Joe Goode, Edward Ruscha. [exh. cat., Balboa Pavilion Gallery, Newport Beach] Balboa, Calif.: Fine Arts Patrons of Newport Harbor, 1968.

Leider, Philip. "Joe Goode and the Common Object," *Artforum* 4, no. 7 (March 1966): 24-27.

Grace Hartigan

Mattison, Robert Saltonstall. *Grace Hartigan: A Painter's World*. New York: Hudson Hills, 1990.

Robert Indiana

Robert Indiana. Philadelphia: Institute of Contemporary Art at the University of Pennsylvania, 1968.

Robert Indiana: Early Sculpture 1960-1962. London: Salama-Caro Gallery, 1991.

Sheehan, Susan. *Robert Indiana Prints: Catalogue Raisonné, 1951-1991*. New York: Susan Sheehan Gallery, 1991.

Weinhardt, Carl J. *Robert Indiana*. New York: Abrams, 1990.

Jess

Auping, Michael. *Jess: Paste-Ups (and Assemblies), 1951-1983*. Sarasota, Fla.: The John and Mable Ringling Museum of Art, 1983.

Burnside, Madeleine. *Jess*. New York: Odyssia Gallery, 1989.

Translations, Salvages, Paste-Ups. Dallas: Dallas Museum of Art, 1977.

Jasper Johns

Bernstein, Roberta. *Jasper Johns' Paintings and Sculptures, 1954-1974: "The Changing Focus of the Eye"*. Ann Arbor, Mich.: UMI Research Press, 1985.

Boudaille, Georges. *Jasper Johns*. New York: Rizzoli, 1989.

Crichton, Michael. *Jasper Johns*. New York: Abrams, in association with the Whitney Museum of American Art, 1977.

Field, Richard S. *Jasper Johns: Prints 1960-1970*. New York: Praeger, in association with the Philadelphia Museum of Art, 1970.

Francis, Richard. *Jasper Johns*. New York: Abbeville, 1984.

Jasper Johns. New York: The Jewish Museum, 1964.

Jasper Johns: Printed Symbols. Minneapolis: Walker Art Center, 1990.

Kozloff, Max. *Jasper Johns*. New York: Abrams, 1972.

Allan Kaprow

Allan Kaprow. Pasadena: Pasadena Art Museum, 1967.

Roy Lichtenstein

Alloway, Lawrence. *Roy Lichtenstein*. New York: Abbeville, 1983.

Busche, Ernst A. *Roy Lichtenstein: Das Frühwerk 1942-1960*. Berlin: Gebr. Mann Verlag, 1988.

Coplans, John, ed. *Roy Lichtenstein*. New York: Praeger, 1972.

Waldman, Diane. *Roy Lichtenstein*. New York: Abrams, 1971.

Claes Oldenburg

Johnson, Ellen H. *Claes Oldenburg*. Baltimore: Penguin, 1971.

Claes Oldenburg: Multiples in Retrospect, 1964-1990. New York: Rizzoli, 1991.

Claes Oldenburg: Skulpturer och Teckningar. Stockholm: Moderna Museet, 1966.

Rose, Barbara. *Claes Oldenburg*. New York: The Museum of Modern Art, 1970.

Store Days: Documents from The Store (1961) and Ray Gun Theater (1962). New York: Something Else Press, 1967.

Mel Ramos

Jones, Harvey. *Mel Ramos: Paintings, 1959-1977.* Oakland, Calif.: Oakland Museum of Art, 1977.

Mel Ramos: A Twenty Year Survey. Waltham, Mass.: Rose Art Museum, Brandeis University, 1980.

Robert Rauschenberg

Feinstein, Roni. *Robert Rauschenberg: The Silkscreen Paintings, 1962-64.* New York: Whitney Museum of American Art, 1990.

Forge, Andrew. *Rauschenberg.* New York: Abrams, 1969.

Hopps, Walter. *Robert Rauschenberg: The Early 1950s.* [exh. cat., The Menil Collection, Houston] Houston: Houston Fine Art Press, 1991.

Kotz, Mary Lynn. *Rauschenberg, Art and Life.* New York: Abrams, 1990.

Robert Rauschenberg. Washington, D.C.: National Collection of Fine Arts, Smithsonian Institution, 1977.

Rose, Barbara. *Robert Rauschenberg.* New York: Vintage Books, 1987.

Solomon, Alan R. *Robert Rauschenberg.* New York: The Jewish Museum, 1963.

Tomkins, Calvin. *Off the Wall: Robert Rauschenberg and the Art World of Our Time.* New York: Doubleday, 1980.

Larry Rivers

Harrison, Helen A. *Larry Rivers.* New York: Harper and Row, 1984.

Hunter, Sam. *Larry Rivers.* New York: Abrams, 1970.

_____ . *Larry Rivers.* New York: Rizzoli, 1989.

Rivers, Larry. *What Did I Do?: The Unauthorized Biography of Larry Rivers.* New York: Aaron Asher Books, 1992.

James Rosenquist

Goldman, Judith. *James Rosenquist.* New York: Viking Penguin, 1985.

_____ . *James Rosenquist: The Early Pictures 1961-1964.* New York: Rizzoli, in association with Gagosian Gallery, 1992.

James Rosenquist. Valencia, Spain: Institut Valencia d'Art Modern, 1991.

Tucker, Marcia. *James Rosenquist.* New York: Whitney Museum of American Art, 1972.

Edward Ruscha

Clearwater, Bonnie. *Edward Ruscha: Words Without Thoughts Never To Heaven Go.* Lakeworth, Fla.: Lannan Foundation, 1988.

Edward Ruscha. Rotterdam: Museum Boymans-van Beuningen, 1990.

Edward Ruscha. Paris: Éditions du Centre Pompidou, 1989.

Edward Ruscha: Early Paintings. New York: Tony Shafrazi Gallery, 1988.

Hickey, Dave and Peter Plagens. *The Works of Edward Ruscha.* New York: Hudson Hills, in association with the San Francisco Museum of Modern Art, 1982.

Peter Saul

Red Grooms, Peter Saul: The Early Sixties. New York: Allan Frumkin Gallery, 1981.

Peter Saul. DeKalb, Ill.: Swen Parson Gallery, Northern Illinois University, 1980.

Wayne Thiebaud

Tsujimoto, Karen. *Wayne Thiebaud.* San Francisco: San Francisco Museum of Modern Art, 1985.

Wayne Thiebaud: Survey 1947-1976. Phoenix: Phoenix Art Museum, 1976.

Cy Twombly

Barthes, Roland. *Cy Twombly.* Berlin: Merve Verlag, 1983.

Bastian, Heiner. *Cy Twombly: Zeichnungen 1953-1973.* Berlin: Propylaen-Verlag, 1973.

_____ . *Cy Twombly: Paintings 1952-1976.* Berlin: Propylaen-Verlag, 1978.

_____ . *Cy Twombly: Das Graphische Werke 1953-1984, A Catalogue Raisonné of the Painted Graphic Work.* Munich: Edition Schellmann, 1984.

Cy Twombly: The Menil Collection. [exh. cat., The Menil Collection, Houston] Houston: Houston Fine Art Press, 1990.

Cy Twombly: Paintings and Drawings 1954-1977. New York: Whitney Museum of American Art, 1979.

Cy Twombly: Paintings, Drawings, Constructions 1951-1974. Philadelphia: Institute of Contemporary Art, University of Pennsylvania, 1975.

Cy Twombly: Works on Paper 1954-1976. Newport Beach, Calif.: Newport Harbor Art Museum, 1981.

Andy Warhol

Crone, Rainer. *Andy Warhol: The Early Work 1942-1962.* New York: Rizzoli, 1987.

Crow, Thomas. "Saturday Disasters: Trace and Reference in Early Warhol." *Art in America* 75, no. 5 (May 1987): 128-36.

De Salvo, Donna, ed. *"Success Is a Job in New York ...": The Early Art and Business of Andy Warhol.* New York: Grey Art Gallery, New York University, in association with the Carnegie Museum of Art, 1989.

Garrels, Gary, ed. *The Work of Andy Warhol.* Seattle: Bay Press, 1989.

Kornbluth, Jesse. *Pre-Pop Warhol.* New York: Panache Press, 1988.

McShine, Kynaston, ed. *Andy Warhol: A Retrospective.* [exh. cat., The Museum of Modern Art, New York] New York: Thames & Hudson, 1989.

Smith, Patrick S. *Warhol: Conversations About the Artist.* Ann Arbor, Mich.: UMI Research Press, 1988.

Warhol, Andy and Pat Hackett. *POPism: The Warhol Sixties.* New York: Harcourt Brace Jovanovich, 1980.

John Wesley

John Wesley: Selected Paintings 1963-1973, New Works. New York: Fiction/Nonfiction, 1991.

General

1961. Dallas: Dallas Museum for Contemporary Arts, 1961.

Alloway, Lawrence. *American Pop Art.* [exh. cat., Whitney Museum of American Art, New York] New York: Macmillan, 1974.

_____ . *Topics in American Art Since 1945.* New York: Norton, 1975.

Amaya, Mario. *Pop Art . . . and After.* New York: Viking, 1966.

Ashton, Dore. *American Art Since 1945.* New York: Oxford University Press, 1982.

252

Baldwin, Carl R. "On the Nature of Pop." *Artforum* 12, no. 10 (June 1974): 34-38.

Banham, Reyner. "Who Is This 'Pop'?" *Motif* 10 (Winter 1962-63): 3-13.

Barthes, Roland. *The Responsibility of Forms: Critical Essays on Music, Art, and Representation.* New York: Hill and Wang, 1985.

Battcock, Gregory, ed. *The New Art: A Critical Anthology.* New York: Dutton, 1973.

Becker, Jürgen and Wolf Vostell, eds. *Happenings, Fluxus, Pop Art, Nouveau Réalisme: Eine Dokumentation.* Hamburg: Rowohlt, 1965.

Calas, Nicolas. *Art in the Age of Risk, and Other Essays.* New York: Dutton, 1968.

Calas, Nicolas and Elena Calas. *Icons and Images of the Sixties.* New York: Dutton, 1971.

Compton, Michael. *Pop Art.* London: Hamlyn, 1970.

Coplans, John. "The New Paintings of Common Objects." *Artforum* 1, no. 6 (December 1962): 26-29.

_____ . *Pop Art USA.* Oakland: Oakland Art Museum, 1963.

Finch, Christopher. *Image as Language: Aspects of British Art 1950-68.* Harmondsworth, Middlesex: Penguin, 1969.

_____ . *Pop Art: Object and Image.* London: Studio Vista, 1968.

Friedman, Bernard Harper, ed. *School of New York: Some Younger Artists.* New York: Grove Press, 1959.

Gablik, Suzi. "Protagonists of Pop: Five Interviews." *Studio International* 177, no. 913 (July-August 1969): 9-16.

Gans, Herbert. *Popular Culture and High Culture.* New York: Basic Books, 1974.

Geldzahler, Henry. *New York Painting and Sculpture: 1940-1970.* New York: Dutton, in association with The Metropolitan Museum of Art, 1969.

_____ . *Pop Art 1955-1970.* [exh. cat., Art Gallery of New South Wales, Australia] Sydney: International Cultural Corporation of Australia Limited, 1985.

Geldzahler, Henry and Kenworth Moffet. "Pop Art: Two Views." *Art News* 73, no. 5 (May 1974): 30-32.

Gibson, Ann. *Issues in Abstract Expressionism: The Artist-Run Periodicals.* Ann Arbor, Mich.: UMI Research Press, 1990.

Glaser, Bruce. "Oldenberg, Lichtenstein, Warhol: A Discussion." *Artforum* 4, no. 6 (February 1966): 20-26.

Greenberg, Clement. "After Abstract Expressionism." *Art International* 6, no. 8 (October 1962): 24-32.

Guilbaut, Serge. *How New York Stole the Idea of Modern Art: Abstract Expressionism, Freedom, and the Cold War.* Chicago: University of Chicago Press, 1983.

Harris, Mary Emma. *The Arts at Black Mountain College.* Cambridge, Mass.: MIT Press, 1987.

Haskell, Barbara. *Blam! The Explosion of Pop, Minimalism, and Performance, 1958-1964.* New York: Norton, in association with the Whitney Museum of American Art, 1984.

Hebdige, Dick. *Hiding in the Light: On Images and Things.* New York: Routledge, 1988.

_____ . *Subculture: The Meaning of Style.* London and New York: Methuen, 1979.

Henri, Adrian. *Total Art: Environments, Happenings and Performance.* New York: Oxford University Press, 1974.

Hess, Thomas B. and Elizabeth C. Baker. *Art and Sexual Politics: Women's Liberation, Women Artists and Art History.* New York: Macmillan, 1973.

Hess, Thomas B. "Collage as an Historical Method." *Art News* 60, no. 7 (November 1961): 30-33, 69-71.

_____ . "Mixed Mediums for a Soft Revolution." *Art News* 59, no. 4 (Summer 1960): 45, 62.

_____ . "U.S. Painting: Some Recent Directions." *Art News* 25 (1956): 74-98, 174-80, 192-99.

Johnson, Ellen H., ed. *American Artists on Art from 1940 to 1980.* New York: Harper and Row, 1982.

Kaprow, Allan. *Assemblage, Environments and Happenings.* New York: Abrams, 1966.

_____ . "Pop Art: Past, Present and Future." *Malahat Review* 3 (July 1967): 54-76.

Kozloff, Max. "'Pop' Culture, Metaphysical Digust, and the New Vulgarians." *Art International* 6, no. 2 (March 1962): 34-36.

Kuspit, Donald B. "Pop Art: A Reactionary Realism." *Art Journal* 36, no. 1 (Fall 1976): 31-38.

Leider, Philip. "The Cool School." *Artforum* 2, no. 12 (Summer 1964): 47-52.

Lippard, Lucy R. *Pop Art.* New York: Praeger, 1966.

Livingstone, Marco, ed. *Pop Art: An International Perspective.* [exh. cat., The Royal Academy of Arts, London] New York: Rizzoli, 1991.

_____ . *Pop Art: A Continuing History.* New York: Abrams, 1990.

Loran, Erle. "Cézanne and Lichtenstein: Problems of 'Transformation'." *Artforum* 2, no. 3 (September 1963): 34-35.

_____ . "Pop Artists or Copy Cats?" *Art News* 62, no. 5 (September 1963): 48-49, 61.

L.A. Pop in the Sixties. Newport Beach, Calif.: Newport Harbor Art Museum, 1989.

Lucie-Smith, Edward. *Cultural Calendar of the 20th Century.* Oxford: Phaidon, 1979.

Made in the Sixties. New York: Whitney Museum of American Art, 1988.

Mahsun, Carol Anne Runyon. *Pop Art and the Critics.* Ann Arbor, Mich.: UMI Research Press, 1987.

_____ , ed. *Pop Art: The Critical Dialogue.* Ann Arbor, Mich.: UMI Research Press, 1989.

Mamiya, Christin J. *Pop Art and Consumer Culture: American Super Market.* Austin, Tex.: University of Texas Press, 1992.

Melly, George. *Revolt Into Style: The Pop Arts in Britain.* London: Penguin, 1970.

Miller, Dorothy C., ed. *Sixteen Americans.* New York: The Museum of Modern Art, 1959.

Modern Dreams: The Rise and Fall and Rise of Pop. [exh. cat., The Institute for Contemporary Art, The Clocktower Gallery, New York] Cambridge, Mass.: MIT Press, 1988.

New Art Around the World: Painting and Sculpture. New York: Abrams, 1966.

New Media, New Forms In Painting and Sculpture. New York: Martha Jackson Gallery, 1960.

The New Realists. New York: Sidney Janis Gallery, 1962.

New York: The Second Breakthrough, 1959-1964. Irvine, Calif.: Fine Arts Gallery, University of California, 1969.

The Object Transformed. New York: The Museum of Modern Art, 1966.

O'Hara, Frank. *Art Chronicles, 1954-1966.* New York: Braziller, 1975.

Pelfrey, Robert H. with Mary Hall-Pelfrey. *Art and Mass Media.* New York: Harper and Row, 1985.

Pelligrini, Aldo. *New Tendencies in Art.* New York: Crown, 1966.

Perreault, John. "'Classic' Pop Revisited." *Art in America* 62, no. 2 (March-April 1974): 64-68.

Pierre, José. *Pop Art: An Illustrated Dictionary.* London: Eyre Methuen, 1977.

Plagens, Peter. *Sunshine Muse: Contemporary Art on the West Coast.* New York: Praeger, 1974.

Poets of the Cities of New York and San Francisco, 1950-1965. [exh. cat., The Dallas Museum of Fine Arts, Dallas] New York: Dutton, 1974.

"Pop Art—Cult of the Commonplace." *Time* 81, no. 18 (May 3, 1963), 69-72.

Pop Art: Evoluzione di una Generazione. Milan: Electa, 1980.

"Pop Goes the Easel." *Newsweek* 61, no. 13 (April 1, 1963), 80.

The Popular Image. Washington D.C.: Washington Gallery of Modern Art, 1963.

Pulos, Arthur J. *The American Design Adventure: 1940-1975.* Cambridge, Mass.: MIT Press, 1988.

Richardson, John Adkins. "Dada, Camp, and the Mode Called Pop." *Journal of Aesthetics and Art Criticism* 24, no. 4 (Summer 1966): 549-58.

Rose, Barbara. "Pop Art at the Guggenheim." *Art International* 7, no. 5 (May 1963): 20-22.

Rosenberg, Bernard and David Manning White, eds. *Mass Culture: The Popular Arts in America.* Glencoe, Ill.: Free Press, 1957.

Rosenberg, Harold. *The Anxious Object: Art Today and Its Audience.* New York: Horizon, 1964.

Rosenzweig, Phyllis. *The Fifties: Aspects of Painting in New York.* Washington, D.C.: Hirshhorn Museum and Sculpture Garden, Smithsonian Institution, 1980.

Rubin, William. "Younger American Painters." *Art International* 4, no. 1 (1960): 24-31.

Rublowsky, John. *Pop Art.* New York: Basic Books, 1965.

Russell, John and Suzi Gablik. *Pop Art Redefined.* New York: Praeger, 1969.

Sandberg, John. "Some Traditional Aspects of Pop Art." *Art Journal* 26, no. 3 (Spring 1967): 228-33.

Sandler, Irving. *American Art of the 1960s.* New York: Harper and Row, 1988.

_____ . "New York Letter." *Art International* 4, no. 10 (December, 1960): 22-28.

_____ . *The New York School: The Painters and Sculptors of the Fifties.* New York: Harper and Row, 1978.

_____ . *The Triumph of American Painting: A History of Abstract Expressionism.* New York: Praeger, 1970.

Schimmel, Paul and Judith Stein. *The Figurative Fifties: New York Figurative Expressionism.* Newport Beach, Calif.: Newport Harbor Art Museum, 1988.

Schimmel, Paul, et. al. *Action/Precision: The New Direction in New York 1955-60.* Newport Beach, Calif.: Newport Harbor Art Museum, 1984.

Selz, Peter. *Funk.* Berkeley: University Art Museum, University of California, 1967.

_____ . "Pop Goes the Artist." *Partisan Review* 30, no. 2 (Summer 1963): 315.

Selz, Peter, et. al. "A Symposium on Pop Art," *Arts Magazine* 37, no. 7 (April 1963): 36-45.

Seven Decades of Twentieth Century Art: From the Sidney and Harriet Janis Collection of The Museum of Modern Art and the Sidney Janis Gallery Collection. La Jolla, Calif.: La Jolla Museum of Contemporary Art, 1980.

Siegfried, Joan C. *The Spirit of the Comics.* [exh. cat., Institute for Contemporary Art, University of Pennsylvania, Philadelphia] New York: American Federation of Arts, 1969.

Six More. Los Angeles: Los Angeles County Museum of Art, 1963.

Six Painters and the Object. New York: Solomon R. Guggenheim Museum, 1963.

"The Slice of Cake School." *Time* 79, no. 19 (May 11, 1962), 52.

Starr, Sandra Leonard. *Lost and Found in California: Four Decades of Assemblage Art.* Santa Monica, Calif.: James Corcoran Gallery, 1988.

Stich, Sidra. *Made in U.S.A.: An Americanization in Modern Art, the '50's and '60's.* Berkeley: University Art Museum, University of California, and University of California Press, 1987.

Swenson, G. R. "The New American 'Sign Painters'." *Art News* 61, no. 5 (September 1962): 44-47.

_____ . "What Is Pop Art?: Answers From Eight Painters, Part I" *Art News* 62, no. 7 (November 1963): 24-27, 60-65.

_____ . "What Is Pop Art?: Part II." *Art News* 62, no. 10 (February 1964): 40-43, 62-67.

Taylor, Paul, ed. *Post-Pop Art.* Cambridge, Mass.: MIT Press, 1989.

Ten From Los Angeles. [exh. cat., Seattle Art Museum Pavilion] Seattle: Contemporary Art Council of the Seattle Art Museum, 1966.

Tomkins, Calvin. *The Bride and the Bachelors: Five Masters of the Avant-Garde.* New York: Penguin, 1976.

Tuchman, Maurice, ed. *Art in Los Angeles: Seventeen Artists in the Sixties.* Los Angeles: Los Angeles County Museum of Art, 1981.

_____ . *The New York School: The First Generation.* Los Angeles: Los Angeles County Museum of Art, 1965.

Tuchman, Phyllis. "Pop! Interviews with George Segal, Andy Warhol, Roy Lichtenstein, James Rosenquist, and Robert Indiana." *Art News* 73, no. 5 (May 1974): 24-29.

Walker, John Albert. *Art Since Pop.* London: Thames and Hudson, 1975.

Wallock, Leonard, ed. *New York: Culture Capital of the World, 1940-1965.* New York: Rizzoli, 1988.

West Coast 1945-1969. Pasadena: Pasadena Art Museum, 1969.

Photo Credits

Photographs reproduced in this book have been provided, in the majority of cases, by the owners or custodians of the works, indicated in the captions. Individual works of art appearing here may be additionally protected by copyright in the United States of America or abroad, and may not be reproduced in any form without the permission of the copyright owners.

The copyright information below also applies:

©Jasper Johns/VAGA, New York 1992 for each work by the artist

©Roy Lichtenstein for each work by the artist

©Robert Rauschenberg/VAGA, Yew York 1992 for each work by the artist

©Larry Rivers/VAGA, New York 1992 for each work by the artist

©James Rosenquist/VAGA, New York 1992 for each work by the artist

©1992 Andy Warhol Foundation for the Visual Arts/ARS, New York for each work by the artist

The following list, keyed to page numbers, applies to photographs for which a separate acknowledgment is due.

2: Douglas M. Parker Studio. 6: Hickey-Robertson, Houston. 8: Squidds & Nunns. 10: Paula Goldman. 18: ©1992 The Museum of Modern Art, New York (photo: Geoffrey Clements, New York). 21: ©1992 Willem de Kooning/ARS, New York. 23: Copyright ©1992 by The Metropolitan Museum of Art. 27: Jim Frank. 28: Paula Goldman. 29: Michael Tropea, Chicago. 30: Paul Hester, Houston. 31: (top) David Sundberg, New York. 32-34: Squidds & Nunns. 35: (bottom) Bruce M. White Photography, New York. 37: (left) Squidds & Nunns; (right) M. Fischer. 38: (top) Squidds & Nunns; (bottom) Michael Tropea, Chicago. 40: Courtesy of Leo Castelli Gallery, New York. 44: Mary Kristin. 46: Robert McKeever. 47: Tom Powel. 48: Robert McKeever. 51 (top), 54: Squidds & Nunns. 55: Courtesy of Statens Konstmuseer. 56-62 (top): Paul Ruscha. 64: Herbert Boswank. 66: Martin Bühler, Kunstmuseum Basel. 71: Geoffrey Clements, New York. 72: (top) ©1992 The Museum of Modern Art, New York; (bottom) Courtesy of The Pace Gallery (photo: ©Ellen Page Wilson, 1991). 74: Courtesy of The Pace Gallery (photo: Bill Jacobson Studio). 75: (top and bottom) photographs courtesy of The Pace Gallery; (top) Al Mozel; (middle) David Sundberg, New York; (bottom) ©Ellen Page Wilson. 76: David Sundberg, New York. 79: (middle) photographs courtesy of The Pace Gallery. 80-81: David Sundberg, New York. 82-83 (top): Robert McKeever. 84: Ed Watkins. 86: Dan Walworth. 88: Virginia Roehl. 92: Dan Walworth. 94: Paula Goldman. 103, 107: Robert McKeever. 108: Squidds & Nunns. 109: David Sundberg, New York. 111: Squidds & Nunns. 113: Rheinisches Bildarchiv, Cologne. 114: Robert McKeever. 120, 123: ©1992 The Museum of Modern Art, New York. 128: Herb Gallagher. 131, 150: ©1992 The Museum of Modern Art, New York. 152: James Prinz. 155: Jochen Litt Kemann. 158: Paula Goldman. 169-170: David Sundberg, New York. 184: Don Myer. 186: (left) Copyright ©1992 By The Metropolitan Museum of Art. 187: (bottom) Lee Staisworth. 188: (left) Rudolph Burkhardt; (right) Copyright ©1992 By The Metropolitan Museum of Art. 197: Copyright ©1992 By The Metropolitan Museum of Art. 198: (left) Rheinisches Bildarchiv, Cologne; (right) Hickey-Robertson, Houston. 202: ©1992 The Museum of Modern Art, New York. 203: Geoffrey Clements, New York. 207: Robert E. Mates Studio, New Jersey. 210-211: Brian Forrest. 212: Paula Goldman. 213: Gene Ogami. 214: Juan Ramon Sanchez de la Peña. 215: Pat Renschen. 216-221: Paul Ruscha. 222: (top) Ferrari Printers; (bottom) David Sundberg, New York. 223, 225: Ferrari Printers. 224: Bill Orcutt. 228-229: Squidds & Nunns. 230: (all but top) Squidds & Nunns. 231: (top left) Rheinisches Bildarchiv, Cologne; (top right and bottom left) Squidds & Nunns; (bottom right) ©1992 The Museum of Modern Art, New York. 232: (top) Squidds & Nunns. 235-236: David Sundberg, New York. 239: ©1992 The Museum of Modern Art, New York. 242: Courtesy of Statens Konstmuseer (photo: P-A Allsten).

ROY LICHTENSTEIN
Knock-Knock, 1961
Ink on paper, 20 1/4 x 19 3/4 inches
The Sonnabend Collection, New York

ROBERT RAUSCHENBERG
Coca Cola Plan, 1958
Combine painting, 26 3/4 x 25 1/4 x 4 3/4
The Museum of Contemporary Art, Los Angeles
The Panza Collection